APOSTLE
IN A TOP HAT

"Rich swine!"

The ragged slum habitant spat out his hatred as two young men passed him in the squalid Rue Mouffetard. For their top hats and frock coats identified them, in the Paris of the early 1800's, as of the generally aloof and unfeeling upper classes.

He did not know that these two were even then on their way to bring help to the sick and penniless. Nor that the younger would soon be uniting his Sorbonne fellow students into an organization whose members would personally and continuously aid the poor.

Frederic Ozanam's Society of St. Vincent de Paul would in his brief lifetime spread throughout France, throughout Europe, and to far lands.

Today, its founding membership of seven has multiplied to 750,000 continuously serving the unfortunate in 112 nations around the globe.

THIS IS THE STIRRING STORY of a modest, gifted young leader who
  —became one of Europe's most influential scholars;
  —championed the cause of the wage slaves of the early industrial age;
  —organized a brotherhood of charity intensely active in thousands of Catholic parishes throughout the world today.

This is the story of Frederic Ozanam, "apostle of charity." It will warm and win your heart.

Cover portrait after a drawing by Louis Janmot (1852). Janmot, a leading French artist and close friend of Ozanam, was one of the pioneer builders of the Society of St. Vincent de Paul.

JAMES PATRICK DERUM

APOSTLE IN A TOP HAT

The Story of Frederic Ozanam

Founder of the Society
of
St. Vincent de Paul

FIDELITY PUBLISHING COMPANY
ST. CLAIR, MICHIGAN, U.S.A.

APOSTLE IN A TOP HAT

NIHIL OBSTAT:
>Gall Higgins, O.F.M. Cap.
>Censor Librorum

IMPRIMATUR:
>Francis Cardinal Spellman
>Archbishop of New York
>July 13, 1960

Originally published by Hanover House,
a Division of Doubleday & Company, Inc., 1960

First paperback edition published by
All Saints Press, New York, N.Y., 1962

Second paperback edition published by
Fidelity Publishing Company,
707 Langley Circle,
St. Clair, Michigan, U.S.A. 48079

Printed in the United States of America

Cover Design: Emilio Rodriguez

Picture section at page 76.

ACKNOWLEDGMENTS

An innate shrinking from spotlights having caused her to deny me the required permission, I am restrained from dedicating this book

TO MY WIFE

—to whom above all others I am indebted for help in its production.

The deep and abiding gratitude with which I acknowledge her constructive criticisms, and patient editing and re-editing, extends also to the following:

The direct descendants of Frederic Ozanam, who supplied information from the family archives, and verses written by their great-grandfather; Monsignor Harold J. Markey, Spiritual Advisor of the Particular Council of the St. Vincent de Paul Society of the Archdiocese of Detroit, who suggested that I write this book; James Fitzgerald, of Detroit, for supplying various books and pamphlets, and for reading the manuscript; John J. Delaney, Editor of Hanover House, whose professionally expert criticisms and suggestions were invaluable; Mlle. Jeanne Terraz, director of the municipal archives of Lyons, who supplied important books and maps, proofread the manuscript, and checked it for accurate rendering of the French scene and mores; Miss Eleanor Brakeman, of Detroit, who put me in touch with invaluable French sources, and supplied translations, including that of the verse written by Frederic Ozanam when six years old; the Religious of the Sacred Heart of Grosse Pointe, and of Bloomfield Hills, Michigan; the Reverend Edward J. Hodous, S.J., of the University of Detroit, for an early editing of the manuscript; Miss Phyllis Ward, of Detroit, who supplied documents, maps, and books, and who proofread the manuscript; Charles Ozanam, of Neuilly-sur-Seine, France, grandnephew of Frederic Ozanam, who directed me to valuable sources including, most importantly, the direct descendants of the book's subject.

Apostle in a Top Hat

CHAPTER 1

DOCTOR OZANAM had one final direction for the woman standing opposite him at the rickety bed on which her fever-ridden husband was lying.

"You are a good nurse, Madame Germaine," he said, as he carefully assumed a straighter posture, for he was tall, and the attic ceiling was very low. "But you must not wear yourself out. Can you get a neighbor to help you?"

"I will try, Doctor," answered the woman, rather hopelessly.

The physician turned toward the chair on which he had draped his greatcoat. Madame Germaine, stepping quickly around the bed, lifted the multi-caped, full-skirted garment and held it for him.

As he shrugged into it she said: "How can we thank you, Doctor? Only the good God knows when we can pay you. Yet you come to us so willingly, and at such an hour! You are the most generous person in Lyons."

The physician tugged his heavy gold watch from a vest pocket, and as if to divert the woman, exclaimed: "Why, bless my soul, it's six o'clock!" He had been at the sick man's side since midnight.

He looked toward the poor room's one small window, now brightening with the day's first dim light. The windowpane was broken, and a rag, stuffed into the opening, kept out the cold March rain that had been falling steadily through the night. He paused a moment in deep thought. Then he said, "Madame, I ask only one reward—your prayers. My youngest boy is close to death. I feel that only a miracle can save him."

1

"Ah, Doctor, I will, I will. I'll pray for him constantly, as I pray for my husband. . . . And to think that you left your son to come to us!"

"I could do nothing more for him," said the physician, "and your husband's health is also my obligation. I will return this evening, or"—he hesitated as the pain of a dread foreboding seared his heart—"if I cannot come, I shall send a colleague."

His hand was unsteady as he held a taper to the room's only candle, then touched it to the candle in his lantern; he would need a light on the tenement's dark stairway.

"In the meantime, madame," he continued, after he had slowly closed the lantern and regained his composure, "let my little Frederic share your petitions. Monsieur Germaine is a strong man; with nature's help, he should soon recover. But Divine Providence alone can save my son."

He bowed a silent farewell, and began to pick his way down the five flights of stairs to the street. He held the lantern well forward—an unnoticed broken step might send him head-long.

When he reached the cobblestone pavement, down which the water ran in scores of tiny rivulets, he snuffed the lantern's candle, then hastened along the narrow street toward his home.

His heart was sick and leaden with the premonition of death. Frederic was now too weak to recover, he told himself—and he would make the eighth they had lost. The others had died in infancy, victims of the dread diseases of childhood. That Frederic had escaped their fate seemed almost incomprehensible; twice before in his six years he had nearly succumbed. . . . How feeble, the father reflected bitterly, were his profession's weapons, and how useless against the typhus which even now was ravaging his son's frail body.

Hurrying through the Place St.-Nizier and the markets of the Place de la Fromagerie, where the marketwomen were already displaying their cheeses and vegetables, he was almost unconscious of the awakening city and the steady rain. His mind was centered wholly on Frederic—Frederic the lovable, the tender-hearted, the precocious—Frederic, whose will was so strong, who could be so insistently demanding, but who

2

was so honest, so sweet, so winning. . . . The thought of Frederic, slipping a little farther from them with every feeble heartbeat, drained him of hope and left him bleak and desolate.

At the Place de la Platière he turned almost automatically toward his parish church of St. Pierre. A priest was celebrating Mass at the high altar, and, kneeling in the family pew, the physician talked to the Son of God in the Holy Eucharist as to an unfailing friend. At the consecration, as the celebrant lifted high the Body and Blood of Him who had offered Himself on Calvary, Frederic's father poured out his heart in supplication.

"Dear Lord," he prayed, "You see how our poor medicines do nothing for my boy. You alone can save him, as You have saved him before. If it is Your will that he go to You now rather than later in his life, may Your will be done. But if it be for his soul's good, and the good of others, again spare him to us. I ask this through Your Blessed Mother's love for You—through St. Joseph's tender care of You—and through Your good servant St. Francis Regis."

Dr. Ozanam and his wife were deeply devoted to the great Jesuit saint of southern France, who had sacrificed himself so heroically for those suffering from spiritual and material poverty, and those persecuted by the worldy and powerful.

As he concluded his prayer, a sense of peace came over him, and he was filled with a calm hope that was almost confidence.

When he drew near to his home in the Grande Rue Pizay the narrow street was still in deep shadow. But there was a light of hope in the father's heart; his trust in God's wisdom and love was absolute.

He had removed his hat and greatcoat and was crossing the parlor, when the room's rear door was thrown open and his wife rushed toward him, her arms upraised, her dark eyes sparkling, her face aglow with joy.

"Beer, my dear husband!" she cried, "our little Frederic calls for *beer!*"

"Beer?" repeated the astonished father.

3

"Yes, my dear Jean! The fever—it seems to have left him. And he calls for beer!"

"Then let him have beer!" shouted the doctor. He was suddenly beside himself with relief and happiness.

"It's a good sign—a great sign," he continued. "He has an appetite. Fever patients often ask for the strangest things when the fever leaves them. Our Frederic is saved!"

"Hurry, Marie," he urged, turning to the middle-aged servant whom the children affectionately called "Guigui." "Bring beer for Frederic. . . . Quickly!" he cried, when Marie seemed to hesitate, "—or by the holy John Francis Regis, I'll run for it myself."

"It was the relic!" exclaimed Madame Ozanam at mention of the saint's name. "St. Francis Regis pleaded for us with our Heavenly Father, and his pleas were heard. I had no sooner placed his relic on Frederic, than the fever left him."

"It's a miracle!" cried Guigui, following him as he strode toward Frederic's room. "I saw it! It is true—as soon as Madame applied the relic, the fever left. . . . But beer! Our boy must have a mighty thirst to ask for beer." And she sped away to bring the beverage.

"Yes, a mighty thirst, and a sanctified thirst," laughed Dr. Ozanam, placing his hand on Frederic's cool brow as the lad smiled weakly up at him. "It was through St. Francis Regis that God cured you, Frederic, so I'm sure the good saint must have inspired this appetite for beer."

For days the doctor had felt far older than his forty years; now, in a moment, he felt almost as gay and youthful as when, a gallant captain of hussars, he had courted and won Frederic's mother nearly twenty years before.

Frederic's startling demand for beer proved to be merely a convalescent's whim, for he turned his head from the goblet after one brief taste. But he ravenously consumed Guigui's stout and savory soup, and almost instantly fell into a deep, calm sleep. He awoke in the early evening, and his mother, sitting by his bed, fed him and he again slept.

Dr. Ozanam came in for a look at him before going out on his professional rounds; he assured her they had now nothing to fear, and urged her to rest. But, though drained of all physical energy, she felt no need of sleep and continued to sit by her child, silently offering thanksgiving from an overflowing heart. Wonder at Frederic's sudden, almost incredible turning back from the margent of eternity grew upon her. God, she felt, had given her child a new birth, and she began very softly to caress his forehead and his silken, chestnut hair, and to sing an Italian cradlesong with which she had often lulled him to sleep when he was a tiny infant in Milan.

She had, she remembered, been singing that same lullaby to him one night six years before in the Italian city when his father burst gaily into the bedroom, wearing the blue ribbon and resplendent decoration the Emperor Napoleon's stepson, Prince Eugene, had placed about his neck but an hour before. It was the government's grateful recognition of his heroic medical services during a typhus epidemic then raging in Milan.

Her voice faded into memories and was still as she recalled how Jean-Antoine had knelt by her side at the sleeping baby's crib and had thrown an arm about her as he kissed her. Then, taking the garnet-encrusted star from his shoulders and holding it up a moment in merry triumph so that it reflected back the light, he had placed it about the infant's neck, saying, "This, little one, is your first decoration. But I'll be much mistaken if, when you come to manhood, you're not the recipient of many another."

She had thought then that perhaps he had stressed the words "when you come to manhood" just a little; he was always trying to quiet her fear of losing the child—she who had already lost so many. Indeed, death was in the air; all about their home the epidemic was still taking its toll. Because of this it had not been until nearly three weeks after Frederic's birth that they had taken him from their home at No. 16 in the street of San Pietro a l'Orto to the old church in the parish of Our Lady of the Slaves for his baptism. She smiled as she remembered how Jean-Antoine, nervously anxious that the record of his son's baptism be correct, had watched over the reverend rector's shoulder as the latter inscribed in the parish register: "Baptized on the thirteenth of May, 1813,

Frederic-Antoine Ozanam, son of M. Jean-Antoine-Frederic Ozanam, Doctor of Medicine, and of Mme. Marie Nantas, married, French, born at midnight on April twenty-third last."

The infant of that evening in Milan—what a strong-willed, precocious child he had become. He had something of his father's features, she thought, studying him as he turned a little toward her in his sleep. But he probably would never be as handsome. She recalled how her heart had raced at her first sight of Jean-Antoine. He had come to their home in Lyons to consult her father about some family business, and he was wearing the brilliant uniform of a captain of hussars. How tall and handsome he had appeared in his high, cylindrical, cockaded cap, and the heavily braided jacket with the loose coat hanging smartly from the shoulder!

Her father had asked her to serve refreshments, but Jean-Antoine ate scarcely anything, so lost had he been in admiration of her. He had managed to become engaged in the shortest possible time, and had resigned his commission at once. . . . She seemed to breathe again the fragrance of that flowery April morning on which they were married. That was twenty years ago, nearly. Twenty years of joys and sorrows, struggles and hardships, disappointments and triumphs.

There had been Jean-Antoine's financial failure in Paris, and the loss of his silk business after he had signed notes for a friend. Napoleon had honored him with the offer of an attractive commission in the army. That would have been an easy way out of their difficulties. But he had decided to study medicine in Milan, though they both knew that would mean continuous poverty during the long period he would be working for his medical degree from the University of Pavia. How sorry she had felt for him as he worked all day tutoring students in French, then poring over his medical books far into the night. . . . And then had come high recognition as a physician in Milan, only to be followed by the sudden loss of that city by the French, and the family's move back to Lyons. Then, again, Jean-Antoine's patient, slow building of a new medical practice.

All their past hardships and disappointments—these now meant nothing; but the thought of the infants that death had torn from her breast would ever bring sorrow and regret. Thanks to the power of prayer, Frederic had been spared to her . . . he would grow stronger now . . . she must see to it that he ate well at every meal. . . .

Almost asleep, she was surprised when her husband entered the room; it seemed such a short while before that he had left the house. She had not realized how long she had been sitting there. He put an arm about her and kissed her, then leaned over the bed to study the sleeping Frederic's face. She was amused to note how closely his motions patterned those of that night in Milan when he had placed the decoration about Frederic's neck. He had been gay and playful then, but now he was very serious as he reached down to take the child's wrist between strong, skillful fingers. He straightened up with a sigh of satisfaction.

"A good, strong pulse—as regular as clockwork," he assured her. "Now, my dear, you must go to bed at once, and get a long night's sleep."

"Did you see the Germaines?" she asked. She always managed to know about his poorer patients, for she often aided them.

"Yes, and the husband's out of danger. He passed the crisis soon after I left there this morning. When I saw him tonight he was sleeping as peacefully as Frederic is right now."

She arose and stood over the sleeping boy, noting with deep content his easy, regular breathing. She leaned over him and kissed him, and asked his Guardian Angel to watch over him, and went to her bedroom for the first unbroken sleep she had had in many nights.

By the middle of May, Frederic, now almost fully recovered, was able to go with his family to a Mass of thanksgiving at St. Pierre's, which was less than a city block from their home. At this time the Ozanam household consisted of the parents; Frederic; Elisa, his eighteen-year-old sister; his brother Alphonse, who was twelve; Marie Cruziat—the prized and priceless Guigui and a second servant.

They lived in a large apartment on the third floor of a six-story building at 5 Grande Rue Pizay—one of a multitude of such apartment buildings facing each other across narrow cobblestone streets. Their home was in the northern section of the peninsula on which older Lyons is built, about midway between the historic Rhône and Saône rivers.

Dr. and Mme. Ozanam governed a family that paid no bourgeois worship to wealth or social prestige. Its members were animated, rather, by an intelligent appreciation of the vast treasures of French and European culture, of human dignity and responsibility, and of the hard work necessary if one were to make the most of God-given talents.

The parents held firmly to the conviction that their first and greatest responsibility was to nourish their children spiritually and mentally; to lead them to know and to love their Creator, and to develop their talents to the full that they might serve Him well. They were truly "domestics of God," and His Spirit dwelt in their hearts, and in their home. Frederic Ozanam's life was to be largely shaped on the pattern of their example.

His early schooling was wholly within the family circle; Elisa now took over a major share of his tutoring, with his father teaching him Latin and his mother religion, and both examining him from time to time to measure his progress. Frederic was devoted to Elisa, obeyed her directions as to study and, as he learned with ease, advanced rapidly in his lessons.

The boy's intellectual development was further quickened by the scholarly atmosphere of the Ozanam home; there conversation was the chief entertainment and recreation. Many learned guests were at home in the Ozanam apartment and at its table. The animated talk, prolonged over delectable dinners and continued thereafter in the Ozanam parlor, was generally above Frederic's understanding, but much of the information and many of the words he heard impressed themselves upon his plastic mind.

Among those who frequented the Ozanam household was the Abbé Noirot, a celebrated philosopher who lectured at the Royal College in Lyons. While at their home one day the Abbé examined Frederic briefly in his studies.

"My faith! Six years old, and making such excellent progress!" exclaimed the Abbé.

"I'm going on seven, Monsieur l'Abbé," Frederic informed him.

"But he really won't be seven for another eight months," Alphonse corrected.

"Well, at that rate, Frederic will surely be ready for the fifth class[1] by the time he's nine years old," responded the Abbé.

"Frederic loves to learn," said Madame Ozanam, "and Elisa loves to teach him. She seems to have a faculty for making any subject interesting."

Elisa flushed with pleasure. She had been a second mother to Frederic from his babyhood. She thoroughly understood him, for her own nature, like his, was fine and sensitive, without his stubborn insistence on having his own way. She realized that, like most children, he responded to honest compliments, and she never neglected to praise him for excellent recitals, and to reward him with little table luxuries she had fallen into the habit of denying herself. Nor did she fail to reprove him by reserved aloofness when he misbehaved.

"Sit still, Minerva! How can I draw your portrait if you move about?"

The small boy at the big carved black walnut desk put down his crayon in unconscious imitation of grown-up exasperation. The big cat on the sofa stretched, yawned, jumped down, looked at the boy with solemn superiority, and walked softly away.

"Perhaps, Frederic, Madame Minerva saw your picture of her and is insulted," suggested Alphonse, who was studying at the big table in the center of the room.

"Why, that's not too bad at all," said Elisa, putting aside her needlework and holding up his drawing with an air of admiration. "I'm certain it will be really good when you finish it."

With a few deft strokes of Frederic's crayon she made the portrait a passable resemblance to the white-faced, white-footed, but otherwise quite black Minerva.

1 Classes were numbered in reverse order; the higher the ordinal, the lower the class.

"See—just one or two touches was all the picture needed," she explained. "May I have it?"

"No—it's for Maman. For her feast day," he explained, "because she got Guigui to keep Lady Minerva when she was a little kitten and Guigui didn't want to because she said kittens were a nuisance."

Frederic had never forgotten the day three years before when he had found the kitten that was to become the present queenly Lady Minerva cowering in the courtyard. It had become a great family favorite, and a particular pet of Dr. Ozanam's. It was he who had named it after the Roman goddess of wisdom.

"I'm writing a poem for Maman, also," Frederic confided, handing Elisa a sheet of foolscap on which he had written several lines. "It's going to be another gift for her feast day."

Madame Ozanam's feast day was Assumption Day, now only a week away. It would be observed in the Ozanam household, as always, with a major celebration.

"This reads very well," said Elisa, perusing the verse. "Maman will be delighted. And I'll help you change just a word or two for better rhythm."

She did so forthwith, but in truth little needed to be done. For even at this early age Frederic had read much, and was revealing a command of words considerably beyond his years.

"Now you must memorize your poem, so you can declaim it to Maman," Elisa said.

"I'll try."

"Oh, you can do it easily. Just read it over and over. When you have it by heart, I'll hear you recite it so you can be sure you have it word for word."

Elisa had arranged a program for Maman's feast day. After a very special dinner, Dr. Ozanam escorted his wife to the chair of honor. Elisa played, and the rest of the family gathered about her at the pianoforte, and sang the old French songs their mother loved. The habitual melancholy that so many sorrows had induced left her, and she joined the singers at Elisa's side—this evening, at least, as joyful as the rest of the family.

Later the family presented gifts. Frederic, his heart beating

10

faster, advanced to his mother's side, holding the drawing of Madame Minerva behind his back. He began his verse and recited it smoothly to the end:

> *Ton Frédéric, chère Maman,*
> *Te présente aussi son offrande;*
> *De son coeur s'il suivait l' élan*
> *Sans doute elle serait plus grande.*
> *Pour mériter tout ton amour,*
> *Je t'offre le mien en partage,*
> *Et je veux à patir de ce jour*
> *Etre plus docile et plus sage.*[2]

With this, Frederic presented his portrait of Madame Minerva. Maman clasped him in her arms and kissed him, and marveled at the "so lifelike portrait of Madame Minerva, and the beauty and perfection of the verse." She pledged herself to cherish both forever.

Again they gathered around the pianoforte. Maman was now at the keyboard, and Dr. Ozanam's hearty baritone was leading the singing, when the rat-tat-tat of the door knocker made itself heard above the voices.

There was a sudden silence at the piano, for all knew this was probably a call for the doctor.

It was indeed, Guigui reported; a little boy living in one of the poorest quarters of the city was dangerously ill.

Madame Ozanam accompanied her husband to the door. "Let us know if the mother needs help," she said.

In less than an hour Dr. Ozanam returned.

"The boy is very sick," he reported. "He requires nursing

---

2 "Your Frederic, dear Mother,
  Presents you, also, his offering;
  If he followed the dictates of his heart
  It would, no doubt, be larger.
  To merit all your love,
  I offer you mine to share,
  And from this day I wish
  To be more docile and more wise."

Verse supplied from the Frederic Ozanam archives in Paris. It bears a note which, translated, reads: "Verse offered to his mother by Frederic Ozanam for her feast day, the 15th of August, 1819. (Aged six years, he was probably assisted by his sister.)"

every minute. And the mother has a sick husband—consumption—and four other little ones."

"I'll go at once," said Madame Ozanam.

"Not without me, Maman," insisted Elisa. "You must have help, or you'll wear yourself out."

Madame Ozanam was already gathering the supplies she generally carried with her on nursing missions. Hurriedly donning poke bonnets over their smooth-combed hair, the two set off for one of the most wretched sections of Lyons.

One afternoon in November of that year, Elisa became seriously ill. Her father, realizing that she had been stricken with meningitis, was in despair. He called in his fellow practitioners, but all efforts were vain. Death came quickly. While her family and the pastor of St. Pierre's recited the prayers for the dying, her soul sped to its Maker.

The fact of death was not unknown to the six-year-old Frederic. A baby brother, Charles Auguste, had died only a year before at the age of ten months. And he was dimly aware of the death of a sister who had died in infancy; he had been three and a half years old at the time. Moreover he knew from family conversation that his father was frequently called to the bedside of many described as "in danger of death"; and that Dr. Ozanam always carried a little book which contained prayers for the dying. He had heard that his father read these prayers beside a patient while awaiting the priest.

But the loss of his adored Elisa, who had been so close to him—this was beyond his child's comprehension. The shock left him utterly desolate and mentally numbed. He seemed to be living in a dream; he wandered listlessly about the house, stared unseeing at pictures on the wall, or out the windows. These pointless movements always brought him to a favorite chair of Elisa's in the drawing room, where she had so frequently sat to hear his lessons. He would kneel down at the chair and lay his head on his arm as if tired; he felt a great emptiness. For weeks, everything and everyone seemed remote, even his parents. It was as if a veil had been drawn between him and the outside world; life was dim and distant and unreal.

For the next three and a half years, the traumatic experience of his sister's death was to make Frederic's training and education a difficult problem to his anxious parents.

CHAPTER 2

GUIGUI, carrying a tray, swished indignantly through the door of Frederic's bedroom and, none too gently, set his dinner down on the little desk at which he was sitting.

She scowled at him as he carefully folded the sheet of paper on which he had been writing, addressed it "To Maman," and held it toward her with a polite request that she deliver it.

"No! I will not deliver your letters to Maman," she scolded. "Instead of writing these letters, why don't you stop demanding your own way and learn your lessons? Then you could eat at the table with the family. But no—you must always have your own way. And when you are punished, you must be always writing your complaints to Maman. You should know by now that these letters of yours change nothing."

She glared at him, but Frederic was unmoved. He was aware that beneath her tightly laced and colorful bodice—she had worn the peasant costume of her native province ever since coming to the home of Grandfather Ozanam at the age of twelve—there beat the tenderest of hearts. He knew that she loved him. Indeed, she loved all the Ozanams as her own, and had pressed her savings on them in their days of poverty; they in turn loved her as a member of the family.

With a final "har-umph," and a hopeless shake of her head, she flounced out, closing the door firmly and somewhat loudly behind her.

Frederic, ignoring his dinner, threw himself on his bed in

that contorted position young boys assume so naturally—one raised knee twisted tightly around the other, arms folded tightly beneath his head. In this tortuous posture he lay for some time, with chin set in stern defiance of his little world, staring at the ceiling. But soon the smell of the onion soup and roast chicken waiting on the desk proved too much for him; he arose and forgot his troubles in the pleasurable experience of satisfying the inner man.

He was being punished because he had revolted against authority when refused permission to go alone to the quays along the nearby Rhône—the fascinating quays with their picturesque river boats and swaggering boatmen. Instead, Maman had ordered him to apply himself more seriously to his studies.

Alas, recitation time—which came just before the 5:30 dinner—had found Frederic totally unprepared. Still rebellious, he had wasted his time. It was then that Maman had ordered him to his room until he had mastered his lessons.

There, still ignoring his books, Frederic had stubbornly set himself to writing a letter of complaint—his sixth under similar circumstances within a month.

Suddenly a far-off clock struck seven, and Frederic roused himself to intense scholarly application; the tender-hearted boy could not bear the thought of ending the day under his mother's disfavor. It was not long before he was able to appear at his bedroom door with the announcement to Maman that he was ready to recite.

These rebellions had begun to occur after Elisa's death: Frederic was unconsciously protesting against a tragedy he could not understand. His devotion to study ceased, and his continuing unhappiness made him a problem. He was by nature strong-willed, determined, and passionate. Before Elisa's death these characteristics had required occasional curbing; now their expression had become more frequent and pronounced. Tempted continuously to yield to Frederic's passionate protests, his mother prayed for guidance and strength—and her gentle but firm disciplining of the lad continued.

During much of this period, Frederic lived entirely within

14

a realm of his own. Older people seemed unreal and remote; the obligations they imposed futile and unimportant. Frederic had his own mysterious interests, and they were paramount.

As his ninth birthday approached, he was jolted awake by a crisis: if he were to gain entrance to the lower school of the Royal College,[1] he would have to apply himself manfully to the required studies. With new-found interest, he threw himself into the task of learning.

Then one momentous morning, about six months after his ninth birthday, he found himself in a classroom of the College, ready for entrance examinations. His ability to learn quickly had served him; he was admitted with a high test average.

If he experienced no setbacks, he would be graduated from the Royal College in eight years, at the age of seventeen.

Frederic's first day of school opened on a sunny autumn morning in 1822. Excited, eager, high-keyed, and somewhat apprehensive, he set out on the great adventure, swinging along proudly beside Alphonse. He felt grown up, for he was wearing the pantaloons and the short jacket that identified him an an "older" boy who had definitely left childhood behind him. With his cap at a rakish angle and his books slung over his shoulder in a strap, Frederic experienced a thrill of new importance as he realized that he was now, at last, a student at the Royal College.

It was a fleeting pleasure. Within sight of the College, his confidence oozed away. These familiar buildings, only five blocks from his home, suddenly loomed stark and grim. Two, three and four stories high, revealing various architectural periods, they rose up mysterious and forbidding. Only the chapel with its cross-surmounted dome seemed friendly and inviting.

This chapel the two brothers now entered.

"Here we separate," said Alphonse, putting a hand on Frederic's shoulder as they paused in the vestibule. "You must sit with your class. Just remember, everyone here started new,

[1] The College included what would correspond to elementary grades in a modern school.

once. You'll soon feel like an old-timer. See you after school."

In a few weeks, Frederic did feel like an old-timer. Gradually he applied himself with increasing devotion to his books. At the end of the term he captured first honors.

In his fourth class, Frederic continued for a little while to stand at the top. But as the weeks passed, he became listless and unambitious. Although still a fair student, he lost the class leadership.

His parents noticed that he had as little appetite for food as for study.

"Frederic must have complete rest, with plenty of fresh air and sunlight," said Dr. Ozanam.

"You mean he must go to the country?" asked his wife.

"Yes, for a few weeks. I shall write at once to my old friend d'Auvergne."

Monsieur d'Auvergne lived in a village not far from Lyons. He was a farmer.

At the d'Auvergne home, Frederic gained strength rapidly. Soon he was strong enough to play with the village boys, who liked this slight, pale, friendly lad from Lyons. For Frederic was now bringing his emotions under control, curbing his stormy protests when he failed to win in games. He was learning to accept defeat as something less than total tragedy.

Frequently his whole day was spent in the fields with Monsieur d'Auvergne and his peasant neighbors. Sometimes he drove the teams that drew the heavy two-wheeled farm carts, thrilling at his mastery over the huge, patient, feather-legged horses.

At the end of the month, his father came to check his progress, and to visit with his friend d'Auvergne, who had been a comrade-in-arms. He found a healthy, bright-eyed Frederic, eager to return to home and school, but the doctor remained three days to enjoy long talks with his old soldier friend.

They recalled at length their adventures together as hussars during Napoleon's Italian campaigns. Again their blood coursed faster as they dashed across the bridge at Lodi, pursued the foe at Rivoli, captured Mantua, and fought on twenty battlefields. Frederic, all eyes and ears, listened breathlessly. But the incident that stirred him most had its origin in

16

his father's attempt, in December of 1794, to rescue Frederic's grandfather, Benedict Ozanam, from prison, and the threat of the guillotine. Hearing of the latter's peril as his regiment was leaving the garrison at Bourg, Jean-Antoine, taking with him d'Auvergne and another friendly hussar, dashed to his parents' home in nearby Chalamont. With his companions he stalked in on a meeting of the town's *Comité de Surveillance*, which had denounced his father. At pistol point, he forced its registrar to sign a retraction of the charges. The young hussar's daring, and the fact that he had dramatically directed attention to what all the townspeople of Chalamont knew to be false charges, worked to his father's advantage. Benedict Ozanam was not executed, and a few months later was set at liberty. In later years, at Frederic's urging, his father wrote a brief account of the adventure.

Returning to school, Frederic found he was far behind in his studies. He missed the leadership of the fourth class by a decisive margin. The next year he studied diligently, and again became the leader.

Dr. Ozanam, still anxious about his son's health, instructed him to walk a goodly distance every day. In his "health walks" about Lyons, Frederic was seldom without a companion. Sometimes it was a book, sometimes a classmate. Frequently it was his father or mother. He accompanied his father on the rounds of his patients and his mother on her visits of charity—and discovered that frequently they were to the same families, for his father attended the poor without thought of fee. Through these excursions Frederic came to know the lives of those who, never far from want, realize daily the full significance of the petition, "Give us this day our daily bread."

His parents' solicitude for the unfortunate impressed him, deeply and lastingly.

Walking with Frederic through the streets of Lyons, his mother frequently related stories of places memorable to her from the days when she had seen the city ravaged and wrecked during the Revolution, and her childhood home destroyed. There were pleasant pauses, too, in the city's squares, and of them all Frederic's favorite was the spacious Place Bellecour, with its tree-lined promenade.

Frederic's walks with his father sometimes led along the charming banks of the Saône, sometimes to the paradise of woods and flowers known as the Ile Barbe. Often they were strenuous exercise for the frail youngster, as when he and his father climbed the high hill to the shrine of Notre Dame de Fourvières. Here, where popes and kings and queens and statesmen had worshipped, he learned increased devotion to the Mother of God amid evidences of the miracles of healing obtained through her intercession. From this eminence, too, he delighted in gazing down upon the city, stretched haphazardly along the banks of its two contrasting rivers.

At these times his father, standing beside him, was given to likening the Lyonnais, with their mixed northern and southern bloods, to the quiet Saône and the dashing Rhône.

"We're a people," he would say, "given to contemplation and dreams, but with the practical ability to realize our dreams."

He would look at Frederic and, studying him fondly, would tell himself that his son was truly one with the people of the ancient city—idealistic, but capable of translating inspiration into achievement.

Another of his father's favorite objectives on their walks together was the great Cathedral of St. Jean. One day as they paused before the looming façade of the ancient temple, Dr. Ozanam, looking up at it, referred to it as "the glory of Lyons, in which ages of art and architecture are united in harmonious praise of God." The scholarly physician always saw the pulsing industrial metropolis against its rich background of past glories and achievements.

"We sons of Lyons are truly elder sons of the Church, also," he would point out. "The Church of Gaul, Frederic, was born amid persecution of the Christians at Lyons under the Roman Emperor Marcus Aurelius 'way back in A.D. 177. You've seen St. Pothinus' statue in the left transept of St. Nizier's—well, he was bishop of the first Christian flock in France. And think of it!—*he* was a disciple of St. Polycarpe, and *that* saint was one of the sub-Apostles who had sat at the feet of St. John, the disciple who stood beneath the Cross. The very stones of this edifice link our Lyons with the early Christian martyrs, for they were taken from the city's Roman arenas. And on the spot on which this cathedral stands there once stood another cathedral that was two hundred years old when a bishop of western France raised Hugh Capet to the Carolingian throne, and France was born. So you see, my boy, we men of Lyons have roots in history."

With his eloquent and learned father guiding him on these walks about a city so studded with richly historic edifices, Frederic realized more and more how deeply rooted was the greatness of his country in the centuries of faith.

Unknowingly, he was being prepared for the vital contribution his future writings were to make toward a new appreciation of the culture and civilization of medieval times.

What he saw and learned during these formative years was to influence him all his life. During these boyhood walks there was born his interest in medieval history, which, expressed in his lectures and books, would one day help change the then fashionable disdain of culture of the Middle Ages to informed appreciation. To the boy, however, ancient Lyons and modern Lyons were one, and the city to him was primarily a vigorous, lively metropolis, teeming with workers and alive with industrial activity.

Yet it was a city still recovering from the savage Revolutionary conflicts of twenty-five years before, and for him its streets and buildings spoke of scenes and struggles in which his parents and grandparents had been participants.

There was, for instance, that crumbling section of the ancient city wall where his Grandfather Nantas had directed artillery fire against the merciless army of Robespierre. And on a street through which they frequently passed stood the very house in whose basement his mother, then twelve years old, had hidden with her parents and sisters from the agents of the Terror. Once, too, when they were on a journey to nearby Chalamont, his father had pointed out to him the road to Bourg—the road over which he had spurred his horse to rescue Frederic's Grandfather Ozanam from the guillotine.

These tales, heard from the lips of his parents, were exciting and historically instructive. But it was the example of his parents, and particularly their solicitude for the poor, that was to have the strongest influence on his character and on his career. The power of this example is evident in the tributes he paid to his parents in letters written years later.

Just before Frederic's thirteenth birthday, his father introduced him to a curious old book which intensified his feeling of intimate relationship to the past. Seated at his desk one day, Dr. Ozanam showed him an ancient tome, worn by time, its embossed leather cover revealing the artful skill of some medieval bookbinder. He opened it, and showed Frederic its contents, starting with the Office of Our Lady.

"This book," said his father, indicating the Gothic characters on delicately illuminated pages, "was lettered by one of the Ozanam family—a nun who lived three hundred years ago. Her name was Elizabeth Hozannam—for our name in her day was spelled with an *H* and an additional *n*.

"You see here the genealogy of the elder branch of the Ozanam family, to which we belong. And note here, where several generations since the sixteenth century have inscribed their names and dates, right down to the names of our own family."

Dr. Ozanam went on to explain that, inasmuch as Alphonse seemed destined for the priesthood, Frederic would probably be heir to the treasured volume.

"It may be God's will," he said, "that you, too, enter the life of religion. If not, you must preserve this treasure for your descendants."

Dr. Ozanam left Frederic studying the ancient manuscript. The boy had from time to time heard reference to his Jewish ancestors. Now, in this old record, the family's history came alive.

On the first pages of the record it was set down that Jeremiah Hozannam, a praetor in the Thirty-eighth Roman Legion, came over to Gaul with Julius Caesar. After subduing Seguvia, a country situated between Jura and the Alps, he received his share of the conquest. It was a canton named Belligum, lying north of Lyons, and later known as Bouligneux.

This territory, wrote Sister Elizabeth, was covered with woods and swamps. Jeremiah Hozannam reclaimed it and founded a small Jewish colony. He died in 43 B.C., the year after Caesar was assassinated.

To Frederic, as he read, the recorded names of his ancestors brought to mind chapters in the family Bible; Jacob, Elias, Abimelech, Jehoshaphat, Shem, Abel, Isaac, Moses, and other great men of the Old Testament. In the Hozannam genealogy, such Old Testament names prevailed down to the seventh century, when the listing began to consist of Christian saints' names.

It was an act of courageous charity by the head of the Hozannam clan which in the seventh century led him and his people into the Church. The family record recounted how St. Didier, fleeing from pursuers who sought to slay him, concealed himself in a forest near the Hozannam village of Bouligneux. The bloody Queen Brunhaut, whose wickedness the holy bishop had denounced, would have ruthlessly put to death anyone who sheltered him. Risking her wrath, Samuel Hozannam, chief of the tribe, offered St. Didier the refuge of his home.

While hidden in the Hozannam dwelling, St. Didier spoke to the family about the rejected Messiah. They listened and, led by Samuel, humbly prayed to the God of their fathers to know the truth. God gave them the gift of faith, and they were baptized.

Down through the centuries, Frederic's ancestors retained the ancient family name of Hozannam. (This, Frederic was to discover when he later studied Hebrew, was a Latinization of the Hebrew for "save now, we pray.") It was Frederic's grandfather who decided to give the family name its French form by suppressing the H and n—quite useless in French pronunciation. Thus Jacques Hozannam, a great-granduncle of Frederic's and the most celebrated mathematician of his day, was known to his contemporaries under the old form.

Shortly after receiving responsibility for the book of family genealogy, Frederic made his First Holy Communion—on May 2, 1826.

He prepared by making the customary retreat. In a notebook[2] he jotted down for future reference a summary of the talks given by the retreat master, and the resolutions they had inspired. For weeks preceding his First Communion he increased his fault-correcting efforts. To discipline himself, to perfect himself for the coming of his Saviour, he gave up many normal pleasures.

The night before his First Communion Day, following a custom common in many French families, Frederic came to his parents as they sat in the living room and knelt before them, entreated their pardon for what he called his "many transgressions" against their commands, and asked their blessing. They laid their hands upon his head and blessed him as the patriarchs of old had blessed their children

Next morning Frederic set off for St. Pierre's, walking between his older brother Alphonse and six-year-old Charles, behind his frock-coated father and his mother in her shoulder cape and wide-flounced dress. Guigui had hastened to an early Mass that she might have time to prepare a breakfast suitable to the great day.

Frederic's clothes were all new—pantaloons, fairly tight and of ankle length, though not strapped under the foot as were those of his father and Alphonse; short, double-breasted jacket with wide, turndown collar; and top hat. The top hat was the customary headgear of young gentlemen, and of older gentlemen, too. It was the sign of the upper classes in an era of formality in dress and manners—but on Frederic's head in his adult years it was to be seen more frequently in the tenements of the poor than in the mansions of the powerful.

The first Tuesday in May was the kind of morning a First Communion morning should be—sun-drenched, with a bracing breeze redolent of spring's new life and hope. That doughty champion of Christianity, St. Athanasius, whose feast day it was, could not have selected a more delightful morning for the First Communion of the youngster who was also, in fulfilling what he considered his duties as a Catholic layman, to devote his life to promoting the acceptance of Christian truth.

2 This notebook was lost during World War II.

22

The bishop himself intoned the solemn Mass, and administered the sacraments. When the great moment came, Frederic advanced to the Communion rail, his parents and brother Alphonse accompanying him. He awaited the administration of the Sacred Host with an overwhelming realization of his own unworthiness, and with gratitude for the infinite love of Him who was about to incorporate Himself with him, Body and Blood, Soul and Divinity. The Bread of Life was placed upon his tongue, and he was one with his Saviour.

The bishop read the boy's intense humility and devotion in his face, and joy filled his heart; he felt that this First Communicant possessed an adult insight into the Mystery of Faith.

Other boys, well trained and devout, also received their First Communion, and were later that morning confirmed in St. Pierre's; among them Frederic's particular friends, Chaurand, Pessonneau and Falconnet; the latter two were his cousins. Later, they were to be among his first colleagues in the St. Vincent de Paul Society.

CHAPTER 3

READING his breviary as he walked back and forth in the college courtyard, the Abbé Noirot lifted his eyes at a sudden burst of laughter from a student group. He smiled appreciatively as he passed them, for he approved of student gaiety.

A few more steps and he encountered Monsieur Legeay, an instructor.

"Ah, monsieur," greeted the Abbé, upon whose prayers thoughts of his beloved students had been intruding themselves, "I've just been noticing some of your Latin pupils— those lighthearted fellows on your left. They're a merry lot. It's my experience that such high spirits betoken healthy minds."

Monsieur Legeay studied the group.

"They're fine boys," he agreed, "and gathered, as usual, about one they admire."

"You mean young Ozanam?" asked the Abbé, peering over his spectacles.

"Yes, Frederic Ozanam. You know his family well, I believe."

"I do—and I've known Frederic since he was knee-high," said the Abbé. "He's an impressive student. He heads the hundred and thirty members of our Rhetoric class in every subject. Yet he's but fifteen."

"He's the youngest in his class," answered Monsieur Legeay. "And he's excellent in Latin. Did you know that he writes rather good Latin verse? I've even saved some of it—it's so well done. I wonder, my dear Abbé, whether you might not find some of the selections worthy of your perusal?"

"Certainly," said the Abbé. "I'd like to read them. I'm particularly interested in that young man."

For a moment or two, both schoolmen studied Frederic Ozanam as he held forth gaily to his laughing comrades. They saw a slim youth of average height for his fifteen years. In his pale oval face, gray-blue eyes were set wide apart beneath eyebrows more straight than arched. The mouth was fairly wide, full and sensitive; the straight, rather broad nose slightly prominent; the forehead high and broad. His chestnut hair—a true chestnut, not at all red—was somewhat long, in the style of the day, and brushed back from his forehead so that it fell to either side with only a faint suggestion of a part.

A bell began ringing inside the college.

"Good heavens, how time outpaces us!" exclaimed the Abbé, looking sadly at his neglected breviary. "Well, monsieur, it's back to our classrooms."

"Yes, youth must be served—in more senses than one!" laughed Monsieur Legeay, adding, "I'll try to bring you young Ozanam's verses today."

If time outpaced the Abbé, it was scarcely more mercurial than Frederic. He was in that golden period of youth when all the world seems fresh and gay and brightly colored, and not the smallest cloud troubles the horizon of the mind. These were the free, the joyful years when most youngsters approaching early manhood are as yet strangers to life's cares, and the still unburdened heart sings with gladness.

Certainly, Frederic had every reason to be happy. He loved, and he was loved by, his parents and his brothers. His schoolfellows gave him their affection and their admiration; his professors regarded him with that high favor reserved for the manly student whose sense of humor renders him modest, and whose sense of responsibility makes him diligent.

He had entered the class of higher studies at fourteen, and —though years later he accused himself of laziness at this time—he was in fact a notably able student. He early fell in love with Latin, and when only twelve he had begun to write Latin verse. It was the most recent of such verses that Monsieur Legeay had praised, and which, true to his promise, he brought to the Abbé Noirot after classes that day.

Sitting alone in his room after the evening meal, the Abbé read the verses with mounting interest. The subjects, highly varied, revealed a soaring imagination, elevation of mind, and a mature penetration into the significance of historical events. They strongly reflected, also, Frederic's devotion to the Church and to France.

"A most gifted young man," the Abbé told himself, as he finally put aside the Latin poems. "May Ozanam always devote his mind and his pen to the honor and glory of God."

How quickly the human soul can pass from joy to agony! Only a few weeks after the Abbé Noirot had commented on his cheerfulness and gaiety, Frederic was walking the narrow streets of Lyons, alone, and almost despairing. He felt old and weary; life was bleak and blank, a burden almost too great to bear.

A spiritual sickness had seized him and was tormenting him as it had tormented innumerable young Christians before him, and as it undoubtedly will torment innumerable others till the end of time. He had awakened suddenly one day to the

25

great questions that can arise when the finite intellect contemplates the Infinite. He had quickly entangled himself, this precocious, intellectual lad of fifteen, in his own unaided attempts to solve his difficulties. These difficulties his highly analytical but inexperienced mind magnified to enormous proportions.

His troubles had commenced a month before. There were at the Royal College skeptical older students who gave free and positive voice to their challenges to revealed religion. Most young men are radicals at heart, and many love to shout their radicalism, whether in politics, religion, or anything else, from the housetops. Day after day, Frederic's ears were assailed by their expressions of unbelief, and one day he suddenly asked himself, "Why do I believe?"

This was no mere adolescent self-questioning. Its basic nature reveals an adult mind. That mind began to try to probe the unfathomable mysteries of God, and theological difficulties, of course, presented themselves. He read books establishing the foundations of the Faith, but though great intellects had met and resolved these same questions time after time down through the ages, the difficulties still tortured him.

When he brought his struggle to the attention of his confessor, the confessor's elucidations gave only momentary satisfaction, for to merely human intelligence no explanation of the Infinite can prove fully adequate. Again Frederic's active mind would begin its questionings, not realizing that faith by its very nature assumed a limited understanding.

He was, in truth, undergoing a major temptation against faith, and to this his restless intellect and limited experience made him singularly susceptible. He resisted with all his will and all the love he had in his heart for his Creator and Redeemer, but the struggle went on and became a ceaseless, savage torture.

Frederic knew, academically, that faith is a gift from God. But he had still to experience in himself how that gift must so often be come by. He had still to learn that man must ask for the gift of faith humbly and prayerfully if he is to receive it, or to retain it.

His difficulties were increased by the formal questionings

which his philosophical studies presented—whether certitude is possible, what is the extent of human knowledge, and by what tests or criteria truth may be distinguished from falsehood. These questions confused him, made him more uncertain than ever.

Over a period of several months, he repelled repeated assaults upon his will to believe. These attacks oppressed him through much of his philosophy course—his final year at the Royal College—and were intensified in their effect by scrupulosity. So savage did they become that in after years he was never able to allude to them without abhorrence.

Toward the end of his last term, the temptations against faith became stronger and sharper; he felt surrounded by impenetrable darkness, and utterly alone.

Many years after this long, acutely painful struggle, Frederic was to write of "the horror of those doubts that eat into the heart, pursuing us even at night to the pillow we have drenched with tears."

[By "doubts" he plainly means "difficulties"—difficulties that can become doubts only when accepted as a negation of Divine revelation. For, as he was to assert long afterwards, he "repulsed the doubt."]

"In this state," he then wrote, "I began my philosophy. The thesis of 'certainty' bewildered me; it seemed to me for a moment that I might doubt my own existence."

In this nighttime of his soul he left college one day, walking aimlessly, scarcely knowing his direction. Suddenly, he became conscious that he was at the Place des Cordeliers, before the Church of St. Bonaventure.

He entered, and drew near the tabernacle. Spiritually exhausted, and with a deep sense of his own inadequacy and need, he knelt and prayed humbly to his Eucharistic Lord. He asked that the Holy Spirit be sent upon him, that his faith might be strengthened, and his mind never again be tortured by difficulties.

He pleaded for the gift of absolute faith; faith positive, perfect, certain, unshakable—the kind of faith which came to the Apostles on Pentecost. He was begging for a great gift—and he made the greatest offering within his power to promise.

He pledged, in return for the gift of impregnable faith, to consecrate his life to God's service.

From St. Bonaventure's, Frederic, now walking briskly and with purpose, returned directly to the college. There, he asked for the Abbé Noirot. Soon he was placing before that master of spiritual counseling all the difficulties that had tormented him through most of his rhetoric year.

The Abbé Noirot was reputed one of the most lucid philosophers of his day; he was, besides, a most able theologian. A master of the Socratic method, his questioning process gently led the boy to recognize that the finite intellect could recognize only remote approaches to Infinite Truth. As he talked, light streamed into Frederic's mind; his plea before the altar of St. Bonaventure's was being answered. Further talks with the Abbé answered that plea fully and finally.

Henceforth he believed, as he later related, "with an assured faith."

Touched by God's goodness, he renewed his vow to spend himself that men might know God and His love for men. From that moment, he held this pledge a most solemn obligation, to be discharged continuously every succeeding day of his life.

Thus Divine Providence strengthened him by struggle and suffering, confirming his faith, and preparing him to serve that faith valiantly in the years to come.

Dr. Ozanam envisioned Frederic as a barrister who would in later years become a member of the magistracy or perhaps a judge of the Royal Court. Frederic's clear, logical mind and rigid integrity would, he thought, make him an honored member of the judiciary, and as such a consolation to his parents in their later years.

While Frederic would have preferred a literary career, he accepted his father's counsel as sound and practical. Normally, he would have set off at once for Paris and its University; it was only there that one could obtain a formal legal education. But Paris in 1830, following the overthrow of Charles X, was a center of violent disturbance. Besides, skeptics and atheists controlled the University of Paris. Its student body, too, was reported to be overwhelmingly anti-Christian.

Frederic, it was determined, should remain in Lyons for two years before going to Paris. By then he would be more mature, the capital would have calmed down, and the University might have become more Christian in spirit. In the meantime, the eighteen-year-old youth would clerk in a law office as practical preparation for his legal career.

The student who loved history and poetry found the copying of briefs and opinions dreary and depressing. Missing the scholarly activities of the Royal College, he undertook at home the study of English, German, and Hebrew; he even dipped into Sanskrit, and enrolled in an art school.

Frederic's dull law office routine was soon disturbed by the blatant boasting of two sex-obsessed law clerks. They detailed their debaucheries boldly and loudly.

Seated one day amid his fellow workers, and intent on his scrivening, Frederic found his ears assailed by the obscene recitals. He turned and faced the two offenders squarely.

"Don't confess your shabby adventures to us," he said, shortly and bluntly. "Your proper audience is a priest in the privacy of the confessional. Try it. You'll feel a lot better."

The brief rebuke was effective.

At art school, too, the naturally reserved Ozanam found his moral courage put to the test. A few students delighted in ridicule of all that Christian men hold sacred. For the first few days after the new session of the art school opened they were somewhat restrained, but it was not long before they went much farther than Frederic thought they should be permitted to go without dissent.

He was busy at his drawing board when one of the ribald students voiced an outrageous insult to religion. Ozanam's pale face became a shade whiter, and his voice vibrated with indignation as he began to speak even while arising from his chair. Yet such was his charity, and his ability to place himself in another's position, that his words were far milder than his manner.

"Messieurs, I have no doubt your family backgrounds are

those of atheism, or at least disbelief in religion," he said. "Otherwise you would perceive how painful it is to us Christians to hear you make the ancient and holy things we hold sacred the butt of your scorn and your ribald jests, even as Our Lord Jesus Christ was made the butt of scorn and jests at the time of his scourging and Crucifixion. It is as if you engaged in coarse amusement at the expense of our mothers. You would not, we know, do that to us any more than we'd do it to you. So we ask you to respect our viewpoint and our sensibilities as you would expect us, in common courtesy, to respect yours."

Léonce Curvier, an industrial apprentice who was a student at the art school, never forgot the scene. He marveled at Frederic's ability to command respect for religion without injuring the feelings of those he censured. All his life Frederic was one of those few who are able to win the liking and admiration of opponents while destroying their position.

In these personal encounters Frederic acted on this simple, practical principle: *Do without hesitation anything that needs to be done in God's service.*

Since his pledge before the Blessed Sacrament in the Church of St. Bonaventure he had acted constantly on that principle, and he was to continue to act on it throughout his life.

CHAPTER 4

"WHY the crowd, monsieur?" Frederic, hastening with his cousin Falconnet toward the Place Bellecour, stopped to put the question to an elderly man coming from that noble quadrangle.

The gentleman pointed toward the square and its huge

equestrian statue of Louis XIV, in whose shadow a man in a blue smock was speaking to a crowd of which he was the center.

"That speaker, as you can see by his blue garb, is a Saint-Simonian," he said. "He spearheads a new invasion of Lyons. A peaceful invasion"—irony edged the old man's voice—"promising sweetness and light, and plenty for all."

"I've been reading about these Saint-Simonians in the press," said Frederic. "They herald a new heaven on earth."

"At least, they've convinced thousands to that effect," returned the gentleman. "They regard Christianity as having been quite all right for past ages, but entirely inadequate to solve the world's present problems."

"Thank you, monsieur," said Falconnet. "We'll go and hear what this bluebird is singing."

As they arrived at the edge of the crowd, the speaker was concluding his talk.

"Do not think we oppose Christianity!" he cried. "In its time, Christianity sufficed. But today we live in a new world. That is why we offer you a new doctrine—a doctrine of progress, of brotherhood, of economic justice. We bring you a new basis for a society that—through industry, through engineering, through science—will guarantee that each of you shall share in the world's wealth according to his production and craftsmanship. That is our message; this is our promise. We invite you to advance with us to its fulfillment."

Excited comment greeted the speaker's conclusion.

"He has made an impression," observed Falconnet. "But at least these Saint-Simonians don't resort to violent denunciations and bitterness, as do the atheists."

"No," responded Frederic, "they use a deadlier tactic. They belittle Christianity, rather than condemn it. They should be answered."

"Why, then, don't *you* answer them?" urged Falconnet.

"I will," said Frederic.

Falconnet was unaware that his impulsive challenge was also a reminder. It recalled forcefully to Frederic's mind that but a few months before he had promised to devote his life to spreading knowledge of God's love and truth.

31

He wrote till late that night, and was at his writing desk early the next morning. Before he left for the law office he had completed an article for submission to *Le Précurseur*, a Lyons newspaper that upheld Saint-Simonism.

Frederic's article appeared in *Le Précurseur*, and was widely read. Despite its clear, strong arguments against Saint-Simonism—or, perhaps, because of them—the editor of *Le Précurseur* failed to answer it, though when accepting it he had insisted he would do so.

His friends urged Frederic to develop the monograph further, and he responded with a hundred-page brochure that won scholarly approval. Alphonse de Lamartine, greatest French orator and poet of the time, owned himself "inspired and filled with admiration by it." Chateaubriand, whose brilliant writings had done so much to repair the ravages that eighteenth-century skepticism had made upon the human mind, referred to the work as "excellently conceived."

All this was heady praise for an eighteen-year-old, and Frederic in a letter to a friend confessed himself "persecuted by a violent desire for publicity." He regarded this desire as a temptation to pride. To combat it, he set himself the ideal of laboring solely to please God.

This working principle heightened his charity toward all with whom he later crossed literary swords. From the very first, good temper was as characteristic of his writings as were wide knowledge, eloquence, and loftiness of thought. He was already thinking of himself as a writer; his whole bent was toward authorship rather than law. Even before the Saint-Simonian article, he had conceived the idea of a monumental work that would examine the chief religious beliefs throughout the ages.

"It would," he told the Abbé Noirot, with the enthusiasm of youth, "go back to the beginnings of religions, and I'd probably have to learn twelve languages, and the history of all religions." In this work, he said, he expected to have the co-operation of scholarly young friends with whom he was already discussing it.

The Abbé smiled benevolently, marveling at the brave and

soaring spirit of the youth who could calmly contemplate learning a dozen languages, and felt more strongly than ever that the young man's confinement to a law office was the wasting of unusual aspiration and talent.

Dr. Ozanam, too, was becoming uneasy over the long interruption to his son's university education, and he decided to consult the Abbé Noirot. The Abbé urged him to send Frederic to the Sorbonne in Paris without further delay.

"Our Catholic students," he said, "must from now on take their rightful part in the University's life. They must train themselves to become members of its faculty. They must rescue the University from the unbelievers. Otherwise, they will be deprived of the higher education necessary to leadership, and that means surrendering France to the enemies of religion."

One morning in November, 1831, Frederic boarded the iron river boat *Swallow* on the first leg of his journey to Paris, and the Sorbonne. He stood at the stern and waved to his parents, his brothers, Guigui, and friends, till the boat rounded a bend in the stream at the Pont de Nemours, and family and friends were lost to sight. He suddenly felt alone, and lonely—still more so when he thought of the University and the strange city of Paris. For to Frederic, Paris was more than the City of Light, center of the world's culture, home of the great leaders in literature, in art, in science. Its University, he felt, was inviting him not only to new studies and learning, but challenging him to combat.

Toward evening the *Swallow* docked at Chalon, whence Frederic took the early diligence for Paris. The air was cool and fresh; the five horses, with three abreast in the lead, pulled well, and the diligence—the driver cracking his whip like so many pistol shots—was soon out of town and rumbling along briskly on the northeast road to the metropolis. The journey seemed endless, but eventually his coach passed the eastern barrier and started slowly through the capital's crooked streets. It seemed hours to the tired and now impatient Frederic before they drew up at the depot. In a few minutes, with his two carpet bags and his small trunk, Frederic was in a cab headed for the *pension* which was to be his home during his university days in Paris.

The *pension de famille* to which Frederic had directed the cab driver was near the Jardin des Plantes. He was astonished that his driver found it with so little difficulty, for the side streets were unlighted, and the night was black.

It was after ten o'clock when Frederic sounded the knocker on the pension door. A tall, scrawny woman in a beribboned dress opened the door a few inches and held a candle to his face, inspecting him shrewdly. Frederic, whose mother had arranged for the pension through a Parisian friend, introduced himself, and the woman bade him enter. She made herself known as Madame Marcel, the *propriétaire de la pension*. In short order Frederic was installed in his room and, thoroughly tired from his journey, was quickly sound asleep.

He awoke too late the next morning for the regular breakfast and, excited at the prospect of his first daylight view of Paris, decided to forgo it. Instead, he set off for the School of Law and the Sorbonne, asking directions from passersby.

He found homself walking through a maze of cobblestone streets, past shop windows displaying boots and umbrellas and garments; past cafés before which sat couples playing dominoes, individuals reading newspapers, and others idly viewing the passing parade; past male pedestrians wearing top hats and frock coats like his own, and women in high-crowned bonnets and bell-shaped skirts. But unlike himself, most of the men wore beards—beards almost as varied in color as their coats; beards long, beards short; beards pointed, beards round; beards like spades and beards as thin as rapiers.

Finally, Frederic came to the Rue de l'Enfer[1] and the Luxembourg Gardens. There he lingered for a few minutes, looking across the beautiful Gardens toward the Chamber of Peers. Before him passed a rumbling procession of carriages, carts, and omnibuses painted green, yellow, or blue, and among the vehicles rode horsemen in frock coats as colorful as the buses.

[1]Today the Boulevard St. Michel. The street names given throughout are those known to the Parisian of 1830—1848. Since those days, the plan of the city has been transformed.

34

Absorbed in all the new life about him, he had overshot the Sorbonne a little, and now, walking back, he found himself standing before the façade of its church, above which rose the great dome. Going inside, he knelt before the Blessed Sacrament, gave thanks for his safe arrival in Paris, and asked a blessing on his labors there.

Young Ozanam had enrolled in the School of Law, and for literary, historical, and philosophical courses in the College of France and the Sorbonne. His fellow students were for the most part from upper-class families such as his own—neither aristocrats nor *petits bourgeois*, neither rich nor poor, but actively interested in artistic, scientific, and literary progress. These upper-class families considered a classical and professional education the most necessary of possessions. From them came the nation's writers, lawyers, educators, architects, physicians, and engineers.

Most of the students lived in the square mile or more known as the Latin Quarter, of which the various colleges constituted the heart. To the superficial observer this historic section would seem an intellectual jungle of ideas and movements, teeming with hot-eyed propagandists for every kind of social, economic, and scientific panacea, and equally tolerant of all. Yet there was one exception.

While the Latin Quarter welcomed every new "ism," there dwelt in its heart—that is, in the University—a power which could not tolerate the age-old idea of a personal God. Against the claims of Christianity most of the University professors waged war, open or disguised. Many Catholic parents refused to subject their sons to such dominating and insidious influence, and Catholic students were therefore a minority.

Indeed, for several weeks after Frederic had started attending the School of Law, he was able to identify only three other Catholics among his schoolfellows. He was on the lookout for more co-religionists, for he felt the need of like-minded comrades; he had been made unpleasantly aware that many of his fellow students were aggressively anti-Christian.

Unfortunately, he was unable to enjoy fully the companionship of the few Christian students he did know, because

Madame Marcel's pension was an inconvenient distance from the center of student life, as well as from schools and library. On other scores, too, he was unhappy with Madame Marcel's. The atmosphere of the house, with the strident excitement of its nightly card games, made study difficult. The blatant hilarity of the players emphasized his loneliness. So did Madame Marcel's practice of serving meat on Fridays and other days of abstinence. Frederic rather sadly found himself dining on bread and cheese while his fellow *pensionnaires* on these days consumed—with irritating gusto—his share of the meat.

Frederic intimated something of these conditions to his parents in a letter asking permission "to make some other arrangement." He was awaiting an answer when, one gloomy Sunday afternoon, he decided to call on a great man, a fellow Lyonnais to whom he had been introduced at a reception in Lyons a few months before. This was the eminent Monsieur André Marie Ampère, France's foremost mathematician and physical scientist. Now in his fifty-sixth year, Ampère was a member of the Institute, and honored throughout the world as the founder of the science of electrodynamics.

Like everyone else in Lyons, Frederic had heard many stories of Ampère's marvelous genius; among them, how he had, before his tenth year, solved highly intricate mathematical problems and read the most serious works of history, poetry, and philosophy. At thirteen, he had applied at the Lyons library for the most difficult books on higher mathematics; finding them written in Latin, he had mastered that language within a month and then proceeded to digest the abstruse volumes few adults could understand.

This towering genius was as simple as a child. He welcomed Frederic wholeheartedly, and inquired with sincere interest into his experiences thus far in Paris. In answer, Frederic detailed his courses at the University.

"And your pension?" asked Monsieur Ampère. "You find it to your liking?"

Momentarily Frederic hesitated for an answer. He disliked burdening such a personage with personal grievances. He became embarrassed, he flushed—and the savant saw at once that his young guest was troubled.

"My dear Frederic," he urged, "feel free to speak of your situation to me as you would to your father. Perhaps I can help you."

With this, Frederic described the disadvantages of his pension.

"On all scores, Frederic, you must move from this distracting pension as quickly as possible," counseled the great man. "Your present arrangement will interfere with your progress as a student."

With this he arose, took the youth by the arm, led him to a door and, throwing it open, disclosed a large, comfortably furnished bedroom. Windows looked out on a pleasant garden, and one wall was lined with books.

"How do you like this room?—it is my son's," queried Monsieur Ampère.

Frederic, puzzled, said that it seemed most comfortable, indeed.

"Then come and take possession of it—it is yours," said Monsieur Ampère, heartily. "Jean-Jacques is studying and traveling abroad; he's specializing in German literature, you know. My son is about twelve years older than you, Frederic, but when he returns to Paris, I hope you will come to know him well. In the meantime, I know he would be delighted to have his room and library at your disposal."

Monsieur Ampère pulled at his side whiskers, smiled quizzically behind his thick-lensed spectacles, and held his massive head, with its thick, wavy hair, to one side as he peered at Frederic.

"I pray you to take it," he said, his tone implying that Frederic would be doing him an immense favor by accepting. "You will make one of my family. And you will have no more difficulties at Friday meals. Also, my sister and my daughter dine with us—that will provide a little society for you. And you'll be close to your classes, and your friends."

"How generous you are!" exclaimed Frederic. "How can I thank you enough? You overwhelm me with your kindness. My parents will be delighted. I shall write them at once."

Two days after he had been installed in the Ampère home, Frederic wrote to his parents, describing his life there:

We breakfast at ten, and dine at half past five, all together—Monsieur Ampère, his daughter, and sister. Monsieur Ampère talks a good deal, and his conversation is amusing and always instructive. Since I have been here (two days), I have already learned many things from him.

His daughter talks cleverly, and takes part in all that is said. Monsieur Ampère is very endearing in his manner toward her, but he never speaks to her of anything except science.

He has a prodigious memory for everything scientific, and in every conceivable department of knowledge, but he never remembers anything in connection with the *ménage*. The discoveries which have raised him to the pinnacle where he stands today came to him all at once, he tells me, by intuition. He is just now finishing a grand plan for an Encyclopedia.

Are you not glad, my dear father, to have me under the roof of this kind and excellent man?—I forgot to tell you that the most perfect politeness reigns in the family. I also forgot to give you my address—19 Rue des Fossés St. Victor.

As a friend—in a sense, a protégé—of the honored Ampère, Frederic became acquainted with some of the most distinguished men of science and letters in Paris. In each of these visitors to the Ampère home he encountered a stimulating intellectual experience.

He had been homesick, but this abated as the thrill of meeting and listening to these eminent savants lent high color and interest to his days. His friends from Lyons, also, were good for his morale; his new, more central location now permitted continuous companionship with them.

To Frederic, Monsieur Ampère's many-faceted genius was constantly a fresh source of wonderment, and the admiration was not entirely one-sided. Monsieur Ampère discovered in his young guest an extraordinary aptitude for mathematics. (He was later to declare that Frederic could have become the first mathematician of his age.) He respected the talented student's mind, and talked often with him, chiefly on philosophy and science. The great physicist was at the peak of his intellectual powers; his penetrating mind ranged the universe. Frederic found his own mental horizon expanding enormously as he followed his illustrious friend to new, high plateaus of scientific speculation and philosophical understanding. His association with Monsieur Ampère became still more beneficial when the latter asked him to act as his literary secretary and amanuensis in the writing of Ampère's *Philosophie des Sciences*.

Monsieur Ampère saw in every new scientific discovery a proof and glorification of the Creator's power, wisdom and love. In a time of rampant skepticism he was the firmest and most devout of Catholics. When the irreligion of Frederic's fellow students and professors weighed heavily on that young man's spirit, as they often did, the rocklike faith of this intellectual giant was a sheltering promontory in whose calm lee he found comfort and peace of heart.

One day—it was about two months after he had come to the Ampère home—Frederic, walking along the Rue de la Montagne St. Geneviève, came to his parish church of St. Etienne-du-Mont. He entered, and walked toward the altar to adore. The church, shrouded in the gathering shadows of a late winter afternoon, seemed empty, and the near-sighted Frederic was almost upon a kneeling man before he saw him. He recognized Monsieur Ampère, and quickly drew back that he might not disturb his friend's devotions, for the savant was praying with that childlike faith which is a prerequisite for entrance into the kingdom of heaven. Into Frederic's eyes there welled tears of contrition for his own disheartenment and self-pity. He sank to his knees, also, and prayed, and his prayer was for greater confidence and courage.

If Monsieur Ampère influenced Frederic by his intellect and life and faith, another great man was to influence him strongly with a word.

Before leaving Lyons, Frederic had been given a letter of introduction to François-René de Chateaubriand, who had been Foreign Minister under Charles X. Now at the height of his dominance as France's foremost literary genius, his writings had powerfully swayed European thought. A converted skeptic, he had championed Catholic truth so brilliantly that he was described as having "reinstated religion in the world."

One Sunday, bearing his letter of introduction, Frederic set out for the Chateaubriand home, arriving just after the great man had come in from Mass.

The distinguished litterateur, with lively interest, inquired as to Frederic's plans, his studies, his tastes.

"Do you like the theatre?" he asked, finally.

"I have not been to the theatre," replied Frederic.

"And do you look forward to attending?" pursued Monsieur Chateaubriand.

Frederic paused, confused. Should he confess to this prince of intellectual sophisticates that he had made his mother what might seem to Chateaubriand an "apron strings" promise not to attend the Parisian theatre? True, the theatre at this period was being brutalized by shockingly immoral plays. But to attend was considered a mark of "intellectual independence."

As Frederic hesitated, Monsieur Chateaubriand's gaze remained bent upon him. Then the young man's courage and love of truth triumphed.

"Before leaving home," he said, "my mother asked me to avoid the Paris theatre. I made her that promise—and I intend keeping it."

Chateaubriand beamed with satisfaction.

"I implore you," he said, "to remain true to your word. You will gain little at the theatre, and you might lose a great deal."

Many times in the next two or three years Frederic was to use this counsel, backed by the towering prestige of Chateaubriand, as indirect suasion against indiscriminate theatre attendance. When "morally emancipated" students urged him to go with them to a play, he would answer: "Monsieur de

Chateaubriand has advised me strongly not to form the habit of theatre-going in these days of a decadent stage."

That night, telling Monsieur Ampère of his visit to Chateaubriand, he commented that even if he desired to frequent the theatre, he wouldn't know where to find the time.

"I'm sure," he said, "that no current play could afford me a fraction of the intellectual interest I find in listening to your conversation and that of your scholarly friends. And what remaining time I have from my studies I'd much rather spend with my schoolfellows from Lyons. You've probably noticed that my books eat up most of my time. I feel that I must study hard to make the most of whatever talents I possess."

Monsieur Ampère answered him with a quotation. "I'm happy, Frederic," he said, with fatherly interest, "to see that you are following the precepts set down in chapter thirty-three of Ecclesiasticus: 'In all thy works, be excellent.' Whatever your chosen profession may be, master it. For through such mastery you will become of the greatest service to your fellow men, and through your fellow men to the God who gave you being, and to Whom you owe your best."

CHAPTER 5

"AT TIMES, Monsieur l'Abbé, I see Paris as a huge corpse to which my youth is chained."

The Abbé Marduel was very old, and very wise, and he smiled understandingly as he regarded the very discouraged young man sitting opposite him in the poor little reception room of his apartment in the Rue Massillon.

"Doesn't Paris seem a little too lively for a corpse, my dear Frederic?" he asked gently.

"Yes, physically lively, but soulless," insisted young Ozanam. "Paris is a spiritual corpse, if one may be permitted to use such a term."

The Abbé Marduel had been vicar of the beautiful church of St. Nizier in Lyons which Frederic knew so well. Formerly, too, he had been spiritual director of Frederic's brother, the Abbé Alphonse. Just before Frederic had boarded the river boat for his trip to Paris, his brother had said to him: "When you reach Paris, let little time elapse before calling on the Abbé Marduel. You will find his counsel invaluable. He dwells close to God."

On inquiring in Paris about the Abbé, Frederic had found that he was well known among the city's Catholics. Old and half blind, he had desired to live in semi-retirement. But his spiritual wisdom drew to him people from all walks of life. They gave him little time for prayer as they crowded into his modest living quarters on the Rue Massillon, in the shadow of the Cathedral of Notre Dame. Frederic had visited the Abbé once before, and now on his second visit was confiding to him his feeling of discouragement.

"There seems so little Christian charity and faith in Paris," Frederic now insisted. "Skeptics and atheists dominate the University. Out of twenty-seven hundred students in the School of Law, I've so far run across only about a dozen Christians—or students, at least, who have made themselves known as such."

The Abbé Marduel possessed that paradoxical, sometimes startling, insight and practicality so frequently found in those who have eliminated from their lives all attachment to the material world.

"You are now fully established in Monsieur Ampère's home?" he asked, surprising Frederic with a question seemingly so far removed from the subject of the University's skepticism.

"Yes, I find my quarters and my life there most agreeable," he answered.

"It's interesting," continued the Abbé, "that out of all the young men in Paris, you should be the one to enjoy such association with this scientific and spiritual man. I have no doubt God has taken you in hand."

The aged priest paused for what seemed to Frederic a long time, his massive head sunk forward on his chest.

"Poor France!" he exclaimed at last. "For so many generations misgoverned by kings and dictators and led astray by confused philosophers in the name of an abstraction they call 'humanity.' But God, Frederic, never abandons His children, even when they abandon Him—though He may seem to do so. You must not despair of Paris, nor of the University, nor of France. You think now that the Catholic students at the University are few. But is it not possible that many are avoiding classroom identification as Catholics? Perhaps they feel themselves too alone to proclaim their faith. Don't let their apparent apathy deceive you. They are, after all, Frenchmen; they'll not turn their backs on a fight, or a crusade. They are, I wouldn't doubt, waiting for a voice—for a leader—to throw down a challenge to the adversary. Continue to speak out, and you may soon find yourself surrounded by other young Christians. They will have learned from your example to be courageous."

He bent his head to Frederic's, keenly studying his face.

"Are you continuing your devotional reading each day?" he asked, referring to a suggestion he had made during their previous conference.

"Right now I'm reading *The Following of Christ*," replied Frederic. "At the start I gave only a few minutes a day to this—now I'm devoting a half hour to the reading and the meditation every morning."

"Good! Persevere in this," encouraged the Abbé. "It's the way to a true inner life in Christ."

He arose, and placed both hands on Frederic's shoulders. Peering through dimmed eyes into his boyish face, he said, "My son, the University is an arena. In that arena you and your fellow students of the faith must fight for the ultimate prize—the mind and soul of intellectual France. There are some who might caution you not even to think of joining battle with the faculty. Those unthoughtful of God's ways might paraphrase to you the words of Saul to David—'Thou art not able to withstand these Philistines, nor to fight against them; for thou art but a boy, and they are warriors from their youth.' But such counselors, Frederic, would be wrong."

Then, as the Abbé walked with Frederic to the door, he said, "So go forth, my David; go forth 'in the name of the Lord of Hosts . . . that all the world may know there is a God in Israel.'"

Within four months after his talk with the Abbé Marduel, and within five months after his matriculation at the University, events proved to Frederic the truth of the Abbé's prophecy.

It was a classroom counter-offensive led by Ozanam that united the Christian students, and led many—a larger number than Frederic had anticipated—openly to take a position in support of religion.

Lack of opposition had led some professors to become reckless in their anti-religious presentations of history. On two successive days, Frederic and his friends detected two of them in the most flagrant misstatements of fact. He addressed formal protests to both. On the part of the Christian students, and in the interest of sound scholarship, he asked retractions. The professors had little choice. They corrected themselves in their classes. They made some effort to explain away their "mistakes," but after that, non-Christian students were less disposed to accept without question professional criticisms of revealed religion.

News of the retractions warned anti-Christian faculty members that their offensive against supernatural revelation must henceforth have at least the semblance of a scholarly basis. As a consequence, the attacks became more guarded and less frequent, but they did not cease.

Soon a more dramatic battle, longer drawn out but even more decisive, further unified and strengthened the pro-Christian group.

The "battlefield," as Frederic termed it, was the Sorbonne's chair of philosophy. The chief antagonist was the celebrated Théodore Simon Jouffroy, foremost among rationalists who were trying to explain away the supernatural.

It was during a lecture in the early part of March, 1832,

that Professor Jouffroy had the effrontery to deny before his students the possibility of "a Christian revelation." Such a revelation, he declared "supposes miraculous intervention by the Deity," and miracles he brushed aside as "mere figments of the theological imagination." They were, he maintained, opposed to nature, which if God created it must be perfect.

As the lecture progressed, Frederic ceased taking notes, and found himself fighting an impulse to refute Professor Jouffroy on the spot. He wanted to ask him why the all-powerful Creator could not reveal His truths directly to man; why revelation should be thought of as opposed to the Divine wisdom rather than as proving the Divine generosity? But an attempt to debate with a professor on such a subject would surely disrupt the classroom. He decided to follow the customary procedure, present his refutation in writing, and request a public reading of it.

That evening he drew up a memorandum of objections to the professor's reasoning, and the next day he presented it to Professor Jouffroy. That gentleman accepted the manuscript with a mechanical "*Merci*," promising to discuss it during his next lecture, three days hence. He delayed two weeks; then, without reading Frederic's objections to the students, he "analyzed" them in a manner slanted to serve his original argument. It was thus his own version of Frederic's objections that he refuted.

Frederic considered the matter as too serious to permit the professor to escape by such a shabby stratagem. He drew up a second memorandum of objections, adding the charge of unfairness. This the professor merely ignored, while continuing to condemn Christianity as the enemy of scientific inquiry and of human liberty.

Thereupon Frederic took a step which demonstrated the advantage of united action. He had already discussed his memorandums with various fellow students; now he asked the students to meet with him to review both protests and the professor's cavalier treatment of them. Paul Lamache, Auguste Le Taillandier, Felix Clavé, Pessonneau, Lallier, and nine others attended. Frederic had drawn up a new protest, which he submitted to them. After some changes, they all approved and signed it.

This protest was more than a refutation of Professor Jouffroy's arguments against revelation and the Church; it constituted, for its signers, a public profession of faith.

Confronted with this unified demand, Professor Jouffroy felt compelled to read Frederic's original refutation. More than two hundred students listened with respect to the young scholar's clear, forceful presentation of Catholic truth—many of them with new understanding.

The professor proceeded to weaken his position further by the bad grace with which he answered Frederic's confutation. He lost himself in confused "explanations"; he declared he had never intended that his words should be taken as an attack on Christianity, which, he asserted, he held in deepest veneration. He promised henceforth to avoid wounding the religious sensibilities of his students.

The student movement that formed around Ozanam surprised him, particularly when he found his schoolfellows looking to him for direction. He was the last person to consider himself a leader and a man of action. Indeed, he acted only when he thought action imperative, and then only when others failed to act—but this reluctance to project himself merely promoted his popularity.

The movement was even more surprising to the anti-Christian professors. They had failed to realize that their intellectual snobbery, and their sacrifice of scholarship to their prejudice against religion, had created a mounting resentment. Unconsciously, the Catholic students had been awaiting the appearance in their midst of one about whom they could rally, and they had found him in Frederic Ozanam.

They followed him, because he spoke with authority. And he spoke with authority because his clear, penetrating mind had grasped firmly the fundamental concept at issue between the unbelievers and the Christians. This basic dispute was over the true nature and destiny of man.

It was at this time that Frederic analyzed the position of the "progressive" professors in a letter to his cousin Falconnet in Lyons. Skeptical philosophers, he pointed out, had created an abstract man and had endowed him with all the attributes they wished man to have. Upon and around their unreal creation they had built their philosophy, professing to find the answer to man's destiny in man himself.

To justify the ideal creation of their imaginations, and to fortify their claim that man was wholly sufficient unto himself, they had rewritten, and were now re-interpreting, history.

In the face of Catholic demands that they present history objectively rather than subjectively, the Sorbonne skeptics were holding forth volubly on their ideas of a new world in which man would worship himself. Against this doctrine, as Frederic pointed out to Falconnet, Catholic philosophers were triumphantly restating the supernatural origin of man, and his dependence upon his Creator. They were proclaiming the divine origin of Christianity, and its beneficent influence on imperfect man's mind and heart and soul. Among these French champions of Catholicism were MM. de Chateaubriand, d'Ekstein, Ballanche, de Bonald, de Montalembert, and the Abbés de Lamennais, Lacordaire, and Gerbet.

Interested in sacred scripture, Frederic had attended one of the Abbé Gerbet's lectures on that subject. The Abbé, only thirty-four years old, had a way with words. He was brilliant, polished, and a respected philosopher; Frederic felt immensely drawn to him. He was prominent in the new Catholic movement which demanded larger political freedom, for the Church as well as for the people—a progressivism in line with the student spirit.

One day as Frederic was leaving the School of Law he began to talk to a few students accompanying him about the Abbé Gerbet, and the group stopped on a footpath near the Rue Soufflot to listen.

"The Abbé's profound, and analytical," said Frederic. "A series of lectures by him could do much to correct the historical caricatures of the Church continuously drawn by some of our professors. I'd like to hear him lecture on the philosophy of history."

Lallier, who made one of the group, strongly urged that they wait on the Abbé at once. When—having agreed to the idea—the little gathering broke up, Frederic and Lallier walked along together, and, coming to a small sidewalk café, sat down to a glass of wine and a lengthy exchange of views. This, their first extensive conversation, was the beginning of a close friendship that they were to cherish throughout their lives.

The Abbé Gerbet agreed to lecture on the philosophy of history every fortnight. The hall the students were able to provide seated only three hundred. Many celebrities came, and the place was jammed at every lecture. But Frederic was disappointed that so few students could be exposed to this brilliant light in the University's theological darkness. He realized, however, that the Abbé's voice was so weak it could hardly have been heard in a much larger hall, and his mind began to busy itself with another picture. It was a vision of a Catholic scholar of more powerful oratorical ability addressing thousands of students in a far larger auditorium.

Several weeks after Professor Jouffroy's apology, Frederic, Le Taillandier, Lallier, and Clavé were lunching at a restaurant near the School of Law, when talk turned to that skeptical philosopher.

"Have you fellows noticed the change in Professor Jouffroy since his apology—or am I imagining things?" asked Lallier.

"His basic concepts do seem to be changing," agreed Frederic. "Who would have expected him to admit that he felt impelled to seek for supernatural light; that material knowledge does not satisfy the mind; that after exhausting all material knowledge a void remains? Perhaps our skeptical philosopher is on the way back to the faith of his fathers!"

"If that turns out to be true, you'll have a convert to your credit!" exclaimed Le Taillandier. "It was you who faced him with the truth."

"We all did that," replied Frederic, "but I doubt whether any of us could claim credit for Jouffroy. The Abbé Marduel says that no one was ever argued into the Church. And that no one was ever given the faith unless he humbly and sincerely asked God for it. Let's hope others of the faculty will be given this grace."

That night, conscious of having achieved a partial success, Frederic and his companions were in high spirits. They were confident of future progress. They would have been even more confident had they been able to foresee that Professor Jouffroy would eventually be fully converted to the faith. As he lay dying ten years later, reconciled to the Church, he was to say: "All these skeptical philosophies lead nowhere. A single act of Christian faith, or one page of the Catechism, is worth a thousand such systems put together."

CHAPTER 6

THE RAGGED, thinly clad man looked up from the pile of refuse he had been stirring and probing with his clawed stick, and scowled at the two top-hatted, frock-coated young gentlemen who had stopped before him.

Pushing back the rimless piece of felt that served him as a hat, and shifting the half-filled basket slung on his shoulder, he sullenly asked: "Why do you interrupt me, messieurs? A *chiffonnier* has no time to loiter—that's for those who can afford fine clothes and idleness."

Jules Devaux gave Frederic Ozanam a glance that said: "You see what I mean?"

They had been walking briskly down the Rue St. Jacques this cold Monday evening in the February of 1832, when they came upon the *chiffonnier*. Against Devaux's caution that they were a surly lot, Frederic had insisted on speaking to him.

Frederic hastened to reassure the ragpicker.

"We interrupt you, my friend, merely to do you a service," he said. "If you will come to my home, 19 Rue des Fossés

49

St. Victor, tomorrow, I will have some clothes and shoes for you."

"Merci, monsieur, I am most grateful," he said, a smile chasing away the scowl from his grimy face. "But that's not my circuit. It belongs to my friend Brosseau. You say 19 Rue des Fossés St. Victor—I'll tell him, and he'll share with me. That's our system."

Placated by the friendly offer, the *chiffonnier* talked readily about his life, and his family. He was married, he said, and the father of three, but hardly ever knew from one day to the next whether his wife and children would have enough money for the next day's food.

"But we're never afraid of going hungry, messieurs," he declared. "When the *chiffe* fails us, or when we have sickness, we can always depend on Sister Rosalie for food tickets, or for nursing. Sometimes, she comes to us herself—but if she can't, she always sends another Sister, or some good person such as yourselves, messieurs . . . Well, one must cover his circuit. Good evening, messieurs, and"—with a bow toward Frederic—"I'll tell my friend Brosseau about the clothes and shoes you have awaiting him at 19 Rue des Fossés St. Victor. Expect him, monsieur."

This was not the first time Frederic had heard casual references to Sister Rosalie and her work. He knew that she was the superior of a convent of the Daughters of Charity of St. Vincent de Paul, an organization St. Vincent had founded more than two hundred years before to care for the sick poor. Her convent was in the poorest district in Paris, a little to the south of the University center. Out of meager resources she had been able to achieve miracles of relief for the destitute.

"Who are these people who help the good Sister?" he now asked Devaux, as they resumed their walk.

"Oh, such as yourself—and myself—for example, just as the *chiffonnier* said," answered Devaux lightly.

Frederic stopped, looking at his friend in pleased conjecture.

"You mean to tell me, Jules, that you are one of her helpers?" he asked.

"I generally lend a hand to the Sisters on my free day."

"When you go next time, let me tag along, will you?"

"Certainly—and you may be sure Sister Rosalie will welcome you. How about tomorrow?"

"Tomorrow it is," agreed Frederic.

Next morning, Jules Devaux called for Frederic at the Ampère residence. In the Rue Mouffetard, only a city block away, they found their pace slowed by the crowds in that narrow, uneven, sloping street. Hawkers were everywhere, ballyhooing their produce, their cheap-Jack merchandise, or their nostrums, while housewives bargained in a strident cackle that rose above the hubbub. Men in faded blouses and patched trousers, fingering the few sous in their pockets, listened idly to the pitchmen.

Frederic and Devaux edged their way slowly through the dense mass of human confusion, stepping carefully to avoid the sewage-filled gutter in the middle of the cobblestone pavement, and the foul and fetid rubbish that strewed the street. They were jabbed in the ribs by women's market baskets and pitchmen's displays; they dodged overflowing drains and gutters.

Wherever Frederic looked, he saw savage and sulky men against a background of ruinous houses, many with broken windows, many doorless. Here and there a roof had fallen in, or a building had collapsed.

"That building crashed six months ago," said Devaux, pointing to one huge pile of rubble. "It killed nine of the tenants. Our Citizen King and his supporters seem devoted to helping the rich get richer. Why don't they compel the owners of these rookeries to tear them down, or to make them habitable?"

They came upon a staggering, gray-haired man whose brutalized features contorted with rage as they passed him.

"Rich swine!" he shouted, and spat toward them. "Robbers of the poor! One of these days we will drink your blood!"

"Ignore him," warned Devaux. "Otherwise we'll have a crowd—and trouble."

They pushed on, both somewhat shaken.

"You can't blame these people for cursing the more fortunate," observed Devaux. "Look at this unrelieved wretchedness all about us."

Frederic had been looking, and his heart was sick. He had seen poverty in Lyons. But never had he seen such squalor and desolation as in these narrow, crooked streets, with their inhabitants packed into damp, airless, crumbling ruins unfit for cattle. Except for sidewalk stalls, and the ambulant peddlers, there were very few markets and shops; the people of the Faubourg St. Marceau were too poor to support businesses requiring much of an investment.

"No wonder," Frederic said sadly, "that these people have been first to the barricades."

"They've nothing to lose except lives of misery," returned Devaux. "They're not nearly the savages they were, though, before several groups of dedicated religious began to work here. Of course, the government won't even recognize the existence of the religious orders, but at least it doesn't interfere. Under Sister Rosalie, particularly, the Daughters of Charity have brought many of these people to realize that the Revolution didn't abolish God, and more of them are coming to accept the fact that they have immortal souls and an inherent dignity as human beings."

"Just how does Sister Rosalie accomplish such wonders?"

"She has faith that God will aid her—and He does, chiefly through the contributions of charitable people who know her work," answered Devaux. "Her system brings the penniless food, fuel in cold weather, and help with the rent. She and the Sisters of her convent work themselves to exhaustion nursing the poor, maintaining a pharmacy for distribution of free medical supplies, and a clothing dispensary. Sister Rosalie has also established a nursery for the children of employed mothers and a day nursery. And I don't want to forget the trade schools which she runs and which are teaching trades that will help the children of this quarter break out of the economic bondage that enslaves their parents. Of course, the Sisters and their lay helpers can do only so much. The poor are very many, and their needs are endless."

Frederic told himself, as they walked through the panorama of this black-and-gray wretchedness, that here was poverty with a difference. In other *faubourgs*, the poor dwelt next door to self-supporting neighbors who might supply relief.

52

Here, poverty neighbored poverty; misery emphasized misery; starvation and disease were the common lot. In this *faubourg,* those able to earn their daily bread faced starvation with the first stagnation in the labor market; they were in danger of freezing with any sudden drop in temperature. These poor lived from hand to mouth, but the hand was often empty. How little, Frederic thought, did Paris as a whole know about these people. How many regarded them as outcasts, beyond hope, and unworthy of help!

"Here we are!" said Devaux, turning into a block-long street leading from the Rue Mouffetard toward the east. "Here's the Little Street of the Wooden Sword. . . . And there's the convent wall, and behind it the house of the Daughters of Charity."

They came to a door in the wall, with a grating at eye level, and Devaux gave the bellpull a tug. Hard upon the faraway jingle the Sister-portress' gentle face appeared behind the grating.

"Ah, Monsieur Devaux!" she exclaimed, and opening the wall door with a welcoming smile, she led them into the convent and to Sister Rosalie's little parlor.

It was a poor, plain, low-ceilinged room, about ten by thirteen feet, with a few pieces of hard-used furniture. The wallpaper—whatever its original color—had been turned to a yellowish brown by age and dampness. On the wall behind Sister Rosalie's desk hung a large crucifix in a deep frame, the garnet-velvet background supplying the room's only note of richness.

To this little chamber came daily not a few of the rich, and many of the poor. The rich came with contributions for the Sister's charities, and often sought her counsel. The poor asked for advice and solace, for bread, clothes and shelter, and for nursing care in family sickness. They were the *misérables*— the wretched, the outcast, the destitute, the forsaken, the despairing. Here they were welcomed gently, as brothers and sisters in Christ.

Frederic's observant eyes had barely noted the room's details when Sister Rosalie, slight and rapid in movement, was before them. Her aquiline face showed signs of fatigue, for she seldom permitted herself sufficient rest; but her maternal smile made them feel at home. Her large dark eyes, seeming darker against the snowy whiteness of her cornet, appraised and accepted Frederic at a glance. Devaux, introducing him, said that Frederic had come to join her band of helpers. Sister Rosalie was warm in appreciation.

"It's to the charity of such as you, messieurs," she said, "that France must look if understanding and peace are to be established among our people."

She went to her writing table.

"For your visits today," she said—Sister Rosalie never wasted time—"I will give you the addresses of three families. One of these, Monsieur Devaux, you have visited before. The other two will be new to you."

She wrote names and addresses on a slip of paper and handed it to Devaux, accompanying it with a briefing on the background of the two new families. She also supplied food tickets for distribution as needed.

"God has already given you spiritual wisdom, or you would not be sacrificing your precious free day to His poor," she said, and Frederic felt she was speaking more for his ears than for those of Devaux. "Because you see Christ in His poor, I know you will approach each one you visit with humility, as His servant. Always remember, messieurs, that if we had lived through the hardships they have had to meet—if our childhood had been one of constant want—perhaps we, too, would have given way to envy and hatred as, I must admit, have many of the poor in this quarter. Be kind, messieurs, and love, for love is your first gift to the poor. They will appreciate your kindness and your love more than all else you can bring them."

As they left, Devaux and Frederic planned their route so that their last visit would be nearest to the convent, for later they would report to the Sisters on the needs of the families visited.

It was Sister Rosalie's method to have the same helpers devote themselves to a few families, whom they would thus

54

come to know as friends. Deavux had thus become well acquainted with the Caron family, first on his present list of three. The Carons lived on the sixth floor of a drafty old wreck of a tenement much like other multifamily houses in the quarter. The entrance led to a small court, on which faced doors to various ground floor compartments and out buildings. Devaux led the way through an arched passage near the living quarters of the concierge, and they ascended a staircase. Frederic stumbled once or twice on the broken tiles of the old stairs, and followed Devaux down a long, dark corridor, feeling his way along a wall from which most of the plaster had fallen.

Treading more dark stairs and corridors, they came finally to the sixth floor. The sound of a rapid tap, tap, tappity-tap led them to the Caron family, for Monsieur Caron was a shoemaker. Monsieur Caron placed two rickety chairs for them, and Devaux spoke to Madame Caron, who was lying on a crude bed.

"Sister Rosalie sends greetings, madame," he said. "She is concerned over the fact that your sickness has now lasted several weeks. She instructs me to say that she will bring the doctor and see you again tomorrow."

"Ah, thank you, monsieur," replied the woman with a grateful smile. She was too weak for many words.

"And Marie," continued Devaux, drawing a five-year-old girl to the light and looking into one of her ears. "Your ear, I see, has stopped draining."

"It doesn't hurt any more," said Marie.

"Good. Be careful not to catch more cold in it; keep it well covered."

"Yes, monsieur."

Frederic noted that the small room, whose sloping ceilings prevented upright standing in most of its area, served as both living quarters and workshop; nevertheless, it was remarkably well-ordered.

As they left, Devaux placed several food tickets on a shelf near the door, and the students bade the Carons farewell. Each of the tickets entitled the holder to a four-pound loaf of bread at one of the nearby bakeries.

The second family, on the Rue Mouffetard, consisted of a husband too weak from consumption to work, two little girls in bed with measles, and a calm, courageous, almost cheerful mother who reported that an older daughter was giving first-rate satisfaction in a dress shop, where Sister Rosalie had found her employment.

Devaux promised both a regular supply of fuel and a full-fledged physician within twenty-four hours.

Search for the third family on the list brought the students to a fourth-floor garret, where an old woman was sitting alone in a chair made comfortable with cushions. She was apparently in fair health, but a broken hip, poorly healed, had made her quite helpless. Madame Blanchard said that she was eighty years old, and entirely dependent upon her eleven-year-old granddaughter.

"She has gone to the Petit St. Thomas," the old lady told them, mentioning a large shop on the Rue du Bac, "to see whether she can get some work. Sometimes they give her dusting cloths to hem; for these she is paid at the rate of ten sous a dozen. It's not much, messieurs—but it keeps the wolf from the door."

"And how long does it take the child to hem a dozen?" asked Frederic. He was finding these slum dwelling places and their inhabitants not entirely dissimilar to those of Lyons, and beginning to feel that he might be able to do his share in helping "Sister Rosalie's poor."

"A dozen makes about a day's work, monsieur."

"But ten sous—does this really suffice for rent and clothes and food and fuel?"

"We are sometimes short on fuel, monsieur. So, too, with food—for Annette is a growing girl with a hearty appetite."

Devaux gave her a generous supply of tickets for food, promising that extra fuel would be supplied and that Sister Rosalie would help obtain more profitable work for her granddaughter.

In talking further with Madame Blanchard Frederic discovered that she had not seen a priest since her accident.

"Would you like a priest to come and hear your confession, and bring you Our Lord in Holy Communion?" he asked.

"That would give me the greatest happiness, monsieur."

"Then," said Frederic, "we will ask a priest to call. I think you may expect him either tomorrow morning or the morning after."

Walking back to the convent with Devaux, Frederic was utterly downcast. His spirit had grown heavier as the visits of that morning progressed; his heart now seemed filled with tears. In the last two hours he had come to realize as never before the needs and sufferings of the poor, and to feel as never before a deep sense of personal responsibility for their relief.

From this time on, Frederic devoted as many hours to this work as he could spare from his studies. To do so, he refused invitations to more than one brilliant soirée.

Thus he passed the winter of 1831-32, a season that revealed to him how winter's cold can be a constant harassment and danger to the undernourished and thinly clad, who must use fuel sparingly when they could afford it at all. But the friendly sun shone a little longer every day, and at last winter, that pitiless enemy of the poor, was in full retreat.

The people of the Faubourg St. Marceau were looking forward to its complete rout, and the coming of spring—not knowing that spring would bring fear and despair, and death on every side.

CHAPTER 7

IT WAS springtime in Paris, but not a springtime of joy and hope. Asiatic cholera, contagious and deadly, was sweeping across Europe and, rumor had it, would soon be at the outskirts of the city.

Hard upon the rumors the pestilence reached the metropolis, and was soon spreading and scattering through the city like fire in a whirlwind. It struck down rich and poor, but it spread most rapidly through the crowded, dark, unsanitary tenements of the slums.

Reports of the plague reached Lyons, and Frederic's parents sent a message posthaste, urging him to return home at once. Dr. Ozanam thought that his son would be less resistant to the disease than more robust young men. He was sure, too, that Frederic would be safe in Lyons. For Lyons seemed providentially protected. A few months before, when cholera had struck in all the towns surrounding that city, its people by the thousands had hastened up the hill to the north of the town. There, at the shrine of the Mother of God—venerated under the title "Our Lady of Fourvières"—they had placed themselves under her protection. She had answered their prayers. The plague stopped at the very gates of the city.

Many students had already returned to their homes, but Frederic decided to remain in Paris unless his parents should command him to return to Lyons. The Sorbonne faculty was carrying on as usual, and he was studying hard for oncoming examinations. His parents reluctantly complied. Had they foreseen how constantly he was to expose himself to the contagion, they would undoubtedly have insisted upon his return.

Several days after the cholera had invaded Paris, Monsieur Ampère said to Frederic, "Should the plague strike me in the night, I will try to attract your attention by rapping on the floor. When you hear my signal, don't come to my room. Instead, run for my confessor. After that, summon my physician."

Frederic asked Monsieur Ampère to do as much for him, and to have him removed to a hospital at once. For he had seen how a plague victim died, and he did not want to burden the Ampère home should he himself contract the dread disease.

A little before, he had sat by the bedside of a suffering student, bathing him to relieve the burning cholera fever, giving him drinking water endlessly to relieve his insatiable thirst. He had seen the student grow cold, seen his skin become dry and wrinkled and purple, his features pinched, his eyes more and more deeply sunk in their sockets as the first, and the second, and the third day passed. He had heard the sick youth's voice reduced to a croaking whisper. Finally, the young man's pulse had faded and died under his fingers, as the heart stopped. But before the student's death Frederic had summoned a priest for the frightened boy. After that the youth, strengthened by the sacraments, had faced death serenely, and a little before he died had whispered, "I'll be thanking you, Frederic, through eternity."

Other friends were stricken, and Ozanam helped to nurse and comfort several. For those who recovered he wrote letters, and procured books for them to read as they convalesced. Among the latter was the Abbé Duchesne, parish priest of historic Notre-Dame des Champs. When the Abbé requested books, Frederic complied by finding for him three works— each describing a plague! One was in the Greek of Thucydides, another in the Latin of Lucretius, and a third in Manzoni's modern Italian. As he handed the Abbé the books, Frederic said with grim humor: "It occurred to me, Monsieur l'Abbé, that these volumes would hold deep personal interest for you."

The Abbé laughed, and observed that the tenderest hearted were frequently the toughest minded. Then, with scholarly appreciation, he proceeded to read all three volumes.

In the tenement districts the cholera claimed its highest percentage of victims, and in the Faubourg St. Marceau Sister Rosalie and her Daughters of Charity labored unceasingly. To help care for the sick, Frederic and other students placed themselves fully under Sister Rosalie's direction. In the history of the Daughters of Charity it is related that among those who assisted them during the plague of 1832 were the same young men who a few months later were to join in founding the Society of St. Vincent de Paul. All of this group were from the School of Law, with the exception of Devaux, who was a medical student. In addition, brave young men of the Polytechnic Institute came to help.

The friendships these students formed as they daily risked their lives in works of mercy were to prove as strong and enduring as ever united soldiers tested together in the trials and dangers of campaigns and battlefields.

As the cholera toll increased, so did the terror of the people. In the Faubourg St. Marceau, death invaded nearly every tenement, and panic seized upon the quarter.

One Thursday morning Frederic and Le Taillandier were harassed by frowns and curses as they walked down the Rue Mouffetard on their way to the convent in the Street of the Wooden Sword.

"*Assassins!*" growled one ferocious looking fellow, shaking his fist at them as they edged their way through the crowds in the narrow street.

"*Empoisonneurs!*" shrieked a tigerish woman, leaning from a second-story window, and throwing a crockery fragment that shattered at their feet.

Clenched fists were raised and shaken, and a mob had begun to gather about them, when suddenly its attention was diverted toward a gentleman dressed in top hat, frock coat, and white neckcloth, and carrying a small satchel. He was obviously a physician, and was following a litter on which two bearers were transporting a cholera victim.

The mob surged around him, separating him from the litter as they turned their cries of "*assassin*" and "*empoisonneur*" against him. The doctor bravely stood his ground, and tried to make his voice heard above the tumult. Frederic and Le Taillandier moved in as closely as possible, ready to attempt a rescue if necessary.

"I'm a physician!" shouted the beleaguered man. "I'm taking this cholera victim to Mercy Hospital. You are delaying us— you may cost this man his life."

"You have been sent to poison us!" shouted the ferocious fellow who had first raised his voice against Ozanam and Le Taillandier, and who was now leading the mob.

"You're an agent of the aristocrats!" cried another. "They say there are too many of us poor. They want to kill us off— and you're helping them!"

"Yes, he's right—you're spreading the pestilence!" agreed a third. "You're in the pay of the rich!"

The doctor attempted to push on, but the mob's ferocious leader whipped out a knife and held it at his throat. The two students started forward, but the physician coolly motioned them back.

Looking his foe in the eye and raising his voice so that it carried to the edge of the crowd, he said, "I am a friend of Sister Rosalie! I am acting for her."

"That's so—I've seen him at the convent," said one of the mob.

There was instant quiet. The threatening knife-wielder muttered an apology, and stuck the weapon back in his belt. The crowd melted away.

"That was close," said Frederic, introducing himself and Le Taillandier as fellow helpers of the Sisters.

"Far too close," said the physician, who identified himself as Dr. Royal-Collard. "But I was at fault. I was so startled that I forgot for the moment that Sister Rosalie's name is magic in this quarter. I had but to call upon it—and you saw how it quieted these panic-stricken people. Every rumor plays upon their ignorance, and their hatred of the better off, whom they think of as their mortal enemies. The latest rumor—of which I was so nearly the victim—is that the rich are spreading the plague in the slum sections to kill off the poor."

A few minutes later, Frederic and Le Taillandier were describing this mob scene to Sister Rosalie. Another visitor who happened to be present in the little parlor overheard them, and spoke out in bitter censure of the poor for attacking those who risked their lives to serve them.

"Ah, monsieur," said Sister Rosalie, "you cannot appreciate the desperate conditions under which these poor people live, or else you would be less quick to blame them."

She spoke gently and sadly, and Frederic thought she seemed tired and taut. He was to learn some time later that she and the other sisters had had only an hour's sleep at a time for the last week. Throughout the epidemic the nuns had slept fully clothed, ready for emergencies.

This experience increased his admiration for the Sisters, and especially for the frail but seemingly tireless woman who led them so calmly, so efficiently, and with such unfailing kindness.

The epidemic raged with mounting intensity for a month before it gradually receded. By August it had burned itself out, having taken thousands of lives, obliterated whole families, and deprived many children of their parents.

In this trial by plague Frederic's devotion to the poor grew and strengthened. More and more he came to see the suffering Christ in his suffering brothers.

In his work among the plague-stricken, he had been sustained by his trust in the infinite wisdom and love of Divine Providence, and by the faith that His heavenly Father called His children to Himself in His own time, plague or no plague. In this confidence he daily exposed himself to the epidemic, and cholera did not touch him. Nor did it strike any member of the Ampère household.

A strange thing was noted. Up and down the street on which stood the Ampère home, the cholera struck heavily along the opposite side. But it never crossed that narrow street; never invaded a single dwelling on the Ampère side, from the Rue des Fossés St. Victor on the north to the Rue de Fourcy on the south.

CHAPTER 8

AMERICAN students would have called him "Dad"; Italian students, "Papa." But as Monsieur Joseph Emmanuel Bailly de Surcy lived in Paris, the students in the University neighborhood of his home called him "Père."

He had founded and still presided over what was left of *La Société des Bonnes Etudes*, but the 1830 revolution had scattered most of the members. Those that remained met in a hall near the Law School in the Place de l'Estrapade. In his commodious home nearby Monsieur Bailly accepted many students as paying guests. But all students were welcome to his fireside and to his extensive library. There they discussed with him the world's problems and their own problems, and they found him, unfailingly, a friend.

"Père" Bailly's paternal benignity suggested an age greater than his actual forty years. His kindness and charity, his selfless interest in his fellow men beamed forth from his florid countenance, bringing comfort and cheer to many a homesick student.

Monsieur Bailly owned and edited a newspaper, *La Tribune Catholique*. From the paper's offices at 38 Rue St. Sulpice, it was issued every other day, Monday through Friday. He wrote for it—frequently far into the night—as a champion of Catholic truth. It served as a training ground, too, for students gifted in the use of words. Provided, of course, their ideas justified the use of words—for Monsieur Bailly set a high standard, and to be published in *La Tribune Catholique* was rightly held an honor.

The paper reflected its owner's nature. Its policy was moderate, midway between the radical and the conservative Catholic political factions. Its circulation was considerably larger than its paid subscriptions; Père Bailly sent the paper free to a list of those he thought *should* read it, including many students.

The *Tribune* was printed in a shop in the rear of Monsieur Bailly's office. In the office lobby stood a magazine and newspaper rack, always well stocked with periodicals from all over Europe. To read these students dropped in at all hours.

One golden day in October of 1832 Monsieur Bailly, his somewhat rotund body supported in an ample "captain's" chair, sat at his great oak desk in the *Tribune's* office. His pen was idle as his thoughts ran to the speedy recovery of Paris from the plague of the previous spring and summer, and to his constant preoccupation—the welfare of the students. He gazed across the office at a trio of young men discussing loudly and with intense animation an historical article in one of the periodicals.

Their conversation, Père Bailly told himself, amounted to a debate—and an idea was suddenly born in his mind.

"Why," he asked himself, "shouldn't the Catholic University students organize themselves into a society to study and debate the great historical and philosophical issues? Yes—particularly history. So many of our professors are seeking to obliterate ancestral traditions. They are using history to teach us Frenchmen to hate one another."

He was wondering whether the students would warm up to his idea, when the street door opened, and Ozanam walked in. Under his arm was a manuscript, for Frederic was one of the students who wrote more or less regularly for the *Tribune*.

"Pull up a chair, my good Frederic," said the publisher. "First, let's read your article and get it to the typesetter. Then I want to tell you about a project that has just occurred to me."

Spreading Frederic's manuscript before him, Père Bailly read rapidly, gathering the sense of whole paragraphs at a glance.

"I like the well-balanced treatment you give a subject," he commented. "Refreshingly different from the extremism of the Abbé de Lamennais. It was largely his immoderation that caused me to establish the *Tribune*."

He headlined Frederic's article and shouted for the printer's devil.

"Now for my idea," he said, as he handed the article to the apprentice and leaned back in his capacious chair. "You and other students, Frederic, frequent this office with the regularity of club members, and discuss history and philosophy here with all the fervor one expects on the debating platform— though perhaps not as loudly. Why not, then, organize yourselves into a society for study and debate? You could meet here—say, once a week—as an association of students devoted to the discussion of history and philosophy."

"This office"—he included the large room in a gesture—"is yours to use. Most of you are studying law. Frequent debates would add to your training for the bar. You will sharpen your minds and your tongues—and on those very historical and philosophical issues your professors so often present falsely. You will thus prepare yourselves to demolish such attacks."

Frederic's eyes were glowing with excitement and enthusiasm.

"You've produced the answer, Monsieur Bailly, to a problem that's been on my mind for some time," he said. "That problem is, how to draw the Catholic students more closely together. A debating society will help us do that! I'm all for your idea, and I'll start talking it up at once. And may I suggest an improvement?"

"What is that?"

"That if we do form an organization, Monsieur Bailly lead off each meeting with a lecture on history or philosophy. Your lecture would instruct us. And by it you could illuminate the subject of debate to follow."

Père Bailly was pleased. He agreed; for he talked well, and he liked to teach.

The "Conference of History," as the new debating association was named, took shape within a few days, and meetings were from the first lively and spirited. The members differed widely on economics, art, literature, and many other topics. From the first, current political subjects were taboo, but the young men held forth on great historical events of the past and discussed philosophical concepts with a degree of understanding that impressed Monsieur Bailly. How enlightening it would be to *non*-Christian students, he thought, could they hear these principles and reasoned arguments. Why not, he asked Frederic and others, admit them to membership? They would, he pointed out, supply an extremely lively opposition, and at the same time learn what Catholics really believe.

The students agreed; they opened the Conference of History to the entire student body. The move proved an immediate success. Devotees of Voltaire, of Rousseau, of the communism of Fourier, and of various socialistic theories all jumped at the opportunity to champion their cures for the world's ills. To do so they were even willing to tolerate Catholic argument.

They began frequenting the debates in such numbers that the *Tribune* office proved inadequate.

As usual, Père Bailly came to the rescue. Out of his own funds he rented a large hall in the Place de l'Estrapade, close to the Pantheon; closer, also, to the School of Law and to the Ampère residence, where Frederic was still living. Soon this hall, in turn, overflowed on meeting nights with young men and their floods of oratory.

The Conference of History set up exacting requirements for membership, but membership continued to increase. It included many of the University's most brilliant students. Some bore family names famed in France and in Europe. Several were widely traveled. A few were learned advocates of the most advanced art theories. A large number were deeply read in philosophy. The majority were devoted to the study of history.

With the admission of unbelievers to the debates, the conflicts over history and philosophy became intense, hard, and heated. The Saint-Simonians, the rationalists, and others, frequently came with prepared papers, and with questions designed to entrap the Christians. The latter, when lacking data on the issues thus suddenly advanced, stood on basic principles to repulse the attacks, and nearly always won the victory. Ozanam gives two reasons for this: They were on the side of truth and were, he wrote, "animated by more order, zeal and assiduity." He himself was one of the most assiduous.

In these debates, he quickly became the leader of the Catholic party. With his well-stored mind, his logic, and his facile command of language, he marshaled the defense against the onslaughts of the anti-Christian champions, and generally turned defense into counter-attack and rout. Frederic proved himself again to be one of those rare persons who can win an opponent's friendship while destroying his arguments. He possessed empathy to a high degree; he was able to put himself in another's place, able to understand almost instantly another's motivating preferences and prejudices. He never failed to show respect for an antagonist, however strongly he controverted his opinions. He never attributed unworthy motives to another, and bore constantly in mind that his opponents were often victims of anti-Christian backgrounds, false sources of information, and inherited bias.

As in most organizations, there were a few in the Conference of History who formed the hub around which its activities revolved. Their common interest in history, in literature, and in Catholic doctrine drew them together. But the strongest bond uniting the members of this little group was their charitable work under the guidance of Sister Rosalie. In their activities on behalf of the poor they had gradually formed firm friendships with one another; they shared each other's problems, misfortunes, good fortunes, joys, and hopes.

A glimpse of their spiritual fineness is caught in a letter Frederic wrote to Ernest Falconnet on March 19, 1833.

> Sometimes, [he tells his cousin] when the air is balmy and the night breeze soft, and the moonbeams are falling upon the majestic dome of the Pantheon, . . . the *sergeant de ville* stops on his beat to cast an unquiet eye on six or seven young men who, arm-in-arm, promenade for hours together in the silent, deserted square.
>
> They discourse concerning many things on earth and in heaven. They speak of God, of their fathers, of friends whom they have left at the old firesides. They speak of their country, and of humanity. . . . The frivolous Parisian did not understand their speech. . . . But I understood them, for I was of them . . . and as I listened to them, I seemed to feel my heart expand; I felt myself a man.

The members of this group were truly young men of talent and character. Their number included Lallier and Lamache, Le Taillandier and Chéruel, Clavé and Devaux, and De la Noue, who was esteemed for his graceful verse. Some, including Frederic, had entrée to Parisian drawing rooms and those brilliant soirées characteristic of the city's intellectual and social life.

Of these gatherings Frederic found those at the Count de Montalembert's home most to his liking. The young count, Frederic's senior by three years, was a graceful host and a well-informed, interesting conversationalist. Among his guests

67

were champions of Catholicism and freedom, including Polish and Irish leaders whose causes the brilliant Montalembert was upholding with his able pen. There were also such guests as Ballanche, the critic and author; Count Alfred de Vigny, the poet and novelist; Savigny the younger; Ampère the elder; and other men of worth.

Discussions at these gatherings touched on a world of subjects: politics, history, science, military tactics, philosophy, economics, the greed of industrialists, the condition of the poor. Frederic mentions in one of his letters to Falconnet some conversation at Montalembert's on the misery of many wage earners.

"It is," he comments ironically, "regarded by many as a very bad omen for the future."

Truly, the misery of the poor was a sad omen for France. It augured ill, Frederic thought, for the political future of the free-thinking Louis Philippe, whose devotion to the interest of bankers and industrialists left little room in his materialistic heart for his humbler subjects. Under him, French industry was forming itself on the English pattern and, Frederic had indignantly observed, was exploiting the wage earner only less outrageously than its English model.

As in England, families found the "high" wages that had enticed them from their countrysides too low to buy sufficient city-priced food, and to pay the rents exacted for their miserable slum dwellings.

These were such families as Frederic had encountered in the Faubourg St. Marceau. Doomed to hopeless indigence despite workdays as long as sixteen hours, the city wage earner's greatest fear, ironically, was loss of his job. That could mean starvation. Under these conditions, many of the powerless victims of exploitation developed fanatical hatred of the rich—and to them anyone who wore a coat instead of a blouse was rich. The industrial worker was a citizen, but a freeman only in the sense that he was free to sell his labor at a starvation wage. He was, in fact, economically enslaved by a political system that deprived him of any means of protest except violence. He was not permitted to vote; he and his fellow workers were forbidden by law even to meet for discussion of their grievances.

In desperate need of friends, the poor found them chiefly among those who had voluntarily become poor; that is, among members of the vowed-to-poverty religious orders of the Church. These religious were assisted in their work by lay men and women, but the voluntary helpers, Frederic knew, were comparatively few. In the dazzling salons, many an intellectual argued the necessity of doing something to combat pauperism, but very few penetrated into the forbidding and repellent slums to aid the *misérables* dwelling there.

Into this salon society—the most fascinating in Europe—Frederic found himself warmly welcomed. Attendance at these delightful and stimulating assemblies in exquisitely appointed homes was poles apart from his visits with poor families huddled in their cold, bare, cheerless dwellings. Frederic was every inch an intellectual, and the salons offered him the literate and cultured companionship he naturally craved. The poor had nothing to offer except gratitude—and many, proud and bitter in their penury, refused even that.

Ozanam might well have been completely captivated by the dazzling charm of a society which drew to itself the most cultivated men and women of Europe. Nevertheless, without entirely putting aside such pleasant and advantageous associations, he found the spiritual strength to sacrifice long and physically unpleasant hours to the poor, week in and week out the year around. At the age of twenty he had already learned spiritual wisdom and developed the habit of using the things of the world in such wise as to promote spiritual health and strength. He was already leading an interior life, trying manfully to live by the example of Jesus Christ. As a result, the Holy Spirit dwelt in him, and moved him constantly toward those activities that united him more closely with Christ.

Without spurning the stimulating intellectual companionship and associations which Paris so generously offered, he struck a balance in favor of charity. He refused to permit the sparkling conversation of salon society or the Conference of History debates to make him a mere man of words, a dilettante in the furtherance of Christian principles, a talker rather than a doer. On the contrary, his experiences in the debating society were now convincing him that words were woefully inadequate substitutes for Christian example.

"This talking," he repeated over and over again to his friends at the University, "this holding our own against our unbelieving opponents—this is all very well as far as it goes. We're forcing them to respect our side of history and philosophy—to admit, at least, that we have a side. But we can't argue them into loving God! That requires example!"

He discussed his concern with his companions in the moonlight walks beneath the Pantheon's dome. All agreed that something needed to be done. Jouffroy's direct attacks had been silenced, but other unbelieving professors continued their sniping at the rock of Peter.

While Frederic had come to look upon the debates at the Conference of History as so much rhetorical fireworks, he still felt obligated to attend, and to uphold the Christian position against the fierce assaults made upon it.

At a debate one March night in 1833, a Voltairian praised Byron as the champion of freedom and blasphemed Christ as its enemy. Then a Saint-Simonian trotted out the tired old calumny that the Church was the friend of the rich, the exploiter of the poor. The attacks grew more bitter, more intense, and in a free-for-all of fiery exchanges the Catholics repelled the charges while Père Bailly rapped in vain for order.

Frederic had sat quietly among the shouting, gesticulating combatants. Now he arose, not only to aid Monsieur Bailly, but also determined to command a hearing. The non-Christians had shown that they knew little or nothing of the Church's friendship for the poor, and he was eager to drive home the historical facts. But to still the voices of his excited opponents called for strategy. As he was searching his mind for some expedient, the speaker who had been occupying the platform gave up his attempts to be heard and stepped down. Frederic advanced at once and took his place. Deliberately pitching his voice so low that those six feet away could hardly hear him, he commenced to talk with intense animation. Curiosity immediately became his ally; the unruly disputants lowered their own voices, striving to hear the gist of Frederic's apparently earnest words. As the room quieted, Frederic allowed his voice to rise to normal, and his audience heard him saying: "Several hundred years ago, a powerful King was about to die."

The history students, particularly, respected the unusual historical knowledge Frederic frequently revealed, and they now listened intently, expecting to hear some ancient, unfamiliar tale.

"This King," continued Frederic, "left to His followers a command—an injunction which they must obey even after His death if they were to be recognized as citizens of His kingdom.

"His command was—'Love one another as I have loved you.'

"And how greatly did He love them? He loved them with infinite generosity and He was about to die for them. For this King was Our Lord Jesus Christ, the King of Kings.

"Now obviously, messieurs, this command by the Founder of Christianity to His followers, to love one another, to love their neighbors as themselves, means that charity is the very heart of Christianity, the source and center of its life."

The unbelievers realized that they had been trapped into a too-respectful silence, and they began to shift about uneasily.

"What other religion, my friends," continued Frederic, "or what philosophy teaches that we must love even our enemies; that our neighbor is the supernaturally adopted son of the Father, and brother, with us, of the Father's Only Begotten Son?

"From the apostolic age to our day, the Church of Christ has declared the slave equal to the master in God's eyes—a teaching which must eventually banish slavery from any truly Christian land. It has taught, and it teaches today, that the rich are but stewards of their wealth for the Supreme Owner, God, and that in giving to the needy, those who have more than they require are but making a just return to God."

The champions of a dozen social and economic theories now began clamoring for the floor. A Saint-Simonian, noted for his eloquence, attempted to interrupt, but Frederic waved him off with a gesture and resumed: "It was these principles that enabled Christianity to triumph over a hostile, pagan world in which the human person possessed no inherent worth.

"And behold the works of mercy to which these principles have given birth! In the time of Constantine, the Church established the first hospitals known to the world—and for centuries, until with the Revolution France became so largely godless, a Christian society recognized its responsibility for its poor. When the rich and powerful forgot that responsibility, Christian leaders never failed to rise up and remind them of it."

Here two or three students again interrupted.

"You talk of the past—what of today?" shouted the Saint-Simonian.

"Do you mean to tell me," asked Frederic in a tone of surprise, "that you have never heard of the Institut de Bon Secours of Paris, whose members devote themselves to nursing the sick poor, and who have been established by the present Archbishop of Paris? Do you not know of the Association of the Holy Family, of the Sisters of the Immaculate Conception, of the Sisters of Hope, and the Daughters of Charity of St. Vincent de Paul? Surely you have heard how during the recent plague they risked their lives day after day caring for the sick in the tenements. But perhaps," he added, permitting himself a touch of sarcasm such as he seldom employed, "you are too patriotic to recognize their self-sacrifice and heroism. For technically these religious operate outside the law. Even their existence is refused recognition by the present government of France."

Frederic was scoring heavily, and the Saint-Simonian, desperately intent on gaining the floor, was by this time almost beside himself with frustration.

"You people put all the burden of relief for the poor upon your religious orders—then you wash your hands of the job!" he shouted. "Don't try to impress us with what priests and nuns are doing for the poor. Tell us, Frederic Ozanam, what are *you* doing for them—you and your fellow Catholics in this room?"

For a moment, surprised by this personal onslaught, Frederic hesitated. Should he tell about the visits to the poor he and a few other students had been making—had, indeed, made the previous day? Should he hide that light under a bushel? But wasn't it a rather feeble light—he asked himself—since comparatively few students were giving themselves to such activities?

"Come!" jeered the Saint-Simonian, "show us *your* works."

"He's right!" shouted a Fourierist. "Just how charitable are *you?*"

"Yes, what about the Christian charity of our Christian students?" taunted a deist.

"Aren't your questions an unconscious tribute to Christianity?" asked Frederic, replying with more assurance than he felt at the moment. "Don't they point up the fact that you expect *us* to practice charity without entertaining such expectations of *yourselves?* However that may be, your accusation that we Christian students fail in practical assistance to the poor does an injustice which I cannot permit to pass without correction. For within my view are several students who to my personal knowledge frequently visit the destitute, bringing them their friendship and what little material help they are able to supply. Would you have have me sound a trumpet for them because they give an alms? Yet, my friends, you are quite right about one thing: It is true that the charity of our Catholic students is, unlike that of the religious orders, quite unorganized, and therefore unrecognized by the student body. And perhaps it should be organized and enlarged."

After the meeting, Frederic, Lallier, and Lamache walked up the Rue de l'Estrapade toward Lamache's hotel. They were silent, thinking over that evening's bitter battle.

"Of all that was said tonight," Frederic finally commented, "four words keep ringing in my ears. They are the words of our Saint-Simonian friend—'*Show us your works.*' He couldn't have asked that if we had formally organized our work for Sister Rosalie. And strangely enough, Le Taillandier and I were discussing such a project in Sister Rosalie's parlor just last Thursday."

They had stopped before the heavy doors of the Hotel Corneille, where Lamache lived.

"Let's hear about it up in my rooms," said Lamache.

Seated in Lamache's tiny living room, Frederic repeated the conversation he'd had with Sister Rosalie and Le Taillandier.

"You and I know how we've benefited spiritually through our small sacrifices for the poor," he began. "Well, that's one of the things Le Taillandier and I were talking about with Sister Rosalie the other day. We agreed that there should be some organized way of bringing more students to share this work and its benefits."

He spoke of the miseries of the poor, the heroic sacrifices of the religious working among them, and the crying need for more lay assistants to aid both the religious and the overworked parish priests.

"We must face the fact," he said, "that thousands of the indigent in Paris have come here from country districts which haven't seen a priest since the Revolution. Is it any wonder they have drifted so far from the Church? And it's not only that they're ignorant of religion; their minds have been poisoned against religion. These people would not listen to a priest, even if there were priests to visit them. And today we've too few priests to care for the religious needs of even practising Catholics. But you and I know that the poor will listen to laymen who reach their hearts through personal kindness and a helping hand. We ourselves have proved that."

Frederic paused. Carried away by his concern for the wants and worries of the poor, he arose and began to pace up and down the little room. His eyes were aflame with an inner light, his voice trembled slightly with emotion. Lamache and Lallier hung on his words, enthralled, for Frederic held them not only by his eloquence, but also by the charm of his facial expression. His gray eyes were particularly expressive; they seemed to become darker and shaded with blue as his intensity increased.

"Formerly," he continued, "a Christian society gave its heart to the poor. But today, to be poor is not simply a mis-

74

fortune. Too many of the well-to-do consider poverty a Divine punishment. An incredibly vicious doctrine, yes—but it's solemnly voiced in England by bourgeoisie who regard their own prosperity as a sign of the Divine favor. It's such heresy we must prevent here in France, else we'll have people starving to death—as a poor woman did in London only a month ago. Starved to death, my friends, in the midst of plenty—in the world's richest city. And solely because society at large, and the officialdom to whom she'd appealed in vain disclaimed any responsibility for her. Cain, in our age, doesn't use a club to kill his victims, but a heart of stone.

"We laymen must do our part to prevent the cold wind of materialism from snuffing out the warm flame of charity in France," he added, as a gust of cold air billowed the curtains and threatened the candles. "We must proclaim through our acts that man is still his brother's keeper. And in doing so, let us heed our old French proverb that says, 'He gives nothing who does not give himself.' Then we will find that the way to the Faubourg St. Marceau is also the way to our own spiritual growth."

"An organization of university students committed to charitable works—that will sound strange to a lot of ears!" observed Lallier.

"Do you have a plan for organization?" asked Lamache.

"Just a rough idea, so far," replied Frederic. "I suggest as a first step that we Catholic members of the Conference of History—as many as care to—form a union of charity."

"It should be easy to start such a union," said Lallier. "Those of us who have been helping Sister Rosalie need simply organize formally to help her on a more regular basis."

"Exactly," agreed Frederic. "We would form a nucleus. And every Catholic student loyal to his faith would be welcomed to membership."

"What's the next step?" asked Lallier, eager for action.

"Let's meet in Père Bailly's office tomorrow and talk this over with him," suggested Frederic. "In the meantime, we can all sleep on the matter—inasmuch as it's high time for sleep, anyway."

The next afternoon, the three met with Monsieur Bailly

in the *Tribune* office. Frederic outlined the idea, describing the organization he had in mind as "a small private association, altogether devoted to charity."

By the word "altogether" he meant that no fund-raising social activities were contemplated. The members of the association were to give *themselves* to the poor. That is, they were to give their personal aid as good neighbors when a poor man or a member of his family was sick, or without funds, or without work, or required legal advice, or was in need of any other service the young men might be able to give. They would finance their charities out of their own pockets and from contributions freely offered by friends.

The warmhearted publisher listened delightedly as Frederic outlined the association's proposed objectives. He was impressed by Frederic's determination to bring the "union of charity" into being at once. Himself a counselor and conciliator rather than a doer, he had special admiration for those who could not only plan, but actualize their plans.

"Let's call a meeting to get this activity under way," suggested Frederic to Père Bailly and his three schoolfellows. "We can count on Le Taillandier, Devaux, and Clavé—Le Taillandier especially. He and I have already talked about it —together, and with Sister Rosalie. As you'd probably expect, she's all for it. I think we can be pretty sure of seven members to start with."

Monsieur Bailly had assured the others that his office was available whenever they might want to use it, and the four agreed to meet there formally the following Tuesday to organize the union of charity.

Frederic Ozanam

His eyes were blue-gray, his hair brown. He was slim, of medium stature, and graceful and quick in movement. His mien and facial features reflect an ardent spirit, high intelligence, and self-discipline.

(Left) House in Milan, Italy, where Frederic Ozanam was born, April 23, 1813, as commemorative plaque records.

(Below) Work table where Ozanam wrote the books and lectures that created a new appreciation of medieval culture.

Lyons in Ozanam's early manhood, viewed from the Pont du Change.

Frederic Ozanam at age twenty, shortly after he had inspired the founding of the "Conference of Charity," soon thereafter to be named the "Society of St. Vincent de Paul".—Sketch by Louis Janmot, a fellow First Communicant of Ozanam's, and an early Vincentian.

Place des Cordeliers, with Church of St. Bonaventure on left. It was in this church that seventeen-year-old Frederic Ozanam consecrated his life to the service of truth and his fellowmen according to God's designs. Almost at once, theological difficulties that had tormented his mind for months, were dissolved. (Pps. 26–28.)

Facade of the Royal College on the River Rhone, Lyons, where Ozanam was a student from his ninth through his seventeenth year.

A few months after her marriage to Frederic Ozanam, June 23, 1841, Amélie sat for this sculpture by her brother, Charles Soulacroix.

Marie, only child of Frederic and Amélie Ozanam, four
years after her birth on July 24, 1845. Sketch by Louis
Janmot.

Frederic Ozanam passed through this imposing entrance to the Sorbonne thousands of times during five student years and twelve years as a professor. In 1840, at twenty-seven, he had become by eight years the youngest professor ever admitted to that university's august faculty.

Pressed to join the Sorbonne faculty after winning a competition of French scholars for the Chair of Foreign Literature in that world-honored institution, Ozanam hesitated. He was planning to marry; the Sorbonne salary was one-sixth the income assured him at the University of Lyons. Before deciding—favorably—he prayed long before the Blessed Sacrament in the Saint-Etienne-du-Mont Church (right).

Sister Rosalie Rendu was a Daughter of Charity—the celebrated "White Caps" founded by St. Vincent de Paul. Ozanam and fellow students made themselves assistants to Sister Rosalie and the Sisters under her direction. Thus they learned, before organizing the Society of St. Vincent de Paul, how to befriend the poor with respect for human dignity.

In his 60 years of priesthood, Vincent de Paul (b. 1581) organized many associations to benefit mankind. All stood time's test excepting an all-male "Association of Charity for Laymen."—Some 200 years later, Frederic Ozanam and fellow students formed a union of laymen to aid the poor. They chose as their patron the great friend of the poor, St. Vincent de Paul.

Ozanam as he appeared in his later years, before his final physical breakdown. Death ended his prolonged suffering on September 8th, four-and-a-half months after his fortieth birthday.

The tomb of Frederic Ozanam, in the crypt of the Church of Carmel at the Catholic Institute in Paris. Here Ozanam had desired to rest.—Mural: "The Good Samaritan," by Rene Dionnet.

CHAPTER 9

MONSIEUR BAILLY looked up as the clock over his office fireplace chimed the quarter hour, and saw that it was fifteen minutes before eight. It was Tuesday evening, the twenty-third of April in 1833, and the clear, golden sunshine that had warmed Paris all through that spring day had failed to leave any trace of its genial glow behind. The editor arose, applied a taper to the waiting fireplace fuel, and stamped about briefly to restore his circulation. In a few minutes he expected a number of young men to invade his office for a meeting called to organize the "union of charity." At Ozanam's suggestion it had been scheduled for eight o'clock.

The publisher placed a few chairs about his desk and was about to resume his writing when Le Taillandier and Ozanam entered. Within ten minutes four other top-hatted, cravated young men in flared-out coats and colorful vests had arrived amid the usual student bantering and skylarking. They laid their hats on the broad, flat top of the railing that separated Monsieur Bailly's work space from the rest of the big room, and seated themselves.

"We're all present, Monsieur Bailly," said Frederic. "Will you take the chair?"

"Gladly," agreed the publisher, "if you'll let me keep the one I'm sitting in!"

He looked over the little group.

"Well, gentlemen, we're all here—all seven of us—to consider Frederic's idea of forming a union of charity, an idea with which, I know, he has made all of you acquainted."

Frederic held up an interrupting hand.

"I feel, Monsieur Bailly," he said, "that we students should begin this meeting by apologizing to Auguste here"—turning toward Le Taillandier—"for not taking action a month ago when he suggested that some of us practising Catholics form an organization whose members would devote themselves to doing good—instead of talking incessantly about who was doing harm."

"I made that suggestion after sitting through one of our long and fruitless debates in the Conference of History," laughed Auguste.

"Ah, but you did make the suggestion," insisted Ozanam, "and we slowpokes didn't wake up to its worth until our Saint-Simonian critic had poured caustic scorn upon our humbled heads."

"Thank you for the clarification," said Monsieur Bailly. "Now we'll start all over again, and this time we'll start right. Let's begin with a prayer for guidance."

He stood, and the others followed suit.

"Come, Holy Spirit," Monsieur Bailly prayed, using the age-old invocation of the Church, "fill the hearts of Thy faithful, and kindle in them the fire of Thy love."

"Send forth Thy Spirit, and they shall be created," responded the six young men.

"And Thou shalt renew the face of the earth," answered Monsieur Bailly, concluding with the petition to God "to instruct the hearts of the faithful by the light of the Holy Spirit."

Surely the Holy Spirit hovered over that little gathering—the first of innumerable future meetings in which Vincentians the world over would pray for Divine guidance before going forth to the poor and the unfortunate.

"And now," said the chairman, when all had again seated themselves, "I think it would help if Frederic would lay before us in greater detail the reasons as he sees them for such an organization as we propose forming."

Frederic leaned forward in his chair and spoke with great earnestness.

"There are two chief reasons why we should join together

for work among the unfortunates of the Faubourg St. Marceau," he said.

"Number one is, that by drawing closer to the poor we draw closer to God. And we students must draw closer to God a little more every day, or we'll find ourselves falling away from Him. Let's face it—we're all subject to temptations. Most of us are far from our homes and the good influence of our families. Through uniting in a formal organization we can strengthen one another in close companionship as we work together to alleviate the poverty that we cannot hope to cure. We'll become better friends of Our Lord as we become more understanding friends of His poor. For while those we visit in the St. Marceau neighborhood may sometimes be our equals in weakness, they will often—and I say this from my experience among them—be our superiors in virtue.

"My second reason recalls the acid criticism we all heard voiced by one of our opponents at the Conference of History a few days ago. We've all been helping Sister Rosalie. But through an organization, however simple its rules, we can assist her and her poor more effectively. And our membership in such a union will bear silent and humble witness to the faith that is in us—a faith that has always inspired its more devoted adherents to work for the good of those the world despises and neglects."

He then repeated and expanded some of the thoughts he had expressed in Lamache's apartment a few nights before.

"Let's hope that the Conference of History," he concluded, "will give birth to an organization given more to action than to words. What we members of the Conference of History have proclaimed, such a body would express in works. Therefore, Mr. Chairman, I move that we form a union of charity."

"I second the motion," said Le Taillandier, instantly.

"Frederic has discussed the idea of a union of charity, individually, with all of us," said François Lallier. "Insofar as I'm concerned, further discussion is unnecessary."

"All in favor of forming a union of charity, say 'aye,'" asked Monsieur Bailly, and a hearty chorus of "ayes" answered him.

"There are obviously no 'no's'!" exclaimed the chairman. "I

therefore declare that the motion that we seven form a union of charity is unanimously adopted."

He paused again, his expression revealing some perplexity, for neither Monsieur Bailly nor the students had given thought as to what steps should be taken next.

"I suppose," he continued, a note of hesitation in his voice, "that we should have a committee to draw up a constitution and bylaws—though it may be that that could well wait on further developments. Also, there's election of officers to be considered, and the matter of formally adopting a name for our new organization."

Frederic gained his attention.

"I think we'd all agree with you," he said, "that the writing of a constitution and bylaws should be delayed until this association has been functioning for some time. Then our constitution and rules will be based on experience rather than theory."

This suggestion was formally approved.

Monsieur Bailly asked: "Are there any suggestions as to a day and a time for our meetings?"

On this question everyone had his own ideas, but it was finally agreed that Tuesday would be the most convenient meeting day and six o'clock the most practical hour.

"That will leave time after meetings for visits to the poor if our studies permit," Frederic said in arguing for the adopted hour. "Though we will, of course, continue to do most of our visiting on our free days, and Sister Rosalie will, as usual, supply us names and addresses of those to be visited."

"What about a name for our organization?" Le Taillandier asked, directing his question to Frederic. "Are you satisfied with 'union of charity'?"

"Well, no," answered Ozanam. "We're an offshoot, in a sense, of the Conference of History—how about calling this association the 'Conference of Charity'?"

This name was adopted.

Frederic proposed that Monsieur Bailly should be made permanent president of the Conference of Charity—a nomination to which all enthusiastically agreed.

Accepting the honor, Monsieur Bailly accompanied his acceptance with a few words of advice.

"If you desire to help yourselves and the poor," he said, "you will gradually raise yourselves to a new spiritual plane; you will attain that degree of humble goodness which will enable you to see Jesus Christ suffering in the persons of the poor. Moreover, if you wish your service to the poor to be efficacious, you must not allow it to become a mere doling out of alms. No—you must make your material assistance a medium of moral assistance; you must be ready always to give aid to the spirit as well as to the body."

"Moral assistance—that's all most of us can afford to give, much of the time!" exclaimed Lamache.

Amid the laughter Frederic arose, turning his pockets inside out and saying mournfully, "How true! . . . But seriously," he continued, "we can't overemphasize what Monsieur Bailly points out should be our first purpose—the spiritual good of those we visit. Yet I learned a lesson three or four months ago—and I know that what I'm about to say reflects the mind of Monsieur Bailly—a lesson that taught me this: To help a person spiritually, we must first rescue him from cold or hunger or from whatever physical distress he may be suffering. This last winter—you'll remember this, Auguste," he said to Le Taillandier, "for we were together—we happened to hear two of the younger Sisters at the convent telling Sister Rosalie that they had come upon a poor man asleep, clothed in dirty rags and exposed to the freezing air. Sister Rosalie asked them what they had done for him. 'Why, Sister,' these inexperienced young nuns replied, 'we began to talk to him about God.' Sister Rosalie shook her head sadly at this answer. She said, 'You made a mistake, my children. You should have cleaned him up first, given him nourishing food—and then, when that was done, talked to him of God.' Let us never forget, my brothers in our new Conference of Charity, that we are but humble servants of the poor. We must never be so egotistical as to expect a hungry man, or one distracted by worry over the rent, to listen to our words about God—when in charity we feel we must give some spiritual counsel—until we have helped to relieve his misery."

"That point is of immense importance," remarked Monsieur Bailly. "Though you budding lawyers can frequently give worldly advice that can relieve a man's misery—even when you can't give francs."

This brought laughter, but the publisher was serious, and said so.

"Many of the poor are victimized," he said, "or fall into distress through circumstances for which there's often a legal remedy. Your legal knowledge will enable you to help such people out of their troubles. Fortunately, all of you have old heads. Though how young in years," he said, surveying the little group—"how young you really are."

The students knew that Père Bailly had their birthdays listed in his editorial calendar, for on those days he generally remembered his student friends with a book from his overstocked library.

"Paul Lamache here," he resumed, pointing at Lamache, "is the oldest of all—and you, Paul, are all of twenty-four. Le Taillandier, you're another oldster—I happen to know you're twenty-two. And Jules—the only medical student among you lawyers-to-be—Jules is twenty-one. Lallier, you are a bit beyond your nineteenth birthday. Clavé, I'm uncertain as to your years—but I'd guess you're twenty, also. And Frederic"—here Père Bailly paused and extracted a book from a desk drawer —"Frederic, you were nineteen years old yesterday, but you are twenty years old today! So with warmest congratulations I present you with this latest volume by that other distinguished son of Lyons, the philosopher Ballanche. With every birthday may you continue to grow in wisdom till you actually are as distinguished as Ballanche. But whether you attain fame or not, Frederic, you'll always have our love and the love of all who know you—and that, as Ballanche himself would tell you, is better than fame."

He handed the volume to Frederic, and then added thoughtfully, "And perhaps, too, it's a good omen that you, and this little new society for charity to whose creation you've given inspiration, have been born on the same date."

There was a burst of applause, and a chorus of well wishes. Frederic, who instinctively shrank from personal acclaim, called his companions back to the business of the evening by reverting to Monsieur Bailly's mention of francs versus advice, and asking the conference president what one should give when a family needed no advice and the visiting member lacked francs?

"The only one of us who thinks that question amusing is Le Taillandier," said Lallier, pointing to the grinning Auguste. "He, lucky rich man, has never had that unpleasant experience."

"I suggest that we pool our charitable contributions, and use the money to buy food tickets from Sister Rosalie," continued Frederic. "If we pool our donations, each can draw from a common supply of food tickets as many as he needs on any visiting day."

"I'm for that," said Devaux emphatically, and there was general assent.

"Then, Jules," asked Frederic, turning to Devaux, "will you take up our first collection?"

"Do you supply a collection plate?" asked Devaux.

"Yes—a capacious one," returned Frederic, pointing to Devaux's hat reposing with the others on the flat-topped railing. "That will do!"

"So it will," agreed Devaux, reaching for it.

With fine consideration, he then held the hat behind him and, walking backward, made the rounds.

The students laughed, but they appreciated Devaux's thoughtfulness.

"An excellent idea!" cried Frederic. "No one excepting God and the giver will know who gives five sous and who gives five francs. Let's take up the collection this way every time."[1]

Devaux was voted the permanent treasurer on the spot, but he and Père Bailly were the only officers elected at this time.

Monsieur Bailly suggested that besides continuing to handle their regular assignments from Sister Rosalie the members take over the care of three families Madame Bailly, at the Sister's request, had been helping. These presented problems

---

[1] This method of taking up the weekly collection at St. Vincent de Paul meetings has become a traditional and a universal practice.

with which she had been unable to cope. Frederic understood why when Père Bailly outlined the unusual difficulties involved.

One family named Arouet, for example, was kept in constant terror by a drunken husband who had threatened violence to Madame Bailly.

"How about assigning that family to Le Taillandier and me?" asked Frederic. "We two have been working together."

"It's yours," agreed the society's first president.

Frederic and other students, counseled to do so by Sister Rosalie, had been visiting tenement families in teams of two. This assured continuity of help to a person or to a household, for if one of the team were unable to make a visit, the other could carry out the assignment. It was, besides, a policy dictated by prudence.

Madame Bailly's other two families were likewise assigned to teams, and the young men began to reach for their top hats.

"Just one more matter," said Frederic, as his brother members were making for the door. "We should inform Sister Rosalie that we're now an organziation. She'll be delighted at the news—and we should get it to her at once."

"I'm seeing her first thing tomorrow morning," said Devaux. "I'm bringing her some new medicine for a woman her sisters are nursing."

"You might tell her that one of these days we'll be asking her for suggestions on our constitution and bylaws," remarked Frederic.

"It's by no means too late for a visit," said Le Taillandier, as he and Frederic stepped out of the *Tribune*'s office.

"And you don't like to think of that Arouet family being terrorized by the drunken father a single hour longer than is necessary," added Frederic, reading his teammate's mind.

"Exactly!"

"Then let's go!"

They stopped at a food store, made a few hurried purchases, then hastened on. Arriving at the many-storied tenement which housed the Arouets, they were directed by the concierge to No. 17 on the fourth floor.

The door to No. 17 was opened by a frail, washed-out little woman.

"Madame Arouet?" asked Le Taillandier.

"Yes, monsieur."

"Madame, we are sent by your friend Madame Bailly. This is Monsieur Ozanam. My name is Le Taillandier."

"Come in, messieurs," invited Madame Arouet, "Madame Bailly has indeed been our friend."

The two students took a step forward, then paused a moment, surprised by the sight of four barefoot children sitting on the floor in the center of the room, each with a pile of feathers between outstretched legs. The youngest was about four, the oldest a girl of perhaps thirteen. To one side, on a pile of old but clean rags, a baby was lying on its back, playing with its toes.

The students' arms were still filled with groceries, which they now deposited on a table near the wall.

"Monsieur Bailly advised us to help you with your shopping," said Frederic, explaining the groceries.

"Thank you, messieurs. Our food is almost all gone, and I have only three sous left after paying the rent."

"Your husband, then, is out of work?" asked Le Taillandier.

"As always, monsieur. He drinks constantly, and often takes from me even the few sous the children and I earn."

"Can't you keep your earnings from him?"

"Most frequently, yes—else we could not live. But when he is crazy for drink, he beats me to give him money. Yes, and he beats the children, too."

The woman was close to tears. Frederic, to divert her for the moment, pointed to the feathers which the children were sorting, and asked, "Is this your occupation?"

"Yes, monsieur. We sort the feathers by size and color."

"And how much does this work bring in, may I ask?"

"The efforts of all of us, monsieur, bring in ten sous a day."

"Three francs a week!" exclaimed Le Taillandier, indignantly. "And who buys these feathers?"

"Milliners, mostly, to decorate the beautiful hats of the ladies of Paris."

"Is there no way, madame, that you can bring your husband to honor his marriage vows, and to love and cherish you and these innocent children?" asked Frederic.

The woman looked uncomfortable.

"Ours was a marriage without vows," she said. "We were not married in any kind of ceremony."

"Then, madame, why is it, not being married, you put up with this man's brutality?"

"I have wanted to escape from him. But he threatens to have me thrown into jail should I attempt it. And then, what would become of the children?"

"But, madame, you are *not* married to him," insisted Frederic.

"He's telling you the truth," said Le Taillandier. "This man is not your husband, either in the eyes of the Church or of the state."

"You are free to leave him at any time," added Frederic, "and to take the children with you. That is the law."

"I should like to believe you, messieurs. But suppose you are not correct? Ah, then my husband would be more of a demon than ever. Who knows what he might do with the children while I was in prison?"

"Would you believe us," asked Frederic, "if we were to bring you a written statement to the truth of what we have said from the *Procureur de Roi?*"

"Certainly, monsieur," answered the woman. "If the king's attorney should say that I am a free woman, it would be like the king himself saying so, and I would have to believe."

"Then, madame," promised Frederic, "tomorrow we will bring you the written opinion of the *Procureur du Roi.*"

Next evening, when the woman had stumbled through the written opinion the two law students had obtained from the office of the king's attorney general, she was like a prisoner released from long confinement in the galleys—overjoyed, yet fearing that her freedom was unreal and might not be lasting. Later she gladly accepted an offer, made with approval of the Conference, of relocation in lodgings where she might avoid the fury of her erstwhile master, who was threatening violence.

"My parents have asked me more than once," she told her two friends from the Conference, "to come back and live with them in our village near Epinal. But they are so poor. And there would be no work there for the older children."

"Would you like to have your three oldest children remain in Paris, if they had good homes and could learn good trades?" Frederic asked.

"That would be wonderful good fortune for them, monsieur."

"We shall see what can be arranged," said Frederic.

Without mentioning their action to the woman, who was bitter toward the scoundrel who had oppressed her for so many years, Ozanam and Le Taillandier sought out the father in his favorite *bistro*, to learn whether there was any possibility of awakening in him a sense of duty toward the woman and children he had so pitifully wronged. To their urgings that he reform his ways, prove himself, and then marry the mother of his children, he replied with abuse. His threats against the woman he had enslaved so strongly impressed the young men that they obtained a police order banishing the brutal fellow from Paris.

Through Sister Rosalie, the oldest girl was placed with a couple who had recently lost an only daughter. Père Bailly offered to take the two oldest boys into his home, and into his printing shop as apprentices. With money collected from their friends, Ozanam and Le Taillandier supplied the mother with stagecoach fare to Epinal and some money for expenses. She was overjoyed that her oldest daughter would have an excellent home and that her two sons would be able to learn a profitable trade.

"They will learn something even more important," Frederic told her. "They will learn about their Creator, and His laws, and they will take instructions in religion so that they can make their First Holy Communion."

"Ah, I remember my happiness on the day I made mine," said the woman, sadly. "But that seems ages ago, and of another world."

"But you are going back to that world," Frederic assured her. "Why not renew that happiness? Our Lord is waiting for you to come to Him in Holy Communion, as He waits and longs for all of us."

"I will, I will—for now I must be worthy of my children, and especially my little Louise here, and my baby, for they will be looking to me," she said, as the young men helped her into the diligence bound for Epinal.

Such were the fruits of the first visit of charity by members of what was to become the St. Vincent de Paul Society, as the account has come down through the years.

CHAPTER 10

NOT LONG after the first meeting of the Conference of Charity, Frederic Ozanam and François Lallier, and Père Bailly, himself, were somewhat nonplussed to find that a majority of the members—in other words, the other four —doubted the wisdom of allowing the little group to increase in number.

"A larger organization," argued a proponent of the *status quo*, "will face problems our group, being small, does not now have to contend with. If we add more members, we'll have to put into effect all kinds of rules and regulations. Why sacrifice our present simple way of operation?"

This attitude caused the three grave concern.

"I agree that we should have stringent membership requirements," Père Bailly asserted. "But I insist that we must welcome more of our Catholic students to our little society."

"Lallier and I agree with you," said Frederic. "We feel that the Conference should be allowed to grow without any limitations whatsoever."

During the next few days, Frederic busied himself with talking to Lamache, Le Taillandier, Devaux, and Clavé. The Conference of Charity, he pointed out to each, must serve the spiritual welfare not only of themselves, but of *all* the Catholic students; therefore, it must be freely open to all.

At this highly critical time in the life of the tender seedling of charity he and his fellow students had planted, Frederic's far-seeing vision and decisive leadership cleared the way for its growth and multiplication.

It was voted that the Conference of Charity should be open to every Catholic student unquestionably zealous in the practice of his faith. This policy prevented the organization going the way to oblivion of innumerable little school societies which are ever being born, restrict membership to a few, live a few months or years, and disappear without a trace.

In presenting his reasons for expanding the membership, Frederic pointed out that requests for aid were already coming from parish priests. The first call was from Père Faudet, newly appointed pastor of St. Etienne's. He had been informed by Monsieur Bailly that the Conference had begun its existence within his parish, though its work was among the poor of a neighboring *faubourg*. Père Faudet was invited to a meeting of the Conference and, curious about this unusual little group, gladly attended. He saw that the members were levelheaded and possessed of humility and wisdom, and therefore qualified to aid him in caring for the destitute of his parish. For this task his many other duties left him all too little time. He was quick, therefore, to ask the Conference of Charity for help.

At this time, membership still numbered only seven. Each one had been devoting his every spare moment to helping Sister Rosalie's poor. Nevertheless, to Père Faudet's request that they aid him, they responded with a generous "We will."

"All we ask, Père Faudet," Monsieur Bailly said, "are your directions. We will try to be your hands and feet—your aides in bringing the charity of the parish to its poor. In return, we will make bold to look to you for spiritual guidance."

Père Faudet thus became the first of thousands of parish priests who were to welcome the co-operation of the future St. Vincent de Paul Society.

Another early request for help came from a house of correction for young offenders. It was in the Rue de Grès, not far from the apartment to which Frederic had moved only recently, upon the return of Monsieur Ampère's son from his travels. In his own quarters, which later he was to share with Le Taillandier, he entertained his fellow students and enlisted the interest of many in the new Conference of Charity.

The first name presented for membership was that of a friend of Lallier's—Gustave Colas de la Noue, a law student, a former Saint-Simonian, and a poet whom Frederic was later to call "one of the chosen spirits to whom God had given wings." He became the eighth member. Soon there were fifteen, then twenty, then twenty-five. Nearly all belonged to the Conference of History, which Frederic had come to look upon as a recruiting ground for his Conference of Charity.

Père Bailly continued to preside over the Conference meetings; he was to be its president for the next eleven years.

For some time after its founding, the Conference of Charity continued to function without a full complement of officers and without a written constitution. It got along smoothly and efficiently enough, for its membership was still comparatively small. Frederic watched the Conference grow to thirty members and knew that the time was approaching when it must have a constitution, bylaws, and a complete staff of officers.

In this early springtime of its life, the thirty or thirty-five members who now composed the Conference of Charity knew how to make even a gay outing serve as an act of faith—as they proved in their excursion to Nanterre.

Early on the Sunday after Corpus Christi, 1833, two young men beat a merry tattoo on the door of the apartment at No. 7, Rue de Grès, which Frederic now occupied with his friend, Auguste Le Taillandier. They had had a long climb to reach that door, for the modest apartment was on the sixth floor. The air was better there, and Frederic enjoyed, he said, being "next to the stars."

Throwing wide the door, Frederic greeted his cousin Henri Pessonneau, and Jacques Janmot, a friend since childhood. Both had been members of his First Communion class, and both were now students at the University and members of the growing Conference of Charity. They had just been to

Mass at the Church of the Sorbonne; Frederic and Auguste had attended the six-o'clock Mass in their parish church of St. Etienne-du-Mont. All were eager to get started early for Nanterre.

The hosts had prepared chocolate and bread and a plate of fruit for breakfast, and the four ate heartily, for they looked forward to a long day. At Nanterre they were to be joined by others from the Conference. They planned to march in the town's Corpus Christi procession, always held the Sunday following the feast.

They stepped out of the apartment house into a golden and glorious morning, walked through the Luxembourg Gardens to the omnibus station, purchased "fresh air" seats on the omnibus roof, and were soon rattling along the Avenue Neuilly on the hour's ride to Nanterre.

The student's excursion to Nanterre was a dramatic and practical protest against the government's proscription of religious processions in the larger French cities. In a meeting on the Tuesday before Corpus Christi Frederic, speaking to the Conference about the government's weak-kneed attitude in the face of anti-Christian truculence, had ended his comments by saying: "Inasmuch as the authorities, intimidated by anti-Christian toughs, forbid Corpus Christi processions through the streets of our major French cities, including Paris, I suggest that we go to some small town near Paris and join in the procession it will have."

The government's proscription did not apply to hundreds of small towns. In these, on the Sunday following Corpus Christi, streets and houses were embowered in foliage and flowers as the faithful marched in procession to pay public homage to the Eucharistic Christ. One of the humblest of these towns was Nanterre, the birthplace of St. Geneviève, the patroness of Paris.

Arrived in Nanterre, the three students were soon joined by twenty-seven more Conference members.

Some of the villagers eyed them narrowly, asking themselves whether these young men had come to scoff or to pray. Their suspicions turned to edification when they saw the students, top hats in hand, walking reverently in the long procession, which now began to move from the church through the town's flower-strewn streets. Crowds lining the thorough-fares on either side knelt and adored as the Blessed Eucharist approached, enshrined in a golden monstrance borne by the pastor of the village. Under the gold-brocaded canopy held by six of Nanterre's leading citizens, he advanced slowly, while two acolytes carrying censers walked backwards, in-censing the Living Presence.

The students sang with fervor the glorious hymn of St. Thomas Aquinas to the Blessed Sacrament as they marched, their strong young voices blending with those of the villagers. The people of Nanterre marveled, and were edified—they had thought that virtually all University students were skeptics.

After the Solemn High Mass, most of the students decided to dine at St. Germain, five or six miles beyond Nanterre. Dividing into groups of three and four, they walked there. The road led through a magnificent forest, and along much of the route wild strawberries grew; the hikers picked and ate them as they went.

At St. Germain, the tavernkeeper agreed to spread the board for forty sous a head, the hearty dinner including a palatable light wine.

Thus fortified, the students set out on the long way back in the cool of the evening, greeting the moon with rousing songs as it rose over the dark woods. Light hearts and light rhythm marvelously shortened the distance to Nanterre—so much so that Pessonneau, Janmot, Ozanam, and Le Taillandier decided to continue the walk all the way back to Paris. It was not till after they had heard the midnight hour strike that they arrived at the Latin Quarter, having discoursed of many things along the way.

Next day, the Corpus Christi excursion to Nanterre was the talk of the University. This dramatic act of faith caused the skeptical students to look upon their Catholic schoolfel-lows with increased respect.

It also increased Catholic student interest in the Conference of Charity. Upright and manly young men are always gen-erous, and sixty or seventy now aspired to join their fellow students in serving the poor. This was fortunate, for many new members would soon be needed when the coming summer brought the usual great student exodus from Paris. Active membership was sufficiently increased to meet the demands for assistance which would be made upon the Conference during the summer.

The long vacation would see Frederic himself absent from Paris. Under instructions from his father, he was preparing to join his family on a tour of Italy.

Dr. Ozanam had written, giving Frederic the itinerary. They were to travel all the way from Lyons to Naples, and back again, by carriage. The tour would be costly, but Dr. Ozanam had been saving toward it for a long time back.

A joyful and excited family welcomed Frederic home from Paris. His father and mother, the Abbé Alphonse, and Charles —now a slim, lively lad of nine—found him matured. He seemed, they thought, more assured, more certain of himself.

The Ozanam family set off on its Italian adventure on a bright, cool morning, across a green land newly washed by a night of rain. The carriage rolled swiftly over the good road behind its four horses, the postillion riding the left rear horse, his whip cracking like a pistol. The excellent highway to Chambéry passed through an immense plain, rich and culti- vated. At the Savoy border, they paused for passport and luggage inspection and were then on their way toward the mountains, and Italy.

At Lanslebourg, they ascended the Maritime Alps beneath snow-capped peaks, and at last beheld the plains of Italy. The scenic beauties of the route demanded many stops; the towering pinnacles, the torrential waterfalls, the lush and peaceful valleys invited much viewing. Each turn of the road presented a new, dramatic beauty—majestic pictures that were to remain with Frederic all his life.

The sight-seers welcomed every pause, for their carriage, though considered commodious enough by the standards of the day, did not provide an unnecessary inch of room. A few jolting, swaying miles, and all the Ozanams were more than ready to descend for a leg-stretching walk.

Stopping at the picturesque inns along the route they found that the food varied with the scenery, each district supplying its characteristic game, fruits, wines and cheese. The Ozanams ordered their meals and gave their directions with much of the familiar ease of natives, for all except Charles spoke Italian.

In Milan, Dr. and Mme. Ozanam renewed old acquaintances and friendships, and the Abbé Alphonse and Frederic met many who remembered them as children.

Posting south toward Florence, they stopped at the bridge of Lodi, where Napoleon had seen his star, and where the young Captain Jean-Antoine Ozanam had crossed at the head of his company of hussars on the way to the capture of Milan. The bullets, Dr. Ozanam recalled, had been whining close that day.

They also visited another scene of battle—Pavia, where Captain Ozanam had fought under the "little corporal," and where too, at Pavia's old university, he had some years later received his medical degree.

By the time they reached Florence, Lyons seemed ages away. Here they stayed at the home of Madame Ozanam's sister.

In this native city of the great poet of the Middle Ages, Frederic steeped himself in Dantean lore. Standing before the painting known as the Dispute on the Blessed Sacrament, he noted Dante's imposing figure and asked himself why a poet had been placed among the theologians. He was to answer that question six years later in one of the most significant literary essays of the time.

Madame Ozanam decided to remain in Florence with her sister until her husband and sons returned from Naples. The latter pushed on toward Assisi, and there another literary seed fell upon the receptive soil of Frederic's precocious mind and fertile imagination. Toward the end of his life, that seed was to grow and flower and bear fruit in his great work on the Franciscan poets.

In Rome the travelers were received graciously by Cardinal

Fesch, the uncle of Napoleon, who though banished from France retained the title of Archbishop of Lyons. But the great event of their visit to the Eternal City was a private audience with Pope Gregory XVI.

Finally their now rather road-worn carriage brought them to Naples. From there they made excursions into all the surrounding country, so rich in historic relics of old Rome's emperors, statesmen and poets. They saw Vesuvius in eruption, and approached to within dangerous proximity of that splendid sight. They visited the dead city of Pompeii, where, eighteen hundred years before, time had stopped. The city was still being excavated. Before the excited scholar's eyes the archaeologists' shovels daily uncovered perfectly preserved scenes from the life of a civilization whose culture had helped shape his modern world. "Be careful!" Frederic would cry, grasping Amélie's arm as they strolled about the ghostly city, "or you'll surely bump into an ancient Latin rounding this next corner."

Even from the most fascinating of vacations there must eventually be a returning; toward the middle of September Dr. Ozanam and his sons started north toward Florence. Here Madame Ozanam rejoined them, and the family began its homeward journey. For Frederic, the carriage wheels now seemed to roll all too slowly. He was eager for Paris—for his student friends, his studies, his work in the Conference of Charity.

CHAPTER 11

"THAT'S the man to confound Jouffroy and his fellow skeptics!" Frederic, his voice vibrant with enthusiasm, was speaking to Lejouteux and Montazet, two fellow students, as they left the chapel of the Collège Stanislas. There they had been listening spellbound as the Abbé Lacordaire delivered the first of a series of lectures on the constitution and the social activity of the Church. His subjects, his arguments, his methods were new. He appealed not only to believers, but to infidels; he adapted his talks to meet the assaults of the day.

"Lacordaire is the man," Frederic repeated, "to bring home to skeptics the significance of religious truth. They'd flock to hear him. How I wish the Collège Stanislas chapel could accommodate six thousand rather than only six hundred."

"I admit the Abbé is a great speaker," said Lejouteux. "But why should skeptics rush to hear him?"

"Lacordaire was once a skeptic himself," Frederic explained, "and therefore possesses deep insight into the skeptic's mind. He sympathizes with the latent desire of many to believe. Moreover, the Abbé is young, and politically, sociologically, and economically a progressive. I repeat, Lacordaire is exactly the man we need. But to influence Paris he must speak to vast numbers. And only one church in Paris is large enough. Lacordaire must speak from the pulpit of Notre Dame!"

"A magnificent idea!" declared Montazet.

"It would certainly startle Paris!" exclaimed Lejouteux. He paused, and a frown creased his brow. "And," he added, "I think it would also startle the Archbishop. He's liberal and courageous, I grant you. But after all, the Abbé Lacordaire is known as having been one of the chief associates of Lamennais. And it is now only a few months since the Holy Father condemned some of the principal ideas advanced in Lamennais's newspaper *L'Avenir*, to which Lacordaire was a chief contributor."

The trio, keeping step as they walked through the Rue de Vaugirard, silently pondered Lacordaire's acceptability to the ecclesiastical authorities.

"The radicals may have forgiven Lacordaire what they considered his conservatism," said Lejouteux, finally. "But I'm sure the royalists and other ultra-conservatives haven't forgiven him his radicalism. There'll certainly be some who'll do their utmost to turn Archbishop de Quelen against him."

96

Frederic declared that the Archbishop of Paris would not be influenced. The prelate, he reminded his companions, had maintained his independence under three kings, including Louis Philippe. Besides, he pointed out, the Archbishop enjoyed strong public support. People were still praising his heroism during the cholera epidemic, when he had turned his seminaries into hospitals and had personally ministered to the sick. Later he had at his own expense established homes for children made parentless by the epidemic.

Lejouteux and Montazet were finally persuaded that the effort to induce the Archbishop to sanction a series of Lenten lectures by Lacordaire in Notre Dame Cathedral was worth a try. They agreed to accompany Frederic the following day on a visit to the prelate.

Next afternoon the three set off for the convent of Les Dames de St. Michel, on the Rue St. Jacques, where the Archbishop had made his headquarters since fire had destroyed his episcopal residence during the 1830 revolution.

Though they had no appointment, Monseigneur de Quelen received them promptly, and his gracious simplicity quickly put them at ease. With the wholehearted earnestness and persuasive eloquence characteristic of him, Frederic presented their plea that the Abbé Lacordaire be named to give a series of Lenten lectures at Notre Dame.

The prelate, impressed by the trio's apostolic spirit, promised to give the suggestion his serious consideration. As he was bidding them farewell, he clasped the three in one embrace, saying, "In your persons I embrace the youth of France."

The Tuesday following their meeting with the Archbishop, Frederic reported on the progress of the proposed Lenten lectures to the Conference. It now numbered nearly a hundred members, and had become a growing influence in the Sorbonne's student body. The idea was enthusiastically received, and all put themselves solidly behind it. During the next several days, "Lenten lectures at Notre Dame by the Abbé Lacordaire" was being discussed wherever students gathered, and a general movement for the proposal developed.

To bring this strong student support to the Archbishop's

attention, Ozanam wrote a petition to him for institution of the lectures. For it he obtained, personally, more than two hundred signatures. Then, accompanied this time by Lallier and Lamache, he carried the petition to the Archbishop.

It was shortly after eight o'clock on a cold morning in early February when they arrived at the prelate's residence just after he had finished celebrating Mass. He had not yet broken his fast, but again he received the young men immediately and was even more cordial than before.

He surprised them with the announcement that all preparations for the desired Lenten lecture series at Notre Dame had been made.

"The series," he informed them, "will be preached by several of our most celebrated pulpit orators. In their sermons, I promise you, the fallacies of skepticism will be exposed and refuted most ably and eloquently."

The preachers he had selected, he told the three students, were even then in the next room, discussing the subjects of the forthcoming lectures. Opening the door, he showed Frederic and his two companions into the room, introduced them to the priests, and suggested that they tell the gentlemen of their own proposal that the entire series be given by Lacordaire! Then the Archbishop went to breakfast.

Ozanam, Lallier, and Lamache now knew their original proposal had gone radically awry, but they sensed that the Archbishop hoped they would be able to give these celebrated and scholarly men of the old school some insight into what young men were willing to listen to in the way of sermons.

Though respectful to the point of veneration—for the men before them were of eminent intellect and learning—the three, with Frederic leading the presentation, began to set their viewpoint before the distinguished orators. Statements and counter-statements, questions and assertions and rebuttals followed. The students and the scholarly clergymen were still arguing the merits of various approaches to the skeptical mind when the Archbishop's reappearance brought an end to the discussion.

The distinguished pulpit orators spoke in Notre Dame according to plan, commencing on February 16, 1834. Frederic, who attended all these occasions, noted that the sermons, which the Archbishop had hoped would appeal to skeptics and to young men, attracted very few of either.

It was during this period—at a Conference of Charity meeting on February 4—that Léon le Prevost suggested the Conference be placed under the patronage of St. Vincent de Paul. Le Prevost, one of the most scholarly as well as one of the oldest members of the Conference—he was in his forties —was devoted to St. Vincent. He was later to found the Brothers of St. Vincent de Paul.

Monsieur Bailly enthusiastically supported the proposal. As a boy he had read much in a notable collection of the saint's manuscripts which his father owned, and his brother was a member of an order of priests St. Vincent had founded.

Le Prevost's suggestion led to a decision to change the name of the organization to the "Conference of St. Vincent de Paul," and in the following year the title "Society of St. Vincent de Paul" was used to designate the organization as a whole.

At the February meeting Ozanam suggested that the Conference be placed under the protection of Our Blessed Lady, and that one of her feast days be selected on which members would unite to pay her special honor. For this purpose, the feast of the Immaculate Conception was decided upon. The Conference also added to the prayers said at every meeting, the *Hail Mary,* and the invocation, *St. Vincent de Paul, pray for us.*

In the midst of these activities, Ozanam and his friends found time to champion the cause of their fellow Christian students in Belgium. The Catholic bishops in that country had decided to establish the Catholic University of Louvain. This would provide for Catholic students a school free from the attacks against Christianity to which they were being constantly exposed in the state university located in that city. Adversaries of religion tried to stop the movement. They instigated non-Catholic students to stage insulting demonstrations before the houses of two of the bishops. The anti-Catholic press took up the attacks.

For French Catholics, the success or failure of the Catholic university venture in the neighboring country could well set a pattern of success or failure for a like venture in their own nation, where education was as yet entirely under state control.

Frederic was selected by his fellow students to draw up a protest. In this he stated: "It should be a cause of rejoicing to the Church, to see raised yet another monument to the immortal alliance of Science and Faith, yet another contradiction for those who announce the early decease of Christianity.—A *free* University: this should be a source of pride for all friends of Belgian nationality, proud of the foundation, in a land too long enslaved, of an institution free from . . . state intervention, worthy of a people who are the true friends of enlightenment and liberty."

He condemned the student riots against establishment of the University, then added: "We even protest in the name of those who, while not professing our belief, desire freedom for the development of all great conceptions, of all noble thoughts, of all useful undertakings."

Noting that he and his friends were students of a state university—the French government permitted none other—he declared: "But we are first and above all sons of the Church. Without ingratitude to our own Alma Mater, we today envy our Belgian brothers the happiness of receiving from one and the same hand the bread of scientific knowledge and the bread of the Sacred Word . . ." In Ozanam's view, religion, philosophy, and science were allies in the service of truth, each explaining in its own way God's plan for man and the universe.

He closed the protest with an expression of hope that, like Belgium, France would some day have its own Catholic University.

The *Univers* and the *French Gazette*, and three Belgian papers printed the protest. To add force and practicality the students subscribed for shares in the new University—each share, however, being valued at only a little over two francs.

A stand for right principle in human conduct can be far-reaching in its effects. This early advocacy of education free from state control prefaced a long battle for that freedom in France some years later, and the eventual establishment of Catholic universities in that country.

CHAPTER 12

"VICTOR GUERINEAU tells me he's engaged to marry," said Lallier, as he and Ozanam seated themselves at a sidewalk table in front of the little Le Grille Café. They had just completed their Vincentian visits.

" 'Marry too soon, and you'll repent too late,' " quoted Frederic, rather sharply.

"If you threw that old saw at Victor, he'd probably throw another right back at you," laughed Lallier, with unaccustomed asperity. "Such as, 'A man without a wife is half a man.' "

"Well, Guérineau is only my age, and I can't see the wisdom of a fellow only twenty-one taking the fatal step. How can he be sure of his real vocation?"

Frederic's question was really subjective. He had recently been asking himself whether he had a calling to a life in religion. This question was to remain in his mind, actively or passively, over the next five years. Having long since dedicated his talents to God's service, his ardent nature made him impatient of half measures. In the event he should not find himself called to a life in religion, he considered marriage a possibility, but a possibility of the vague, indefinite future. He was in no haste to come to a definite decision either way, for his filial duty, as he saw it, required that he become a lawyer and ease his parents' declining years. Fortunately for one with such responsibility, he was not subject to the stormy passions of youth. In such a sense he had never been young, despite his boyish face and bearing. In thinking about marriage, his analytical mind balanced disadvantages against advantages, and the advantages seemed heavily outweighed.

In the silence that succeeded Frederic's question, each busied himself with the *blanquette de veau* which was one of the specialties at Le Grille. At last Lallier said: "A lot of fellows our age know they have no religious vocation—and I'm one of them."

"You're quite sure?"

"Yes, I am, and I told my mother so not long before she died, for after my father's death she had been quite anxious about my future," replied Lallier. "I told her that I had long admired a girl whose family and mine have for years been friends, and that someday, if a marriage agreement could be arranged, I intended asking her blessing upon our betrothal. Before Mother died, she reminded me of this, and said she hoped that the match would soon be made. The young lady smiles on me, and I think her family would be favorable. So, Frederic, I'm thinking of taking steps to become engaged."

"What!" exploded Frederic. "You, too? At *your* age!"

Lallier was a year Frederic's junior.

"Understand, François, I've nothing against marriage *per se*," Frederic continued. "But you're so young. . . . How would you live?"

"Oh, I expect to retreat to our family land, and farm it."

"What a life! You'd forsake your friends—your studies— your work for the poor—to go off into the country and raise turnips. François, that's suicide!"

"Someday you'll marry, too," returned Lallier, nettled. "Then you'll change your tune."

"Good Lord!" exclaimed Frederic. "To be tied endlessly to a chattering female, with her moods, demands, petty tyrannies, light-headed whims—the thought appalls me!"

"I tell you, Frederic, you don't know what you're talking about," declared Lallier stoutly. He was beginning to enjoy his friend's exaggerated horror of youthful marriage. "Someday you'll meet the girl God intended for you—and you'll fall

102

like a ton of cobblestones. Then you'll look back on this talk and wonder how you could have thought of all girls as useless scatterbrains."

"I didn't say they're useless," objected Frederic. "I'll admit there are many fine women, and that the one you've set your heart on may well be one of them. And for the sake of the Mother of God, and my own mother, I can pardon every feather-headed daughter of Eve her aimless prattle, her capriciousness, her lack of ability to follow through in discussing an idea."

Lallier laughed and asked: "You think I'm too young for an engagement. When *do* you think a man ought to marry, Frederic?"

"When he's earned the right to," said Frederic. "When he has thoroughly established himself in his profession or business."

"Frederic," insisted Lallier, seriously, "you've never known the attraction of a sweet and serious-minded girl, as I have—but you will. And when you do you'll find it hard to believe you'd ever held these crusty bachelor opinions."

Frederic gazed commiseratingly at François, shaking his head. That Lallier was uttering a true prophecy was the thought farthest from his mind.

Seated atop the Lyons-bound diligence, Frederic Ozanam swayed with the heavy coach as it rattled through the crooked streets of Paris.

It was a late afternoon in August of 1834. He had just bade Lallier farewell, and still felt the sadness of the parting. For François Lallier was Frederic's ideal of all a man should be— loyal, trustworthy, and capable; generous and dependable; pure in mind, strong of character; highly intelligent. "Ah," he thought, "if only François were less in a hurry about this marriage business!" For miles his thoughts, as the coach lurched along, were concerned with Lallier and his other university friends, and with all his poorer friends of the Faubourg St. Marceau.

Suddenly, the heavy vehicle hit a rut, jolting Frederic nearly out of the coach and all thoughts of Paris out of his head. For now the country was opening before him, and he began to think of his family and of the weary miles he must travel before he greeted his parents and brothers.

Frederic found Lyons sadly changed. During an attempted insurrection about five months before, cannon-fire had destroyed several houses. The hills were now "crowned with brand new fortresses, with green slopes and white walls, and cannon of the finest bronze," he wrote ironically to Lallier. There was little trade; workmen were emigrating to Switzerland. He told Lallier that he thought the "splendid garrison, reviews, practising of firearms, patrols and sentries at every step" a sorry exchange for the ruin of commerce, the loss of workmen fleeing the city, and overflowing prisons.

In this uneasy Lyons he foregathered with schoolfellows also home from Paris on vacation—with De la Perrière, Chaurand, Dufieux, and others—all, as it happened, fellow Vincentians.

One day Dufieux surprised him with an unexpected invitation.

"You are invited to St. Point," Dufieux informed him. "Monsieur de Lamartine wants to meet you."

"Monsieur de Lamartine!" exclaimed Frederic, puzzled. "Why, he doesn't remember me."

"Yes, he does," Dufieux assured him. "He recalls your brochure on Saint-Simonism. And I've related to him how you inspired us all in the formation of the Conference of History, and in establishing the St. Vincent de Paul Society. I've told him, too, how you've tried so valiantly to start a lecture series by Lacordaire in Notre Dame."

"There's no one in France I'd like more to meet than Lamartine," said Frederic.

Poet, philosopher, orator, statesman, Lamartine was acclaimed throughout France. Frederic, in common with thousands of others, had read and reread the beautiful lyrics in which the poet sang soaring songs of the spirit.

It was Madame de Lamartine, an Englishwoman, who welcomed the two students when they arrived at the château. A convert to the faith, she was intensely interested in things

Catholic and, somewhat to Frederic's surprise, inquired as to the progress of the St. Vincent de Paul Society. Though she was that day entertaining numerous guests, including a family from her native land, she succeeded in making Dufieux and Frederic feel that they were her major concern.

Monsieur de Lamartine himself—tall, commanding, ascetic— soon came to greet them with utmost warmth. He was close to his forty-fourth birthday and at the summit of his powers.

"I read your brochure refuting Saint-Simonism," he said, as Dufieux introduced Frederic. "Indeed, I remember sending you a congratulatory note about it. You did a scholarly job. I was surprised to learn later that you were but eighteen years old at its writing. You displayed the mental maturity of a much older man. What are you writing at present?"

Lamartine was always ready to assume that anyone equipped to write for the benefit of his fellow men was actually using his talent; he thought expectation the most effective form of encouragement.

"My studies give me little time for writing while I'm at the University," replied Frederic. "But since I returned home for the long vacation, I've started a critical political essay which I'm thinking of titling *The Two English Chancellors*. It contrasts the characters and careers of Thomas à Becket and Francis Bacon. It will develop the theme that the former— who sacrificed position to principle—was a product of Christian philosophy, and that Bacon—who sacrificed principle to ambition—was a victim of rationalism."

"He certainly was opposed to Christian philosophy," returned Lamartine. "It's difficult to tell what he believed in; he's pretty confused. But there's little doubt as to his theology," he added, sarcastically. "A man originally without fortune, he became what we call a self-made man, and thereafter he worshipped his maker, for he was enormously egotistical. But tell me—where do you expect to publish this new work?"

"I've already sent the first three chapters to the editor of the *Revue Européenne,* and he writes me that he will soon begin publishing it serially. He also informs me that he showed the chapters to Monsieur de Coux, a former editor of the *Revue,* who says he may be interested in publishing *The Two*

Chancellors as a book—after he has seen the entire work, of course."

The next day, Lamartine showed Dufieux and Ozanam his extensive estate and pressed them to remain a week. When they pleaded that they must return to Lyons the next morning, he made them promise to visit him in Paris during the winter. They left regretfully, completely charmed by France's leading poet and orator.

Frederic had three reasons for returning to Lyons without undue delay. He was concerned about his mother's health, he was eager to resume work on *The Two English Chancellors*, and he was expecting his old friend Léonce Curnier to arrive from Nîmes.

Curnier and Ozanam had been fast friends since the day when Frederic—then a youth of seventeen—had arisen in art school and rebuked a blaspheming student. In occasional letters he had told Curnier much about the formation and progress of the St. Vincent de Paul Society, and Curnier had shown some interest in the possibility of starting a charitable organization in Nîmes.

Talking with Frederic in Lyons, Curnier emphasized the great need of poor relief in his city.

"Then why not start a St. Vincent de Paul Conference there?" urged Frederic. "You can follow our rules. They're the result of experience and should be as practical in Nîmes as in Paris."

"We have no fund for charitable work," objected Curnier.

"Don't let that stop you," said Frederic. "Our Society in Paris has only the money it collects from members every Tuesday meeting and the alms some of our friends contribute. And oh, yes—our cast-off clothes. Yet since we started in May of last year—that is, seventeen months ago—we have distributed about two thousand four hundred francs, some books, and a pretty fair quantity of clothes."

Frederic told Curnier that the Paris Conference would number a hundred or more with the start of the new scholastic year.

"We're getting unwieldy," he said. "So we must divide into two or three Conferences. And your group in Nîmes, Léonce,

106

can be considered another Conference. I suggest that you consult your pastor, and if he approves, plan to form a St. Vincent de Paul organization in your parish. I'll write at once to our officials in Paris, and suggest that they authorize you to do so—I know they will—and that they maintain a regular correspondence with you."

Frederic, again back in Paris, obtained the central body's unanimous approval for a Nîmes affiliate. Writing this news to Curnier, he pointed out that the great body of the poor, in their times, had—like the traveler in the Gospel—been seized upon by robbers, who had despoiled it of the treasure of faith and love and then left it naked and moaning by the wayside.

"Let us," he wrote, "poor Samaritans that we are, draw near to the wounded man. Perhaps he will . . . let us try to probe his wounds and pour balm into them, breathe words of consolation and peace into his ear. Then, when his eyes are opened, we will place him in the hands of those whom God has constituted the guardians and physicians of souls. . . . This is the task that is before us, this is the divine vocation to which Providence calls us."

Frederic's ardent spirit, which led him to encourage and inspire Curnier and others, drove him to long hours of study as well as a heavy round of outside activities. He was constantly whipping himself to intense effort, and the equally intense reaction brought weariness of spirit. Eventually he fell into a languor from which he could not rouse himself. He felt weak of will and weak of purpose. When he tried to write for publications to which he had promised articles, his pen weighed like lead.

This breakdown in nervous energy affected his religious devotions.

"Piety is a yoke to me," he wrote to Dufieux, "prayer a mere habit of the lips. It's the last branch I cling to, so as not to roll to the bottom of the abyss—but the nourishing fruits of which I do not cull. I see young men of my age advancing proudly in the path of real progress, while I hang back, despairing of ever following them, and spending in idle lamentation the time I should be up and doing."

It is probable that Frederic was on the verge of what is now known as a "nervous breakdown."

If he had been middle-aged his nervous sickness would probably have been more serious and longer lasting. But he was only twenty-two, surrounded by generous and high-spirited young men who were his unfailing friends.

They helped him with their affection and care and encouragement, by conspiring in various ways to take his mind off the responsibilities he had assumed, and by persuading him to give his mind a vacation from study. Gradually he worked his way back again from the edge of the "abyss," and in two months he was his old self again—the optimistic young man whose good nature and delightful sense of humor were among his most notable attributes.

CHAPTER 13

PERE BAILLY shook his head hopelessly at Frederic Ozanam and François Lallier as the confusion of voices from over a hundred members of the St. Vincent de Paul Society filled their new quarters in the Place de l'Estrapade. It was the evening of Tuesday, December 16, 1834, and the rotund president of the Society was about to call its regular weekly meeting to order.

"One can scarcely hear himself speak," he complained to his two younger friends, looking out over the crowd of University students gathered in the hall.

"The Conference has become too big, too unwieldy," said Frederic. "We get in each other's way. We can't conduct our weekly business effectively when so many members have to be dealt with. We must split up," he concluded, positively.

"I'll second such a motion if you'll make it," promised Lallier. "What's your opinion, Monsieur Bailly?"

"I must admit the present difficulties, but I hesitate to advise splitting the Conference," answered the president. "Will such action not weaken us, and perhaps change what is a success into a failure? Besides, many of our most valued members are utterly opposed to such a step."

The meeting now got under way. The leaders tried to give necessary attention to the reports of members concerning families visited the previous week. But so many were the reports to be made, so many the problems to be discussed, that the meeting lasted far beyond a reasonable hour. There was little time left for that night's visits.

Frederic saw concern on many faces as the meeting was prolonged. He judged conditions favorable for introduction of a proposal that the Conference be split—a proposal he had had in mind even before talking with Curnier in Lyons three months before.

Rising, he obtained President Bailly's permission to bring up "a matter of greatest importance to the good of the Society."

"It has long been apparent to all of us," he began, "that our Conference has grown unwieldy. The remedy is obvious. It is to divide our Society—to form a second Conference—but to make this division in such a way as to strengthen rather than weaken the Society as a whole. Such division is natural and beneficent. The human hand grasps more strongly, more effectively, more flexibly, because it is divided into fingers which act individually, yet in concert. This principle is applied in nearly all large bodies of men. They are divided into smaller bodies that they may operate with effective order. We, too, must increase our effectiveness—yes, and our unity—by dividing into units of manageable size."

There was a loud murmur of dissent from various parts of the gathering, but Frederic continued: "I therefore formally propose that this Conference of St. Vincent de Paul divide itself into two or more sections, each distinct from the others, but all united as links in a chain. These sections would communicate with each other through regularly scheduled central

109

meetings—general meetings—to be held once a month. In this way, we would multiply our strength. We could grow without limit, to the increased benefit of the poor and to all who might join our ranks now and in the future."

Lallier quickly seconded the proposal, but many voices were raised in protest. "No!"—"Never!"—"We must not divide!" was heard from all sides, and the protests grew in volume. Le Taillandier and Paul de la Perrière were seen to be among the strongest opponents of division. Lallier and a few others strongly supported Frederic's proposal.

Père Bailly, caught in the midst of the storm, arose and held up his hands to quiet the tumult.

"This proposal," he said, placatingly, "is plainly too important to be debated until after a period of private consideration on the part of all of us. I suggest we postpone discussion for one week, and that in the meantime a committee study the motion and make a report next Tuesday evening."

A committee of six, three supporting and three opposing the proposal, was appointed.

During the week there was much discussion of the motion among groups of members. Père Bailly himself maintained a noncommittal attitude, but was said to be against the measure. Like La Taillandier, he feared division of the Society might weaken and destroy it. Neither could envision a growing organization, spreading its beneficent work and influence from parish to parish, perhaps from city to city.

The debate continued during the next meeting on December 23, and a decision was again postponed.

On Christmas Eve Vincentians gathered to assist at midnight Mass in the Carmelite church. After Mass, they sat down as a family of brothers to the Christmas feast. The Abbé Combalot, who had celebrated the Holy Sacrifice, was present, and he grasped the occasion to advance several reasons for the division of the Society into smaller groups.

Sister Rosalie, too, had been informed of the debate going on within the Society, and she lent all her influence to the Ozanam position. But the opposition remained strong and determined.

At a third meeting, on December 30, resumption of the

debate failed to settle the question. Yet all agreed that it must be decided with all possible rapidity, and the members voted to hold a special meeting the following day—New Year's Eve.

At this meeting, after several others had spoken, Frederic was called on; he was the last to speak. As he arose, his heart went out in sympathy to Le Taillandier and others who were so sincerely opposed to division.

"It is only too true," he agreed, "that splitting into three divisions will deprive many of us of weekly association together—we who have been the closest of friends and co-workers and who must, on division, become members of separate Conferences. No one can regret this more deeply than I. Yet I am certain that this personal sacrifice is demanded of us. For how else can this Society multiply its activities? It has become increasingly plain that we can work more effectively in smaller groups, in parish groups, rather than in a large but unwieldy body.

"There is fear that through division we may become a weaker factor in the life of the University. My answer is that the Society by seeming to weaken its influence will multiply it. For it is by division that we shall assure new life—a life renewed and stimulated on many fronts.

"Yet even when divided, we shall still be one."

An amber circle in a stained glass window at the front of the hall had caught and was radiating the rays of a light in the next room.

"As divergent rays emanate from the same center," he said, pointing to the luminous amber disc, "so should our efforts, extending to different points, resolve themselves into the same motive and proceed from the same principle. When we divide—and I sincerely hope we will—we must continue to be united in such wise that each Conference strengthens all the others and receives strength in return. We must have frequent communication with each other, so that we may all be stimulated by the individual success of each Conference. We will periodically hold a common meeting, and be ruled by guiding principles emanating from a central source. Our division will assure continued growth in every direction, while our organization from the center will assure unity."

Frederic's eloquent plea did not completely dissolve the opposition. A confusion of comment and suggestion arose the instant he concluded his appeal.

The hour was nearly midnight. As the clock struck twelve, and the bells of Paris began to ring in the New Year, President Bailly, demanding order, said, "These discussions and uncertainties are breaking down my health. I am unable to continue them any longer. A new year is commencing. Let us shake hands and leave it to me to find a way of satisfying everybody."

Frederic arose, and walking swiftly across the room to De la Perrière, embraced him, and wished him a Happy New Year. The members applauded, repeated the gesture amongst themselves, and agreed to entrust solution of the question of division to Monsieur Bailly.

On February 24, he announced the decision. The Conference was to be divided into three sections.

The unlimited extension of the Society was assured.

At first only two sections were formed, named St. Etienne-du-Mont, and St. Sulpice. Early in 1835, Felix Clavé proposed that those Vincentians visiting in the Faubourg du Roule meet at his home, which was closer to that quarter. This suggestion, acted upon favorably, brought about the establishment of the third Conference, named St. Philippe du Roule. Toward the end of June a fourth section was established for a like reason, and from then on the multiplication of Conferences continued.

It was early in 1835 that Frederic learned the sequel to his failure to have the Archbishop of Paris name the Abbé Lacordaire as Lenten lecturer in Notre Dame Cathedral.

Through an exchange of letters with Lacordaire, the Archbishop had become directly acquainted with the young Abbé's social and political views, as well as his deep devotion to the Church and to the welfare of all men. As a result, shortly before the Lenten season of 1835, Frederic heard electrifying news: The Archbishop had offered the Abbé Lacordaire the pulpit of Notre Dame for a series of lectures during Lent!

The announcement was a bombshell. It dumbfounded some politicians and religious leaders, and instantly became the most discussed topic throughout the University, and, for that matter, throughout Paris. Paeans for Lacordaire's matchless eloquence were opposed by storms of criticism of him as a "soap-box orator." Some declared him heaven-sent to restore France to Christianity; others denonunced him as an enemy of the Church. The conflict in viewpoints aroused curiosity to fever pitch, and assured an overflow audience at the first lecture.

The lectures were, of course, front-page news, and Ozanam agreed to cover them for the *Univers*. For this, he was to receive twenty-five francs a lecture.

At the first lecture the crowd crammed the enormous temple. Not a pillar but supported the backs of as many men as could stand around it. Not a jutting ornament, balustrade of a side altar, or any other point of advantage but swarmed with humanity. And wonder of wonders!—in a Paris where women sometimes predominated in the church congregations by a ratio of twelve to one, the crowd was mostly men. Still more marvelous, the majority were young men.

At every *conférence*, as the lectures were called, the crowds began coming in at every door fully two hours before services. The whole of the enormous nave of Notre Dame was railed in, as was the custom on Easter Sunday. As the lectures were primarily for students, women were not admitted to that part of the cathedral; they were restricted to the side aisles.

To each lecture members of the St. Vincent de Paul Society marched in a body, and took seats in the nave. Frederic noted that Monseigneur de Quelen honored every lecture with his presence. At the final *conférence*, the prelate expressed his heartfelt gratitude to the Abbé Lacordaire and named him a canon of the cathedral.[1]

Frederic, trudging the dusty road that ran from Mâcon to

---

[1] The annual Lenten Conferences, or lectures, at Notre Dame have continued year after year and today are an honored Paris tradition.

Lyons, envied the carefree and earth-free birds that sang and flew above him.

"Oh, to have wings!" he muttered to himself through dust-dry lips. His throat was dust-dry too, and dust covered his clothes. It seemed to him three days instead of three hours since he had set out from Mâcon, and three months rather than that many days since he had boarded the diligence from Paris. That vehicle had brought him to Mâcon on the eve of Assumption Day, and was scheduled to leave the next morning just too early for him to assist at Mass in Mâcon on the holy day. His inquiries established the fact that it would arrive in Lyons just too late for him to attend Mass in that city. Under the circumstances, his status as a traveler might have excused him from hearing Mass at all on this "holy day of obligation," but he gave that possibility not a thought. Instead, he set about trying to find some other carrier that might be departing for Lyons a little later in the morning. His search brought only disappointment.

He began to feel almost unbearably frustrated, for Assumption Day being his mother's feast day, he had been looking forward to taking part in the family celebration. This year he was particularly eager to do so, since letters from home had caused him to be deeply concerned about his mother's health.

After assisting at early Mass, he again sought high and low for some kind of vehicle—any kind of vehicle—that might be headed for Lyons. He found none.

Finally, he decided to walk, hoping to be picked up on the road.

Plodding the thirty-mile road toward Lyons, he asked himself, as he passed by the inhospitable blank walls of wayside houses, "Why do our French villages seem to turn their backs to the wayfarer?" Thinking such thoughts, he had just walked wearily through Belleville—it was mid-afternoon—and had given up hope of reaching Lyons before night, when he heard the sound of hoofs upon the road behind him. He turned to see a team of horses pulling an old cart, badly tilted on one side, but lightly loaded.

The driver, a young man in a nondescript hat and a brown smock, brought his horses to a halt.

"Could I be of assistance?" he asked.

Frederic, observing thankfully that the horses were of a breed noted for endurance and ability to maintain a steady speed, said that if the driver was going toward Lyons, he most certainly could be of assistance.

"I must be in Lyons by early evening," answered the driver, "though I have been warned to stay away. You are most welcome to ride with me, monsieur, as you also seem unafraid to go to Lyons."

Frederic had heard in Paris that cholera had appeared in the south of France and had been advancing steadily northward.

"Has the cholera reached Lyons?" he asked, as he gratefully seated himself beside the driver.

"Not quite, monsieur," said the driver, cracking his long whip again to start his team. "That is, it hadn't a week ago when I was there. But by now, I have no doubt, it's killing off citizens right and left."

"Our Lady of Fourvières saved the town three years ago," Frederic reminded him. "Perhaps she will again."

"Perhaps, monsieur," said the driver. "Let us hope so. For the rabble-rousers plan a blood bath for the city if the plague strikes. They've convinced thousands in the poorer quarters that the rich are poisoning the drinking water, and they're planning riots and insurrection."

"Poor Lyons!" said Frederic.

"Well, there's a brighter side," said his companion, suddenly flicking his whip to pick off a giant horsefly that had settled on a horse's back. "Thousands of the faithful besiege Our Lady of Fourvières, singing hymns in the church during services—and outside, too, for the church cannot begin to hold them all. And more than fifteen hundred of them have already signed up to nurse the poor should the cholera come."

Shortly before eight o'clock Frederic bade his benefactor farewell before his home in the Grande Rue Pizay, the driver having gone well out of his way to bring him there.

Frederic's mother had been seriously ill, and now, as he kissed her, he noted with a sense of shock how drawn and thin her cheeks were, and how weak she was. Nevertheless, she still continued her charities. She had even volunteered, against the remonstrances of her family, to help nurse the cholera victims should the plague strike Lyons.

Happily, her services were not needed, for the cholera again stopped at the city's boundary.

As Frederic wrote to Lallier: "The name of the Dame de Fourvières no longer brings a smile to the lips of the skeptic, who cannot but think that to her protection he perhaps owes his life."

CHAPTER 14

"LOOK, Henri, walking chairs."

"They must be going to a masked ball, these merrymakers. Very smart, Marie—if the ball is crowded, they are still sure of a place to sit!"

Henri and his Marie were two of a score or more who, standing in doorways along the Rue de Grès, gazed with smiling bemusement on a sight strange even for the Latin Quarter. Eleven young men marched along the street through a slanting rain, each carrying on his head a chair and over all an umbrella.

It was after the dinner hour—the young men might well have been, as Henri thought, on their way to a *mascarade*. The fact was, they were bound for Frederic Ozanam's sixth-floor rooms for what, to these intense intellectuals, was more exciting entertainment—an evening of conversation.

With sublime disregard of the size of their quarters and its equipment of only five chairs, Frederic and Le Taillandier had invited twenty-two guests, asking those who lived nearby to bring a chair or two. But these guests were late in arriving, and it became urgent that more chairs be procured at once.

116

In this emergency Lallier, who lived only a block away, went into action.

"Volunteers, fall in!" he cried. "Follow me! Forward—to my apartment! Onward—to more chairs!"

Frederic, Chaurand, and Biétrix grasped their umbrellas—for rain was falling—formed behind Lallier, sped with the light feet of youth down five flights of stairs, and hastened to Lallier's rooms. As they were returning through the rain, each with a chair and an umbrella over his head, they met De la Perrière, Janmot and other promised chair-bringers, similarly encumbered. Suddenly realizing the grotesque picture they presented to the little world of the Rue de Grès, each contingent stopped to laugh at the other, and at itself.

Somewhat winded, the chair-bearers were soon gathered in Frederic's apartment, and within minutes were absorbed in lively talk.

There was some light jesting at Frederic's expense; his first book, *The Two English Chancellors*, had just appeared, and everybody wanted to know how it felt to be famous.

"Frederic," cried Lamache, "I demand, as one of your closest friends, that you dedicate your next book to me. That's the only way I'll ever see *my* name in print!"

"Buy a copy of this one, then—and assure me of at least one sale," retorted Frederic.

"Oh, you needn't worry about your book's popularity," declared Le Taillandier. "Your *Two Chancellors* will sell like hot cakes. The rationalists will buy it to disagree with what you say about Francis Bacon as a victim of rationalism, and the Christians, to read your praise of St. Thomas à Becket as a product of Christian philosophy."

"Now, Frederic, you can give up law for literature," said Clavé.

"You wouldn't say that if you realized the struggles *The Two English Chancellors* cost me," answered Frederic seriously. "Those 170 pages required more research, more study, and more painstaking writing than I ever dreamed a book could demand."

"You're too conscientious, Frederic," commented Jules Devaux. "To make a fortune at literature, you must produce with the abandon of a Dumas."

This brought a ripple of laughter; there could be no one as utterly opposite to the money-making, universally known, and vastly popular Dumas both in income and in his attitude toward authorship, as Frederic. Yet the latter, though comparatively unknown even among scholarly authors, had received many congratulations on his book.

One of the first to call upon him with words of praise was the younger Ampère, whose father had introduced him to Frederic some time before.

Jean-Jacques had taken an immediate liking to the much younger Frederic. He was attracted to the modest student by Ozanam's spiritual maturity. Frederic had long since committed himself to the essentials of a life of faith; shallow ambitions vexed his spirit not at all. Jean-Jacques was later to write that Frederic was as deep and serene as a quiet mountain lake—and quite as refreshing.

Frederic found Jean-Jacques Ampère a pleasant and polished man of the world, who had achieved standing in the literary field. A literary critic of no little prestige, his opinion of a book counted. His reviews were looked forward to, his judgments respected in the most exclusive salons. Even more important, he was a highly regarded friend of the two great literary potentates of Paris—Chateaubriand and Madame Récamier. The latter, childless, regarded the younger Ampère almost as a son. He had as an immature young man conceived a romantic passion for the clever and gracious woman—who was old enough to be his mother. With understanding and skill she had diverted his ardor into a devoted friendship, and his friends were always welcomed to her salon.

When Ampère called on Frederic after the appearance of *The Two English Chancellors,* Jean-Jacques bore a message from the great lady.

"A week ago, while conversing with Madame Récamier," he told Frederic, "I spoke to her about your new book. Naturally, she was interested in the good work of her fellow Lyonnais— she is intensely loyal, you know, to her native city. She is now reading your book, and she has instructed me to persuade you to come to a reception next Thursday at her apartment in the Abbaye-aux-Bois. Will you be able to attend?"

Frederic was immensely flattered, and said so, but declined because he was in the midst of preparations for an important examination—which would determine whether he was to receive his doctorate in law.

"Then, my friend," said Ampère, "I'll see to it that you are invited again, after the examinations. You're a literary man, Frederic—you must make friends with those in Madame Récamier's circle."

There was every reason an aspiring writer should jump at such an invitation. Entrée into the Récamier drawing room meant entrée into the most illustrious literary group in Europe. Assisted by the interest of its members, a young man of talent might find the road to literary fame wide and smooth.

It was not examinations alone, however, that kept Frederic from the celebrated salon. At this time he was conferring continuously with Monsieur Bailly and Lallier. As President, Monsieur Bailly had instructed Lallier to draw up a rule for the St. Vincent de Paul Society; he himself was writing what he called an "Introduction" to the rule. In this important work, Frederic gave his friends all the assistance within his power.

On April 13, 1836, Frederic won his doctorate in law by ably maintaining two theses, one in Roman law, another in French law. Few students advanced as far as this degree, which alone conferred the privilege of lecturing to higher classes as a member of a university faculty. At this time Frederic had no idea that within a few months he would find the degree of practical value. He stood for it only because he desired to be, in the greatest possible measure, a master of his profession.

To obtain a realistic concept of a lawyer's everyday activities, he talked with leading barristers in Paris. Nearly everything they told him increased his doubts that he could be happy in the legal profession. But he was determined, as a matter of duty to his parents, to make it his career.

Perhaps it was his reluctance to commence life as a barrister

119

that led him to stay on in Paris after receiving his law degree. He continued at the University, studying for a doctorate in literature. He could not bear to tear himself away from literary studies until the moment for entering upon his career as a barrister had arrived, and that would not be until the fall of the year.

A second invitation to Madame Récamier's came to him through Jean-Jacques Ampère at the beginning of May, and this time Frederic gratefully accepted. He anticipated his attendance at the famed salon, however, with apprehension, for there he would be conversing with some of the greatest minds in France.

Madame Récamier was one of those intellectual Frenchwomen who, presiding over salons frequented by brilliant writers and artists, statesmen, scientists and savants, have inspired and even directed creative genius and have had an influence on political developments.

She was regarded as the most charming hostess in all Europe, and her sympathy, understanding, and selfless devotion to her friends had won the allegiance of some of Europe's most powerful personalities. Inevitably, she wielded great influence. A writer of real talent, aided by her interest, would find his climb up the usually tortuous pathway to success assisted by many helping hands.

At this time, Madame Récamier was fifty-eight years old. When sixteen she had been married to Jacques-Rose Récamier, a banker twenty-six years her senior and originally from Lyons. His magnificent style of living had been the talk of Paris. Several years later, he lost his fortune, and for more than twenty-five years Madame Récamier had been living on her own modest inheritance. She occupied a very old but ample first floor apartment in the Abbaye-aux-Bois—an abbey conducted by the nuns of Notre Dame, the Canonesses of St. Augustine. In this simple environment, her place and influence in literary society continued to grow.

On the day of the reception to which Frederic was invited, Jean-Jacques called for him at his apartment and, the afternoon being fine, they walked to the Abbaye, a building of severe and simple style within whose enclosure monastic quiet prevailed. Jean-Jacques led him toward the wing that housed Madame Récamier's apartment and ushered him into the drawing room. Several ladies and gentlemen had already gathered, some surrounding Chateaubriand, others gathered about a tall woman, the singular sweetness of whose countenance made an instant impression. It was Madame Récamier, who looked their way intently as they crossed the room toward her.

"Her sight is failing," Ampère whispered to Frederic.

It was not until they were halfway across the room that she was able to distinguish Jean-Jacques, and with an exclamation of welcome came forward to meet them.

Madame Récamier's warm words and manner conveyed to Frederic that the distinguished circle of literary men about her would have been incomplete without him. Through the magic of her personality the shy young man quickly felt at home in that august company, which beside Chateaubriand and the younger Ampère included Sainte-Beuve, Lamartine, Ballanche, and the talented Countess d'Hautefeuille.

"I read your *Two Chancellors* immediately after its appearance," said Madame Récamier. "Our friend Jean-Jacques brought it to me. I found it excellent."

"You both are good to me far beyond my desert," murmured Frederic.

"You have deserved well," insisted Madame. "It was a very real pleasure for me to read your scholarly appraisals of Becket and Bacon. Your analysis of each is so keen, and clothed in such a fresh, lively, interesting style. Let us hope you are not letting your pen lie idle."

"I have been too busy with my law studies to devote myself further to literature," answered Frederic. "That was why, too, I was—though deeply regretful—unable to accept your first invitation to come here."

"Yes—Jean-Jacques conveyed your regrets," Madame Récamier replied. "But he did not tell me," she added in a tone that mingled sadness with reproof, "that you intended forsaking literature for the law."

"I do so most reluctantly, madame," said Frederic. He explained his obligations toward his parents in the matter of selecting a more surely remunerative profession.

The great lady motioned to a servant, who brought a small table and placed it before Ampère. The latter was seated well toward the front of the room.

"Why do you prefer literature to the law?" resumed Frederic's hostess.

"Because writing gives me the opportunity, while enriching my own mind, to enrich the minds of all men who read," answered Frederic. "I wish to help make men more sensible of their great heritage, and of their great dignity as children of God. I should like to bring any readers I might have, to know the truth that makes men free; I mean the truth that frees man from the ugliness and corruption growing out of false philosophies that bring hatred, and misery, and every evil into the world."

"With you, Monsieur Ozanam, I see that the truth is a passion," observed Madame Récamier.

"As it must be, madame," returned Frederic, "with every intelligent person devoted to the faith."

"Would that serving the truth were a passion with all writers—yes, and with all professors, too," observed his hostess. "But of course, monsieur, you can serve the cause of truth manfully in the law, also. Yet"—again with a touch of sadness in her liquid tones—"surely much less widely than through authorship."

Frederic saw Chateaubriand, who was carrying a thick package enveloped in a silk handkerchief, withdraw the covering, disclosing a manuscript. This he handed to Jean-Jacques.

The latter had told Frederic something of this manuscript on their walk to the Abbaye, but had not said that he, Jean-Jacques, was to be the reader. It was Chateaubriand's *Memoirs from Beyond the Grave*, so called because they were not to be published until after the author's death. Invitations to the weekly readings of the *Memoirs*—which for some time had been a feature of Madame Récamier's receptions—were eagerly desired by the most distinguished people in Paris.

The reading was about to commence, and Madame Récamier excused herself to direct the seating of her guests. She placed them—they numbered about twenty—around the reader in two semicircles, the ladies closest to him, the men in the rear. As Jean-Jacques read, Frederic's attention, despite the prestige of the author, wandered. His eyes first rested on Chateaubriand's wonderfully expressive countenance, and then took in the room's exquisite furnishings. From his seat near the fireplace he could study, on the opposite wall, a celebrated painting of the Grecian poetess Corinna by Gérard, who was among those present. Above him on the mantel, flowers in great vases scented the air. From another side of the room windows looked out upon a garden, their white silk curtains softly diffusing the sunlight. Through one of the windows he could see something of the surrounding gardens, which were so spacious that their expanse removed the Abbaye from the sounds of Paris.

Frederic listened to Ampère's voice and Chateaubriand's words as in a dream. Here he was, a mere student, he reflected, associating with the most glamorous literary figures of France. To continue his association with this distinguished and influential circle, all he need do was to remain in Paris, pursuing a career as a writer. Why return to Lyons, that city of commerce and factories; why leave the "city of light," the intellectual center of France, of Europe, of the world—this exciting, resplendent Paris? Must he give up this delightful society, a writer's career, and quite possibly fame? Must he surrender it all—and for what? To haggle in Lyons courtrooms over the suits and countersuits of tradesmen, each trying to obtain a petty advantage over the other. Or to plead for the liberty of those who had taken liberties with the law.

He listened with only half his mind to the charmed words of Chateaubriand, for thoughts of his career persisted. He must think this out fully and finally, he told himself, and then do what his conscience dictated. Whatever the decision, he determined not to be unhappy about it. After all, he reflected, there were brave people in the Rue Mouffetard who would be amazed that anyone so situated as he could be unhappy. Thoughts of the Rue Mouffetard brought to his mind the St. Vincent de Paul Society and the great need of a Conference in Lyons.

The reading came to an end, and so at last did the reception. In bidding him farewell, Madame Récamier said she would expect him soon again.

"I will take advantage of your kind invitation," he replied, "when I have achieved something to make me less unworthy of it, and of association with your distinguished guests—and that, madame, may be years from now."

His answer surprised him, as it did his hostess. Had he all unconsciously, he asked himself, reached a final decision to return to Lyons?

Madame Récamier, who assumed that he was merely being modest, answered: "Ah, my fellow Lyonnais, let us be the judges of your merits, for we can judge you more objectively than you yourself. You must come again, and soon—we will not hear a 'No.'"

When he found himself back in his humble apartment, large questions continued to impose themselves strongly upon his mind.

That evening, and on many succeeding days, these conflicting thoughts tore at his spirit. His filial duty argued that he should return to Lyons and take up the practice of law. Every other logical consideration urged him to remain in Paris.

Reluctantly, with deep regret at giving up what he was convinced was his true calling as a writer, he decided on the course he knew would be most pleasing to his parents.

Shortly before he left, André Marie Ampère died, reciting to himself pages from *The Imitation of Christ*—a work which the marvelous memory of the great scientist is said to have retained in its entirety.

The passing of his eminent benefactor seemed to Frederic to emphasize the death of all those aspirations he himself might have realized by a literary career in Paris.

CHAPTER 15

SEVERAL of Frederic's Lyonnais comrades were to finish their studies six months before he would complete his course. Responding to Frederic's urging, they established, soon after their arrival home, a St. Vincent de Paul Conference in Lyons.

When, a few days after his return to Lyons in July, 1836, Frederic attended a meeting of the recently formed Lyons Conference, he found twenty-one present. The majority were former members of the Paris Conferences. To his surprise, he found himself called upon to fill the President's chair. "We have reserved the Presidency for you, with title of Founder," Chaurand informed him. "For truly, you were the founder of this Conference *in absentia*."

A few venerable priests encouraged the young Conference, but some laymen asked themselves: "What novel—perhaps inflammatory—ideas might not these youths, freshly returned from radical colleges in Paris, be spreading among our poor, under the cloak of charity?" These honest burghers had agonized through more than one bloody civil uprising, and they knew that revolution generally traveled under a disguise. Their opposition was active and continuing.

Nine months after the founding of the Lyons Conference, Frederic wrote to Lallier that "the Society here has never ceased to be an object of vexations; the bigwigs of orthodoxy, fathers of the council in dress coats and strapped pantaloons, declare modestly—putting themselves in the place of Our Lord—'whosoever is not with me is against me.'

"You would hardly believe the tricks, the caviling, the insults, the meanness we have had to bear from these people, who are all in perfectly good faith. The most estimable have been carried away by the general feeling, and we have had a great deal to suffer even from those who love us.

"Chaurand and I, as chief founders and promoters of the work, have been continually in the breach, and find it a very wearisome post. One's spirit must imbibe a certain bitterness, charity must more or less suffer, in the conversations one is forced to have on this subject."

He added that at its weekly meetings the Conference was reading the life of St. Vincent de Paul "better to penetrate ourselves with his maxims and traditions. A patron saint should not be a mere signboard to a society, like St. Denis or St. Nicholas over the door of a tavern. A patron saint should be regarded as a type on which we should strive to pattern ourselves, as he patterned himself on the Divine type, which is Jesus Christ."

From Lyons Frederic continued to help mold the Society. There is no mistaking the tone of his letters of counsel to Lallier in connection with the Society's management and policy. His is the voice of primary responsibility. He speaks to the secretary-general as a founder who feels it his duty to guide, to admonish, to inspire.

"Our little Society," he writes Lallier, "has become sufficiently important to be regarded in the light of a providential fact. See that you are present as often as possible at the particular meetings. Call on the presidents from time to time. Take an interest in the meetings of the board of direction.

"I fully approve of your idea of speaking in a forthcoming letter to presidents of St. Vincent de Paul Conferences of the exterior spirit of the Society, the absence of secrecy, and the necessity of remaining in the background. It would perhaps be well to lay down this principle, that humility is obligatory for associations quite as much as for individuals. That you might illustrate by the example of St. Vincent de Paul, who severely reprimanded a priest of the mission for speaking of the Society [of the Missions] as 'our holy society.' "

To Lallier—who as secretary-general was stationed, of course, in Paris—Ozanam even addresses a mild rebuke because the latter failed to appreciate the importance of maintaining regular correspondence among the various Conferences.

Under Frederic's leadership, the Lyons Conference by its humble practice of charity gradually silenced its critics. The Conference grew, and was divided into two parish units—one in Frederic's old parish of St. Pierre, the other in St. François parish.

The Vincentians also opened a club for the many soldiers garrisoned in the city. There they taught reading, writing and arithmetic, and quickly built up a club library of more than five hundred volumes. Each Sunday a priest gave the soldiers an instruction in religion and led them in saying their night prayers in common. Paris headquarters took up the soldiers' library idea, and followed Frederic's suggestion that the vicar of St. Valère, near the Invalides, act as chaplain.

Opening of court sessions in November found Frederic enrolled as a barrister. His heart was still not in legal practice, but he gave himself to it with all his will. Where he could serve justice, he saw the practice of law as a privilege.

In one of his first cases he represented a man too poor to engage counsel, whose conviction was regarded by all—including the judge—as a legal formality. But Ozanam threw himself into the defense with an ardor that forced judge and prosecutor to accord his client as much consideration as if he were a leading citizen. Instead of being found guilty and hurried off to a long prison term the accused saw his rights protected at every step, and he was soon restored to liberty.

Few cases, however, enabled Frederic to protect the clear-cut rights of his fellow man. He could not "acclimatize" himself, he said, "to the atmosphere of chicanery, and to discussions that turn solely on pecuniary interests."

During a court session in 1837, he pleaded twelve cases and won them all. He was praised for his logic and eloquence; he was proving himself a strong and persuasive advocate, and this phase of the law attracted him. Still, substantial fees came only with difficulty, and the growing feebleness of his parents increased his disappointment at not being able to add more liberally to the family income.

Frederic's solicitude for his parents was increased by their lack of concern for themselves. Despite failing health, Dr. and Mme. Ozanam continued their visits to the sick and to the poor. Frederic pleaded with them not to overdo, not to climb too many flights of dark, broken stairways in their visits to the needy. This, he realized, was fatiguing to tired hearts and could result in damaging, even fatal, falls.

The aging couple finally admitted to themselves the wisdom of their son's advice; they endeavored to restrain one another. Through mutual persuasion, Dr. Ozanam and his wife arrived at an agreement: On their errands of mercy, they promised each other they would climb no higher than *four* flights of stairs!

But soon charity proved stronger than their agreement. One day Dr. Ozanam, climbing to a sixth-floor room to visit a penniless patient, came face to face with Madame Ozanam, who had come to nurse the woman. Hearing from another source about the sufferer's friendless plight, she had hastened to her bedside. Husband and wife looked at one another across the woman's cot, their guilty embarrassment mingling with amusement at the other's discomfiture. Together they ministered to the invalid. Then the tall, gray-haired doctor and the sweet-faced woman helped one another down the dark stairway, each warning the other of the dangers of broken steps—a hazard even to the sure feet of youth. Madame Ozanam urged her husband, as she had before, to retire from practice, but he shook his head. There were too many sick poor in the city, he said, to justify him in such self-indulgence.

Frederic felt that if he could increase his income, his father might be induced to retire. With his pen he attempted to supplement his meager income from the law. He also devoted many hours to literary study.

In April of 1837 he went to Paris, expecting to remain there a few weeks while he prepared for an examination for a doctorate of letters.

He had been in Paris three weeks when he received shocking news: His father, descending a tenement stairway after visiting a patient on the upper floor, had tripped on a broken step. He had fallen headlong, and had died within a few hours.

Frederic returned home posthaste to join his brothers in comforting his mother. She seemed dazed by her husband's death, and weeks were to pass before she recovered.

The three Ozanam brothers, too, were immeasurably shocked and grieved. They had loved their father deeply; they revered him as a model of the Christian virtues, were grateful to him for his example and inspiration, and respected him as a scholar.

"Through revolutions, adversities, and in the soldiers' camp his nature remained noble," Frederic was to write many years later. ". . . When he left the hussars he had read the Bible of Dom Calmet from one end to the other; he knew Latin as few of us professors know it nowadays."

Shortly after his father's death he wrote to a friend: "If ever your indulgence found anything in me worthy of esteem or love, attribute it to my father, to his advice and example."

When Frederic undertook the duty of looking into Dr. Ozanam's accounts he found that one third of his professional visits had been made to the "recognized" poor without remuneration.

Frederic now added other activities to his small law practice. He became a tutor to three young men who desired to learn law but who, he noted with amusement, "were too grand to sit at the desks of a school." He wrote for the *Univers* of Paris. He authored a scholarly brochure on *Church Property* and a larger work on *Origins of French Law*. The latter book —originally a series of articles in the *Univers*—answered an effort of the eminent Jules Michelet to undermine the Catholi : faith. In this work, Ozanam showed a command of his subject remarkable in a writer of twenty-four years. He also lent his pen to promoting the Society for the Propagation of the Faith, founded in Lyons sixteen years before by Pauline Jaricot. While he lived in Lyons, Frederic was a director of this Society.

Toward the end of 1838 he again went to Paris to take the examinations for Doctor of Letters, which his father's death had interrupted. He delivered one thesis in Latin and another in French before an examining board of nine professors. His Latin thesis was acclaimed; he had displayed such eminent scholarship in his answers to one of the professors that the latter abruptly halted his questioning as if in acknowledgment that he had met his peer.

His thesis in French was a literary and an oratorical triumph; it won the unrestrained applause of examiners and audience. More important, this thesis, of which Dante was the subject, revealed the towering Florentine as a poet-theologian whose influence upon the faith of his countrymen had been strong and enduring. This was a new concept to French men of letters.

Later, Frederic was to expand the Dantean thesis in a work published under the title *Dante and Catholic Philosophy of the Thirteenth Century.*

From his triumph at the University in Paris, Frederic returned to creeping tragedy at home. Since her husband's fatal accident his mother's health had declined rapidly, and it seemed to Frederic that her strength now failed a little every day. Her eyesight grew dimmer. Particularly disturbing to Frederic was the fact that she had become prey to anxieties common to enfeebled old people. This took the form of constant concern for the future of Frederic and his younger brother, Charles.

His continued inability to add more adequately to the family income was a further harassment to the young barrister. The word got around that this strange Ozanam served justice first and his clients second, and it was a rare litigant indeed who wanted his interests placed second to justice. The result was that Ozanam failed to build a profitable law practice.

Such noble failures are sometimes rewarding. To obtain more income Frederic was compelled to turn from the courtroom to the schoolroom. Soon his principal income came from teaching law rather than its practice; he became a member of the faculty of the University of Lyons. It was not long before he was being considered for the chair of commercial law at that institution. The Municipal Council voted him the appointment on February 21, 1839.

In the meantime he had received from Victor Cousin, Minister of Education, the offer of the chair of philosophy at the University of Orléans. This he felt it necessary to decline, though he preferred philosophy to law. His mother's poor health made it imperative that he remain in Lyons.

Upon receiving his refusal, Monsieur Cousin wrote that he wanted him for his "own regiment," and that he would refuse to despair of that possibility.

Anxious to provide more amply for his mother, Frederic had looked forward to the professorship of commercial law at Lyons and the larger income it would assure. Monsieur Cousin gladly confirmed his appointment to the local post, but the increased revenue the new position brought with it came too late to be of much help in supplying the care the sick woman required. Soon after the confirmation it became plain that his mother's death could be only a matter of weeks.

Certainty that his mother soon would be beyond his helping brought the question of his vocation before his mind with a new sense of exigency.

He felt himself drawn toward the Dominicans—largely, it seems evident, through his admiration for Lacordaire. The latter, preparing to join the Dominican order, was already taking the lead in plans to re-introduce it into France from which it had been expelled during the Revolution. He and Frederic had been corresponding, and the Abbé had written that he and two other candidates for membership in the Order of Preachers would leave Paris for Rome and the Dominican novitiate there on the feast of the Order's brightest luminary, St. Thomas Aquinas. On their way, they would stop over in Lyons.

To welcome the celebrated Lacordaire, Frederic called together the city's Vincentians. The Abbé greeted them as brothers, and later conferred privately with Frederic regarding the latter's vocation. After reaching Rome, Lacordaire maintained a correspondence with Ozanam. In his letters Frederic urged that Lacordaire obtain permission from his superiors to resume his Lenten lectures in Notre Dame. Ozanam's persuasion was probably effective, for some time later the great

Dominican was able to do so. Frederic also described to Lacordaire the growth of the St. Vincent de Paul Society, whose members under Ozanam's leadership had been so influential in bringing about Lacordaire's first series of lectures in the great cathedral.

"Next year Paris will count fourteen Conferences," he tells the Dominican, "and we shall have a like number in the provinces."

He speaks to Lacordaire of his Commercial Law professorship as "a position which filial duty alone led me to seek," and then adds, "Uncertainty as to my vocation returns with increased anxiety.

"I commend to your charitable prayers this interior trial, from which I have long suffered; for, if God deigned to call me to His service, there is no army in which I would more gladly serve than that in which you are enrolled."

Lacordaire replied promptly, inviting Frederic to visit for a week at the Dominican novitiate in Rome, that he might judge for himself whether his vocation lay with that order. Because of his mother's failing health and the urgent necessity of going to Paris for several days on family business, Frederic did not accept. He returned from Paris about the middle of August, 1839, to find that during his brief absence his mother's illness had become critical.

She grew steadily worse. Day by day, Frederic watched her fail, and the sight of her suffering was a continuous emotional torture. In a month she was dead.

To Frederic the shock was deep.

"What so crushed me," he wrote Lallier, "was the long illness that I beheld day by day destroying her, and which—shall I say it?—seemed as if it were going to dishonor the sacrifice before consuming it, by quenching the intellectual faculties. . . . Just at the end, the energy of her soul revived, and Christ, in descending into the heart of His beloved servant, left there strength for the supreme struggle. She remained for three days calm, serene, murmuring prayers, or acknowledging our caresses and services by a few words of indescribable sweetness.

"At last the fatal night came; it was I who was watching.

I suggested to my dear mother the acts of faith, hope, and charity—the same that she taught me to lisp after her as a child."

He summoned the family, including the Abbé Alphonse Ozanam, and the last consolations of the Church were given.

"There were no convulsions, no agony," he tells Lallier with a note of relief. "Only a slumber that left her countenance almost smiling, a faint breathing that grew gradually fainter, until at last it ceased, and we rose up orphans."

His mother's death left a great emptiness in his life, though for many months thereafter he was conscious of her spirit hovering near and smiling approval in the distance when he had done anything for the poor, "whom she loved so tenderly." At times, too, when he was praying, he fancied he heard her voice praying with him—"as we used to do at the foot of the crucifix every night."

He was living alone—except for Guigui—in a lonely house. The Abbé Alphonse was absent on the missions; his brother Charles was away at school, studying medicine.

Frederic's days were busy with the course of law he had inaugurated at the University of Lyons. His lectures were crowded. From the day of his first lecture more than two hundred and fifty students occupied every available space in the small hall to hear him.

What they heard were no dry-as-dust discussions of subtle judicial problems and points of procedure. The young professor treated law as a branch of philosophy. He placed the law in an historical context. He discussed its literary aspects. He taught principles without compromise, but he seasoned his lectures with a humor that lightened the heaviest subjects. He aimed, this wise teacher of twenty-six years, at making his auditors good men, as well as proficient, soundly grounded lawyers.

The University's rector was enthusiastic; he thought Ozanam worthy of a still higher position, and wrote as much to the authorities in Paris.

CHAPTER 16

EDGAR QUINET, who occupied the chair of foreign literature at the University of Lyons, had been promoted to the Collége de France in Paris.

Toward the end of 1839, shortly after this news had become public property, Monsieur Soulacroix had a talk with Frederic Ozanam.

"You are excellently qualified to take Quinet's place," the University's rector told Frederic. "You are familar with English, Italian, German and Spanish literatures in the orginals and are a writer of reputation; you would find the chair of foreign literature thoroughly congenial. But between you and the appointment there are two obstacles. One is the fact that I hesitate to ask you to resign the chair of law, where you have achieved unusual success and popularity. Of course, you are young. You are used to hard work. And I have no doubt that if you desired to carry the double burden, you could do full justice to both courses."

"I have mastered the content of my lectures in commercial law," said Frederic. "I think I could handle both courses. And I agree with you—I would find the chair of foreign literature extremely congenial."

"Good!" exclaimed the rector. "I'm happy that you agree— for I have already recommended you to the Minister of Education for Monsieur Quinet's place."

"Thank you—thank you very much!" returned Frederic. "I hope you'll never have reason to feel that your confidence in me has been misplaced. But," he continued, puzzled, "you mentioned *two* obstacles."

The rector remained for some time in deep thought, as if reluctant to go on, and Frederic, always prone to exaggerate his shortcomings, began to fear that Monsieur Soulacroix was hesitant about mentioning some personal deficiency of his as the second obstacle.

As if in answer to his thoughts, the rector said: "The other possible obstacle has nothing to do with either your ability or your character. It has to do with powerful educators who have the ear of Monsieur Cousin who, as Minister of Education, has to get along with them. Monsieur Cousin, I know, respects your scholarship. He is disposed to be friendly to you. You're the kind of man he needs to help achieve his ambition—which is, to bring university education in France to a supremely high level. But we must be practical, my dear Ozanam. And therefore, we must face the fact that several men in our educational system would not applaud replacement of the anticlerical Quinet by a recognized champion of Christianity and the Church such as yourself. To retain their dominance of education, they must prevent such appointments."

"To name names," said Frederic, intent on making sure who the opposition might be, "you mean that theologically, philosophically, and politically I'd fail to meet the approval of Villemain and his friends."

"Precisely," confirmed Monsieur Soulacroix. "And only Monsieur Cousin can help you surmount such opposition. For these are dedicated men, who know their target is the Catholic Church—and know how to hit it. Look, for example, how they are working to destroy the Jesuit order. Naturally, these men will want to see Quinet's place taken by one who agrees with their anti-religious and political views.

"So, Frederic," concluded Monsieur Soulacroix, "I urge that you go to Paris, and talk with Monsieur Cousin. He is, above all, a scholar—and I'm sure he places scholarship above partisan prejudice. Your brilliance in the examination for the doctorate of letters has already impressed him. I feel quite confident that his closer, firsthand acquaintance with you will overcome any prejudicial influences that might be brought

135

against your appointment to the chair of foreign literature at the University of Lyons."

During the Easter holidays, Frederic traveled to Paris and called on Monsieur Cousin. The Minister of Education, after lengthy conversation, promised Frederic the chair of foreign literature at Lyons—on one condition.

"Five months from now," he explained, "we are to have a competitive examination of candidates for professorships in the Sorbonne. In the future, no candidate for a professorship will be considered unless he has taken part in such a competition. I have just issued a decree to that effect. Because the competition for this *Agrégation de littérature* is a new institution—and also, I must confess, because it is my own creation—I have set my heart on its being a success."

He replenished Frederic's wine glass and his own and then leaned forward earnestly as he resumed.

"I want you, Monsieur Ozanam, to enter that competition," he said. "It's not that you could reasonably hope for success. You are a very young man—and you would be competing with a selected group of veteran scholars. Most of them are eight or ten years older than yourself, and therefore with eight or ten years more of study behind them. But I desire this competition to reveal, particularly, our strength in young men of genius, and I feel that your wholehearted participation in the competition will help toward that end.

"Do me this favor—and I in turn promise, no matter what your standing in the competition may turn out to be—to appoint you to the chair of foreign literature at Lyons."

Frederic realized that once he was committed, preparation for the competitive examinations would mean a grueling five-months' grind. His planned literary projects and contemplated vacation travel in Germany and Switzerland would go by the board, and he would have to slave over books as he had never slaved before. "And for what?" he asked himself, for he had now no incentive of family obligation, and honors would mean little to one who might soon be in a Dominican novitiate.

"Your invitation," he told Monsieur Cousin, "is flattering. I should like time to consider it."

While in Paris, Frederic sought out his friends of the St. Vincent de Paul Society. He found the Society flourishing. Six hundred members attended one meeting at which he was present. The majority, he noted, were students, but he also observed leading citizens in the gathering, including a peer of France, a councillor of state, army generals, and several distinguished writers.

On Easter morning he received Holy Communion in the midst of a hundred and fifty members of the Society, many of whom belonged to the original Conference.

At a General Conference he was gratified to hear letters read from Conferences active in fifteen French cities, and news that another fifteen new Conferences were being started. A total membership of more than two thousand was reported.

St. Vincent de Paul Conferences were urgently needed throughout France. Pauperism was increasing, and with it, Frederic observed, there was increasing desperation and a spirit of hatred against society. "With a moneyed aristocracy whose bowels of mercy have grown hardened," he wrote, "it is well that there should be found mediators who may prevent a collision of which no man can foretell the horrible outcome."

The bloody revolutions which had lacerated the nation during the previous years made him—and most Frenchmen of his time—dread another.

After his return to Lyons, Frederic's reluctance to enter Monsieur Cousin's competition continued. He knew that the contest, written and oral, would stretch over eleven days— seven devoted to the examinations themselves and four days during which contestants could study subjects announced during the examinations. From each competitor would be expected a mastery of Greek, Latin, English, Italian, German, Spanish—he knew little of that language—and a thorough knowledge of each literature in the original. Besides, of course, a profound knowledge of French literature. In Lyons, too, he would lack the wealth of research material that was available in Paris, and would have to carry on his course as professor of commercial law.

But if Ozanam had hoped that the Minister of Education would forget his request, he was disappointed. Through various friends Monsieur Cousin sent him messages, all urging him to participate in the *Agrégation de littérature*. In addition, the chief of the French educational system enlisted the influence of Monsieur Soulacroix. Finally, he invited Frederic by formal letter—and this decided the matter; it made a refusal virtually impossible.

Knowing the severity of the coming trial, Frederic was grateful that it was set for five months away, and proceeded to prepare himself as best he might to meet it.

To concentrate on study for the competition he became more of a recluse than ever. He was not buoyed up by hope of capturing first honors—that would have seemed unrealistic. His aim was to attain a degree of success that would disgrace neither his own scholarship nor Monsieur Cousin. Yet he speculated also as to whether this contest that had been forced upon him might not possibly hold the answer to his prayers for certainty as to his vocation. If by some wild chance he did win top place, he asked himself, might not that unimaginable triumph indicate that he was to serve Divine Providence not as a religious, but as a layman in the teaching profession?

Whether Ozanam should teach and write as a religious or as a layman—on this question the Dominican Lacordaire and the Abbé Noirot were in total disagreement.

From Rome Lacordaire continued to write to Frederic. Eight gifted young Frenchmen had joined him in the Dominican novitiate; he hoped that Frederic would make the ninth. His letters radiated happiness, and Frederic was impressed.

The Abbé Noirot was also counseling Frederic. Much older than Lacordaire, the Abbé was more experienced in reading young men. He had known Frederic intimately from his boyhood, and he realized his need of the tenderness and sympathy and encouragement a devoted wife could give.

Nevertheless, he kept his opinions to himself until one day

138

Frederic confided his uncertainty to him. His forthright answer surprised the young professor; the Abbé was so positive in his opinion as to discourage further discussion.

"Marry, my dear Frederic!" declared the Abbé, roundly. "You must marry! You are not fashioned for monastic life. And you can do as much—perhaps even more—for God and His Church as a devoted layman."

The fact was, Frederic's youthful fear of matrimonial bondage had passed. He was still in doubt as to his vocation. But he was praying that, if his vocation were marriage, he might meet a young woman who, as he put it to Lallier, "might be much more worthy than I . . . as ardent in the things of God as I am lukewarm . . . and sufficiently charming."

The Abbé Noirot, too, was praying—but with a more definite objective. He had in his own mind picked a proper wife for Frederic and he was asking the Blessed Mother to guide his shy young friend to the demoiselle. He was even considering the advisability of recommending the young lady —who of course was totally unaware of the Abbé's hopes—to Frederic's consideration. But he feared that any direct attempt to play Cupid would cause his friend to bolt like a frightened colt.

It was not long after the Abbé confided the task of matchmaking to Our Lady that Frederic called upon Monsieur Soulacroix concerning some business having to do with the University's law library. He paused to say a few polite words to Madame Soulacroix, who had greeted him at the door, when his eyes fell upon a girl who had just entered an adjoining room, pushing a little boy in a wheel chair. As the young lady leaned over the child's shoulder to point to a page in the book he held, Frederic thought her smile the sweetest he had ever beheld.

Madame Soulacroix, explaining that her husband would be in shortly, asked him to be seated. Doing so, he carefully selected a chair from which he could gaze upon the entranc ing girl in the next room.

He noted that her face, when she was not smiling, wore an expression of reserve. Her hair, dressed in classical style, was parted in the middle over a fine, full forehead. Her eyes were large and expressive, her manner charming as she entertained and waited upon the little cripple in the wheelchair.

Monsieur Soulacroix came in, and the law library matter was disposed of all too soon. But Frederic, enraptured by the sight of the fascinating creature in the near distance, had no intention of allowing the rector to terminate the conversation immediately.

"Do you think, Monsieur Soulacroix, that I am stressing the philosophy of law too strongly as against its technical problems?" he asked, knowing full well that the rector was heartily in accord with his subject matter.

The stratagem worked handsomely. Monsieur Soulacroix launched into a lengthy defense of the philosophical as against the technical position, while Frederic continued to look in admiration upon the picture framed by the doorway. As the rector concluded his response, the young professor came to with a start.

"And as to my treatment of the law in relation to history monsieur—do you have any comment?" he asked, not in the least concerned as to what the rector's comment might be. Monsieur Soulacroix went off on another small lecture, complimenting Frederic upon the wisdom of his teaching, while that wily dissembler again lost himself in contemplation of the lovely girl in the adjoining room.

He wished that she might look his way; again, he was filled with dread that she might turn suddenly and find him staring. He realized that his interest would be inescapably obvious should she chance to look toward him, for he was so nearsighted that his eyes narrowed noticeably when studying any object as much as twenty feet distant.

Monsieur Soulacroix was bringing his second justification of Frederic's teaching to a close, and Frederic was about to ask another time-killing question, when the girl wheeled the boy from the room. Whereupon Frederic arose, and bid Monsieur Soulacroix adieu.

"Come with your problems or questions at any time, my dear Ozanam," said the rector. "I do not conceal my admiration for your lectures; they do great credit to our University of Lyons. But whenever you think a little talk with me might help, do not hesitate to come in for a visit. You are always most welcome."

Thereafter Monsieur Soulacroix was rather gratified at the number of "little problems" about which Frederic felt it necessary to consult him.

The Abbé Noirot, who also visited the rector often, noted Frederic's frequent presence—and he too was gratified. He guessed the real reason, and he thanked the powerful patron to whom he had prayed on Frederic's behalf. For the girl who unwittingly had fascinated the most timid bachelor in Lyons was the very one the Abbé had in mind. She was Monsieur Soulacroix's daughter, Amélie.

Frederic's frequent "professional" visits to the rector's quarters had extended over some weeks, and the Abbé Noirot was growing impatient for word of some development in the one-sided romance. He had kept himself informed; by this time, he knew, Frederic had met Amélie Soulacroix, and had on several occasions conversed with her. He knew, too, that both her parents regarded the young professor highly. He was sure the young man was in love—yet Frederic made no move.

Frederic was, indeed, very much in love. His admiration of Amélie had grown with every meeting. Here was a young lady, he told himself, in whom good sense was combined with sensibility, who was both intellectual and practical, and in whom spiritual strength found expression in womanly tenderness.

All this the Abbé saw, or sensed—and finally felt sufficiently sure of Frederic's mind and heart to venture a bold move. He decided, without saying a word to Frederic, to act as a father might, and speak to Monsieur Soulacroix. Such action taken by one less close to Frederic both personally and spiritually would have been an intolerable impertinence, but the event proved that the Abbé knew his man and his unspoken desire.

Monsieur Soulacroix agreed with the Abbé that Frederic would make his daughter an excellent husband, and the good priest went straight to Frederic and told him so. Frederic, surprised that the Abbé knew he was attracted to Amélie, was even more astonished by the Abbé's action, but he was delighted that he had acted.

The Abbé advised him to have an informal talk with Monsieur Soulacroix.

"Tell him," he said with a gentle smile, "that you have another 'little problem' you'd like to discuss with him."

Frederic, realizing that the Abbé had detected his maneuvering, smiled sheepishly, but armed with new confidence hastened to visit the rector. He found Monsieur Soulacroix all kindness.

"Thanks to the Abbé," said the rector, "you already know my disposition in this matter; I approve. But I must speak to Madame Soulacriox—who, being an American, thinks that a marriageable young lady should have absolutely free choice in the selection of her future husband. And then, of course, Amélie must agree. I will, if necessary, plead your cause, for I think this would be an excellent match."

Frederic's heart bounded with joy.

"Amélie is, as you probably know, very well educated," continued Monsieur Soulacroix. "So she is well fitted to be a scholar's wife. And from childhood she has shown a serious interest in literature. But we must not be precipitate. You are in the midst of your preparations for the competitive examinations in the Sorbonne in September. I propose, then, that we postpone going further with this matter in a formal way until after you return from Paris. For your peace of mind I will ascertain the attitude of my wife, and of Amélie—and then we'll let the whole thing rest until September. After that," he added, "will come your appointment to the chair of foreign literature here—and this, with the chair of law, will assure you a total income of 15,000 francs. A handsome income, indeed, for a young man, and quite sufficient to support a household."

Frederic's heart sank, but he could not dispute the logic of Monsieur Soulacroix's position. After all, it would mean a wait of only three months before a formal engagement. During that time, he promised himself, he would devote himself to study as never before. He felt like a young knight, training to win a tournament for the lady of his heart.

In preparation for the September contest in Paris, he studied until—as he told a friend—his head seemed to burst. He managed to "devour an enormous quantity of Latin," and devoted much time to Greek texts. Yet he felt that his preparation for the great test was lamentably inadequate. He had given to studies connected with the coming competition as much time as he could spare, but this, he was sure, was all too little. He could not, in conscience, slight even in smallest measure his duties as a law professor. He would not curtail his activities as a member of the St. Vincent de Paul Society. The Society for the Propagation of the Faith also took some of his time. One of his tasks for this organization was the writing of a lengthy article on the missions; this appeared in its *Annales*. He was working as much as eighteen hours a day.

He was overburdened, he was worried, he was fearful of the coming contest—but at the core of his being he was happy. Amélie had given him assurance of her love.

CHAPTER 17

BEHIND HIM, as he took his seat in the examining room in the Sorbonne, Frederic heard the door close and felt that its closing symbolized the fact that he was now a prisoner of circumstances created by the Minister of Education. He managed an expression of calm indifference, but he wondered whether other competitors felt as miserable as he.

His duties had kept him in Lyons until the last minute; he had come a three days' journey with hardly a wink of sleep. He was thin and pale, and he felt feverish.

He looked at the five eminent scholars who constituted the examining board. Among them was his friend Jean-Jacques Ampère, professor of French literature at the College of France; he was the only one, thought Frederic, who looked at all friendly. Even the examiner he most admired, the great Monsieur Fauriel, who looked far older than during Frederic's student days at the Sorbonne, seemed forbidding. He wished he could command the assurance exhibited by the seven well-known professors of the colleges of Paris who were his competitors. They *should* look assured, Frederic told himself; were they not among the most brilliant younger educators of the French University system? And hadn't they been preparing for this extraordinary test of scholarship a good six months before Monsieur Cousin had thought to tell him about it and insist on his participation?

Well, here he was at last, after five months of punishing study. And now, he said to himself, there was only hope— that he wouldn't disgrace himself, and that he'd be lucky in his assignments.

He heard the voice of the bearded professor as he read from the slip of paper in his hand. The voice seemed to come from miles away; it was announcing the first day's assignment.

"Your Latin dissertation," the remote voice was saying, "will be 'On the Causes which Arrested the Development of Tragedy Among the Romans.' "

Ah, he knew a great deal about that, thought Frederic, as he wrote down the title in his fine, small hand. His familiarity with the subject reassured him.

It was Ozanam's custom to write slowly and painstakingly, to correct and polish; the end of the eight-hour examination found him still hard at work, with his copy still in the rough. Crude as it looked, he had no other course than to hand it in. Its untidy appearance humiliated him; he hoped its roughness would not entirely discredit the content. But he felt defeated.

After the ordeal he met Monsieur Bailly by arrangement and set off with him for a restaurant. As they walked through the familiar streets, Bailly directed their conversation to the problems of the St. Vincent de Paul Society. He wanted Frederic's counsel, as always, but he also wanted to distract him from the examinations, and he knew that the interests of the Society could not fail to drive all other considerations from Frederic's mind. After dining they strolled for a while through the Luxembourg Gardens. By the time they said good-night, Frederic was completely relaxed mentally and very tired physically. That night he slept soundly.

It was well he did, for the next morning he and his fellow contestants faced another eight-hour session. The test was a dissertation in French "On the Historical Value of Bossuet's Funeral Orations." Again, at the end of the eight hours, Frederic found himself handing in rough copy. Such papers, he knew, were unworthy of himself and of the examining board. His depression over what he considered his certain failure became so great that he determined to withdraw from the competition.

This thought was uppermost in his mind the next morning as he was hurrying through the Sorbonne. Deep discouragement was written on his face as he encountered Ampère. Jean-Jacques saw at a glance that anxieties were torturing his young friend.

"Be of good cheer, my dear Frederic," he greeted him, smiling. "When one starts favorably, one has a good chance of finishing well."

Ampère hastened on and, greatly heartened, Frederic headed for the library. He would have a day before each of the coming tests in which to prepare himself. These would consist of three oral argumentations on alternate days, in Greek, Latin and French texts.

This kind of examination brought him face to face with the jury, and enabled him to judge the reactions of its members. These were, he thought at the conclusion of the examination, quite favorable. This impression increased on successive test days, as he went from Greek, to Latin, to French. He dealt with Euripides' *Helen;* with a fragment of the Rhetoric of Dionysius Halicarnassus; with Lucian, Pliny and Caesar, and the evolution of religious doctrines among the Romans. During his French test he deliberately compared Montesquieu and St. Thomas Aquinas in such wise as to make unmistakably clear his adherence to Catholicism.

Following this the contestants were invited to show their familiarity with German, English, Spanish and Italian literatures by discussing in those four languages such authors as Schiller, Klopstock, Shakespeare, Dante and Calderón. This part of the program was optional. Ozanam was surprised, however, after he had finished his translations and critiques, to find that none of his competitors appeared. The examiners looked about questioningly, decided that the other contestants preferred not to participate in the foreign literature program, and retired. Ozanam had come off very well. He had won a marked success even in Spanish, in which language he had taken only ten formal lessons, devoted chiefly to pronunciation and idioms.

To complete the competition, each entrant was now required to deliver two lectures on subjects to be assigned—one twenty-four hours, the other only one hour, before the test. When the candidates drew lots for their first lecture subjects, there fell to Frederic a theme that dismayed him—"The History of the Greek and Latin Scholiasts." The audience laughed, rather commiseratingly, for no drier, less familiar subject could have been assigned than that of the annotators of ancient manuscripts. Frederic was to refer to this popular impression the next day when in discussing the subject he mentioned that the scholiasts were thought of "by ignorant commentators as so many worms gnawing at the manuscripts of the past."

During the last week he had been without a sound night's rest, with the exception of that one blessed night after the first day's examination, and had labored under an enormous strain. He was feeling profoundly discouraged, when new hope and encouragement came unexpectedly from two directions. His brother the Abbé arrived from Lyons, bringing a message from Amélie that she was praying fervently for his success. A little later, Professor Emile Egger, one of his rivals in the competition, generously passed on to him three books on the unfamiliar subject assigned him. Thankfully bearing these

146

treasures, Frederic returned to his quarters for a night of study.

Late the next day he dragged himself again to the Sorbonne. He had driven himself almost to the breaking point; he was exhausted in mind and body. His face was pale and worn, and he hoped he would not appear as utterly spent as he felt.

As he entered the lecture hall through a little door in the rear of the room, he found himself before more than three hundred scholars sitting in twelve semicircular rows of chairs. Some, he sensed, were ill-disposed toward him. He felt his body grow rigid in panic; his lips seemed paralyzed, and all memory of his subject deserted him.

In this extremity he made—as he afterwards related—"an act of faith in God such as I never had made before, and never was I so rewarded."

He arose, and slowly—as was his speaking habit—began his preparatory remarks. His voice carried hardly ten feet. As he spoke, however, he felt his strength and assurance growing; within a minute or two he was holding forth on his newly acquired information with a freedom and mastery that astonished him. He won and held the minds of his judges and of the entire audience. When he concluded, all—even those who had shaken their heads commiseratingly the day before—stood and applauded in tribute.

The next day he drew as his subject—with an hour for preparation—"The Literature of the Reign of Louis XIV," with the task of delivering a criticism of it. Here he was entirely at home; he spoke with deep insight and authority; he felt, for the first time, completely confident; he "indulged himself"—as he was to write some years later—"to my heart's content."

The ballots had been gathered and scrutinized. The spokesman for the judges arose, a slip of paper in his hand. He praised the contestants for their learning and their eloquence. The judges felt the great difficulty—yes, the distressing burden —of having to choose one from among men of such deep scholarship and brilliance. But it was necessary that a winner be decided, and it was now his duty to announce the decision.

He paused, and then, uttering the words slowly and in a

higher voice, he said, "The vote of the judges awards first place in this *Agrégation de littérature* to Monsieur Frederic Ozanam, of the University of Lyons."

There was a long moment of silence, then a burst of applause, and Frederic found himself surrounded by a score of scholars, heaping their congratulations upon him.

He himself was too stunned for elation. The judges had overruled his own secret verdict, and his mind was trying to re-focus on this new reality. He might now, with some hope, expect a call at some time in the future to the Sorbonne. In the meantime, his position in Lyons was secure. He could surely become formally engaged to Amélie Soulacroix; yes, he could marry within the year. He would continue to lecture in law, and to this he would add the professorship of foreign literature at the University of Lyons. He would receive an ample income—an income that would provide a life of comfort for Amélie, and for the children with whom God might bless their marriage.

Next day, Frederic was surprised to receive a note from Monsieur Fauriel, professor of foreign literature at the Sorbonne, asking him to call at his earliest opportunity.

Charles-Claude Fauriel was now in his sixty-ninth year. He had long been recognized as one of the great minds of France. He had made known to the French people the merits of Ossian and had greatly increased their appreciation of Shakespeare. He had assisted his countrymen in a new valuation of German literature. He had popularized the Romance literature of the Middle Ages. He had gathered the remnants of the ancient Basque and Celtic languages, and had made many other contributions to French appreciation of foreign cultures.

Frederic found the great man slumped in a large chair, and noted that he gained his feet with difficulty as he greeted him. He was pale and worn; it was evident that the old professor was yielding to the years.

"My doctor has ordered me to let up a bit," Monsieur Fauriel confided to Frederic over a glass of wine, "and, Monsieur Ozanam, I have decided that you are the man to serve as my supply professor. Will you accept the position, beginning with the new term? The salary will be a little over 2500 francs a year."

In these few words Professor Fauriel suddenly faced Frederic with the necessity of making the greatest crossroads decision of his life.

To accept the offer would mean immediate risk and hardship.

To refuse it would be to reject the opportunity of taking his place at once at the heart and center of French and European scholarship.

To accept, he would have to sacrifice his life tenure in two Lyons professorships for an uncertain supply professorship, subject to termination the moment Professor Fauriel decided that he had recovered his health.

He would be going from a university where he enjoyed unquestioned popularity with students and faculty to one in which his uncompromising Catholicism might excite hostility. And hostility at the Sorbonne could express itself in student riots and other manifestations that might rob his teaching of effectiveness and eventually even result in dismissal.

He faced still greater risk—a risk that made his heart sink when he thought of it. This was the possibility—or what seemed to him to be the possibility—of losing Amélie. She was not committed to him by a formal engagement; there was so far only a tentative understanding between Frederic and Monsieur Soulacroix. The latter, as a loving and sensible parent, naturally was insistent upon seeing his daughter well provided for. Frederic's assurance of a 15,000-franc income undoubtedly had been a factor in the rector's favorable attitude toward his suit. How would he react when Frederic informed him that he could now offer Amélie only one sixth of that amount?

These thoughts tumbled through Frederic's mind while he sat as still and silent as a statue and Professor Fauriel waited on his word. Finally, he said: "Monsieur, your offer is the greatest professional honor any man has ever paid me. Acceptance, however, might have certain consequences of a personal nature, and to these I must give some thought. May

I have the rest of the morning to analyze my position? I can give you my decision this afternoon."

Monsieur Fauriel bade him take all the time he might require. Frederic promised to call on him at three o'clock with his decision. Then he went at once to the Church of St. Etienne-du-Mont, where he knelt for an hour before the Blessed Sacrament, praying for light to see the right way and for strength to follow it.

He left the church and walked aimlessly until, coming to a little café, he sat down at a sidewalk table and ordered food. He toyed with it, so deep in thought that he hardly realized it was before him, until his waiter solicitously inquired if it were not to his liking.

He was thinking of Amélie. All his natural longing for an early union with her, all his manly desire to surround his loved one with the good things of life, argued powerfully that he turn down Professor Fauriel's offer. Why not defer teaching in Paris, he asked himself, until after he had saved a substantial sum from the handsome double salary he would soon be receiving in Lyons? That, surely, would be the safe, sane, sensible thing to do. Was not a probable deferment of marriage, with the possibility of eventually losing Amélie, entirely too much to ask of any man? After all, wouldn't the Minister of Education invite him, sooner or later, to come to the Sorbonne—and at a far more adequate salary? Yes, stay in Lyons for a while—that was the sensible compromise. Continue to teach the young men destined for the factories and the counting houses and the law courts of Lyons. True, the field was of minor importance compared to that offered by the Sorbonne. There he would be forming the professors, the writers and the statesmen of tomorrow—the men who would lead in forming French thought and policy in the next generation. He had dedicated his talents to the advancement of Christian truth—beyond doubt it was in Paris, at the Sorbonne, that he could serve that truth more effectively. If the decision was left to Amélie, would she not urge that he accept?

He called the waiter, paid his account, and hastened to Monsieur Fauriel's apartment.

150

"Monsieur," he said, when a maid had ushered him in, "I accept your offer."

What Frederic Ozanam did, he did wholeheartedly. In his new professorship he was to teach German literature of the Middle Ages. He decided to study the country of the *Nibelungen* and the *Book of Heroes* firsthand. Instead of setting out directly for Lyons, he traveled east by way of Aix-la-Chapelle and Cologne and descended the Rhine. He reveled in the Rhineland's romantic landscape and legends, but he was far from satisfied with this flying excursion. To fit himself for his new work he wanted to live in this country, to absorb its history, its traditions, its fables, until they were a part of him. But time pressed; many matters must have his attention if he were to be ready to take up residence in Paris by the year's end. Above all, he must secure his formal engagement to Amélie—if Monsieur Soulacroix would now permit it.

Frederic had written to him, presenting his resignation from the faculty, and informing him that he had accepted Monsieur Fauriel's offer of a supply professorship at 2500 francs. His letter eloquently set forth the reasons for his decision, and voiced the hope that it would not adversely affect Monsieur Soulacroix's approval of him as his future son-in-law.

As his German excursion drew near to its end, he became desperately anxious to reach Lyons and to hear from the lips of Monsieur Soulacroix his response to the letter.

CHAPTER 18

WALKING beside his brother, the Abbé Alphonse, Frederic followed the familiar way to Monsieur Soulacroix's apartment. It was the day after his return from Germany. Though still fatigued from his Sorbonne ordeal and the roundabout journey home, he had asked Alphonse to arrange an interview with the man he hoped would accept him as his son-in-law-to-be. The all-important matter of formalizing his engagement to Amélie had been uppermost in his mind from the day he had left Lyons. Now he was eager for, yet fearful of, the interview.

Monsieur Soulacroix seemed as well disposed toward Frederic as ever; he welcomed him warmly. Alphonse came quickly to the objective of their call; as the eldest member of the Ozanam family, it was his duty formally to request the alliance.

"In making his formal request for your daughter's hand," said the Abbé, "my brother expresses the hope that the recent radical reduction in his income will not affect your acceptance of his proposal."

"A decrease in income?—but that's impossible!" cried the rector, turning toward Frederic. "With your two professorships here at Lyons your income will be increased."

"Didn't you receive my letter?" asked Frederic, surprised and embarrassed. "I wrote you from Cologne that I had accepted the supply professorship of foreign literature at the Sorbonne, commencing with the new term."

"Your letter has not reached me," replied Monsieur Soulacroix. He was regarding Frederic with an air of startled dismay.

"It miscarried, or is still on the way," interjected Alphonse. "There's room for improvement in the foreign mail service."

"You say you have agreed to become assistant in the foreign literature department at the Sorbonne?" asked Monsieur Soulacroix, somewhat recovered from the first shock of Frederic's announcement. "That means you will be supplying for Monsieur Fauriel."

"Yes," answered Frederic. "I feel that he has done me a great honor."

"I recognize the honor," said Monsieur Soulacroix. "But I gather that it entails a financial sacrifice."

"The salary," replied Frederic uncomfortably, "is 2500 francs."

"My dear young friend," said Monsieur Soulacroix, regarding Frederic sadly, "you overwhelm me. At a single stroke you deprive me of my most prized professor, and my daughter of the financial security and the comforts that your increased income here would have provided her."

"Before making my decision," explained Frederic, "I asked myself what Amélie would have me do. And it seemed clear to me that she would have urged me to sacrifice comfort and ease—yes, even her own comfort and ease—to grasp this opportunity."

Monsieur Soulacroix shook his head solemnly.

"Ah, Monsieur Frederic," he said, "you are brave—and I hope not rashly so. As a father, I am troubled. Yet I recognize that heroism, also, has its rights in this world! And I must confess that I have unlimited confidence in your energy and in your talents. Still—2500 francs a year! On that small income, you would be asking my daughter to practice unusual austerity."

In these words Frederic saw his opportunity.

"Why not let Amélie decide?" he asked Monsieur Soulacroix.

The rector, leaning his head on his hand, considered this proposition.

"Amélie?" he said at last, looking at Frederic with a shrewd but kindly smile. "I think you know she would be a most tender and perhaps prejudiced judge. Yet—she is the one who is most concerned. Do you go to her, Frederic," he said, placing a hand affectionately on his shoulder, "while the Abbé and I discuss other matters."

Amélie did not hesitate in her agreement. Placing her hands in Frederic's she said: "Your decision, Frederic, is mine. You have a mission in the world. At the Sorbonne, you will be able to pursue that mission on a higher level. I would have it no other way."

Monsieur Soulacroix must have been quite certain of his daughter's answer. While Frederic was talking with her, he discussed the matter of dowry with Alphonse. It would amount to several thousand francs, and Monsieur Soulacroix would pay it in installments several months apart.

"They will need it," said the Abbé.

"Yet their enforced frugality," said Monsieur Soulacroix,

"will have a salutary result, I feel, all through their married lives. It will constitute a discipline, and a thorough schooling in the ways of thrift."

It was now November. The wedding, it was decided, would be in June of the next year.

When Frederic and Amélie whispered their farewells on the eve of his departure for Paris they exchanged gold medallions, each containing a lock of the other's hair. They were to wear these medallions constantly as long as they lived.[1]

"Six months of exile are before me," wrote Frederic to Lallier the day before he left Lyons and Amélie for Paris and the Sorbonne.

It was an exile that under ordinary circumstances would have passed with almost insufferable slowness, relieved only by the letters he received from and wrote to Amélie. The circumstances, however, were far from ordinary.

Arrived in Paris, Frederic Ozanam stepped from the Lyons diligence into the midst of a battle over the monopoly of education by the French University—which was virtually a governmental agency. Almost ten years before, the Catholics had solemnly declared war on the monopoly. At that time Count de Montalembert, who had campaigned for freedom on many fronts, had defied governmental restrictions on freedom to educate by opening a primary school. For this he had been fined by the House of Peers, of which he was a member. Now, in the struggle against the central government's control of education, he and the Catholic party of which he was a leader were clashing with forces led by Villemain, who had succeeded Cousin as Minister of Education. Villemain could depend upon the support of the majority of the University professors, and he certainly was in no mood to overlook opposition from any faculty member; indeed, opposition from that quarter was the last thing he expected to encounter. Not once in the fifty years that had passed since the Revolution had a professorial voice been raised in the Sorbonne's ancient halls to uphold the Christian viewpoint.

1 These medallions, with other keepsakes, are in the custody of Frederic Ozanam's descendants.

With the opening of the fall term, Villemain was startled and shocked by an astonishing event. Frederic Ozanam, the new, stripling supply professor from the provinces, was with consummate scholarship revealing the enormous debt that European culture owed to Christianity, committing himself beyond retreat to a course which seemed certain to bring him into conflict with those controlling higher education.

He had no tenure, and he might reasonably have adopted —at least until he was more firmly established at the Sorbonne —a less aggressive position. He might have reasoned: "Why add to the initial disadvantages that circumstances impose upon me?" Was he not, he might have asked, facing difficulties enough in trying to fill the place of one of Europe's most distinguished scholars, in trying to meet the extremely high standard set by the eminent savants who were the Sorbonne's professors? He had weighed the risks, but had rejected compromise. Unbelieving professors felt free to make their courses serve their anti-religious bias—he would exercise equal freedom in examining factually and fairly the Christian contribution to society insofar as it came within the scope of his course. He would trace European literature to its Christian background and sources, and in doing so he would necessarily refute the errors to which students had been exposed.

From his first lecture he stood before his audience as a bold and masterly expositor of full historical truth, proclaiming the Christian heritage of each European country whenever to do so came within the scope of his subject.

Some years before, under Frederic's leadership of the Catholic students at the Sorbonne, the more outrageous attacks on Christian belief had been reduced in number and recklessness. Yet skeptical professors continued the process of de-Christianizing France through control of the education of its future intellectual leaders. They were backed by the government of Louis Philippe, which as a matter of policy welcomed demonstrations against any assertion of the rights of the Church.

That even the slightest challenge or threat to their control should alert the faculty was to be expected. Yet faculty politicians and the student body remained strangely quiescent in the face of Ozanam's single-handed assault upon the entrenched anti-Christian position.

Ozanam's youth was doubtless disarming. Guizot, before Ozanam the youngest man ever admitted to the august Sorbonne faculty, had been thirty-five years old; Ozanam was twenty-seven. Ozanam's scholarship, too—wholly remarkable in one so young—won him, almost immediately, stature and respect. His students recognized in him a scholar of seemingly inexhaustible erudition. Through long hours of analysis and reflection, his mind transmuted the common clay of knowledge into the gold of creative interpretation. He stripped each subject to its essentials, condensing and simplifying, and laying bare its inner structure. Then, filling in, he gave life and solidity to the literary period he was discussing, painting in its background in glowing colors. His manner was fresh, simple, and spontaneous and—except for the first two or three sentences at the beginning of a lecture—animated and expressive. His retentive memory, his thorough organization of material, his clear and colorful language contributed to a sustained eloquence that charmed his hearers. He was easy to listen to—with the exception, always, of those first few labored utterances. Throughout his career he suffered from nervousness approaching "stage fright" when about to open a discourse; the blood seemed to drain from his head, leaving him deathly pale; his blue-gray eyes grew almost black and wandered over the room as if he feared to look upon his audience; his voice seemed to choke in his throat. Then the inspiration of his subject broke through the psychological dam holding back the words, and flowing eloquence streamed forth, crystal clear, yet reflecting in sparkling colors the brilliance of his mind. The students, enchanted, gave vent to their admiration in bursts of applause as he proceeded. No one ever left an Ozanam lecture until the final word had fallen from his lips.

God had endowed him with talent approaching genius, and he improved his natural gifts by endless study and thought. He was never satisfied with merely reviewing a subject, no matter how thorough his mastery of it. Instead, he devoted the evening and the morning preceding a lecture to arranging

156

his material and to meditating on it, until his mind penetrated to the basic significance of the matter.

When students entered his lecture hall, they knew they must be alert to every word, for he had the true scholar's ability to compress a whole chapter into a sentence. They learned to listen with particular intensity to his preliminary outline, for to this he always rigidly adhered. They recognized in this a mark of respect for them as persons; it was obvious that he valued his students' time too greatly to cause them to waste an instant of it through any slackness in his teaching effort.

The fact that he was not attacked was above all a tribute to his charity. His love for his fellow men shone through his words and disarmed even those most envenomed against religion. This was felt even more in his conferences with individual students.

To these qualities was added superb command of the teaching art. He possessed a true genius for stimulating curiosity, arousing interest, imparting knowledge, and inducing students to think, to search, and to speculate. Following the Socratic method, he led his pupils but at the same time compelled them to exercise their minds and imaginations, so as to make the most of their latent capacities and to develop the priceless habit of hard work.

Whatever the reasons, the opposition Ozanam expected, and had seemed almost to invite, failed to materialize, and his lectures gained rapidly in popularity until they were among the best attended in the Sorbonne.

During the Easter vacation of 1841 he returned for two enchanted weeks to Lyons. At this time, he and Amélie discussed plans for their wedding and the months of travel that were to follow. Like betrothed young people the world over, they were moved by an instinctive desire to retreat from the society they knew and were known by. Like birds prior to the responsibility of a nest and nestlings, they wanted to fly freely about for a while, rejoicing in the beauties and wonders of far places before settling down.

"For a whole six months from our wedding day, Amélie, we'll be as free as gypsies, wandering where we will," said

Frederic, "and wherever we wander will be paradise, for you'll be there."

"Not quite six months," laughed Amélie, who was already thinking as a homemaker. "Only five months, for we must have four or five weeks in Paris to set up our new home."

"Very well, then—only five months," agreed Frederic. "And it's you who must decide where we're to spend those hundred and fifty golden days."

"I don't care where we go—as long as we go there together!" cried Amélie, merrily. "But if *you'd* say Italy, I'd agree."

"Mind-reader!" exclaimed Frederic. "How'd you guess I'd say Italy? Can you read my thoughts?"

"Only to a degree—as yet," answered Amélie. "But I can read your thesis. And when a man who had won his doctorate in literature with a thesis on *The Divine Comedy* talks so glowingly of Italy's charms, where he'd like to travel is as clear as crystal."

"You're right, Amélie—and Italy it shall be! But there's another reason for Italy. The University has offered me a subvention for a report on Greek colonial influence in Sicilian architecture. What a help *that* will be! But even with that financial aid, we'll not be traveling like English millionaires."

Frederic returned to Paris, his hard work, his brilliant lectures, and the excitement of the never-ceasing battle for the truth that makes man free—until the day he had so eagerly looked forward to, the day he would leave Paris for Lyons and his marriage to Amélie, arrived at last.

CHAPTER 19

THE ABBE ALPHONSE had coached Frederic as to the moment he was to step forth from the sacristy and advance to meet his betrothed.

"When the organist starts playing," Alphonse had said,

158

"that will be your signal. But," he added, pausing in humorous despair, "no bridegroom, my dear brother, ever hears the organ. You'll be far too excited for that."

Frederic thought the statement preposterous, but the Abbé continued: "No— we must leave that matter in the hands of Falconnet, who fortunately will be with you."

"Falconnet," he said, turning to their cousin, who was grinning broadly at the flustered Frederic, "*you'll* hear the organ. When it starts up, please remember that our Frederic will be in a state of shock—or at least of unconscious animation, something like a sleepwalker. Simply place your hand firmly on his shoulder, point him in the right direction, and give him a gentle shove. Remember he is a bridegroom, and all bridegrooms are practically paralyzed just before the ceremony. He will come to life—at least partially—when he sees the white vision of his Amélie advancing up the aisle to meet him!"

"What gross exaggeration," thought Frederic, and joined in the laugh.

But the Abbé was not exaggerating. Frederic was now, as the ceremony began, at least partially in a daze. He did not hear the organ, though some of the congregation thought that the organist was playing a trifle loudly. Falconnet did start him toward the main aisle with a gentle shove. And he regained full consciousness only when he beheld Amélie coming up the aisle on her father's arm—the "white vision" his brother Alphonse had foretold. She was, it seemed to Frederic, an ethereal being enveloped in a luminous cloud, floating lightly toward him as he advanced to meet her.

The wedding guests—somewhat more detached and analytical—saw a beautiful and modest girl, her dark hair, parted in the middle and arranged in delightful little curls at the sides, cunningly visible beneath her bridal veil. Her gown—a dressmaking triumph, whispered the ladies—had a tight, small bodice, a slim, pointed waist and a full skirt of satin; it was enveloped in gauze and lace—the fleecy cloud within which, to Frederic's charmed gaze, she seemed to float.

Frederic felt his angel's hand placed in his as her father withdrew, and found himself escorting her to a prie-dieu, where he knelt beside her.

He received the ring from the Abbé, realizing that this act signified that he was receiving this pure soul into his keeping from her Creator. He placed it on her finger, his mind dwelling for a moment on the little circle of gold—that circle of infinity which, again, signified their spiritual union throughout eternity.

As he knelt there, he felt a moment of keen regret that his parents were not present to bless him and his bride, and as the Divine Blessing of their marriage descended upon them he could scarcely restrain his tears.

There had been a last-minute change in their travel plans. Frederic had for some time been afflicted with a persistent laryngitis, and a few days before the wedding Amélie had persuaded him that they should pause for a few weeks at the curative springs of Allevard, in the nearby Dauphiné.

"The treatments there will benefit you, I know—and then you'll enjoy traveling and sight-seeing all the more," she had urged.

"A month at a spa—when we could be seeing Italy!" Frederic exclaimed protestingly.

Yet he knew Amélie's suggestion was sound, and at the Allevard Springs they remained a month. His persistent throat affliction disappeared—that is, all but the slightest trace of it. Indeed, his "laryngitis" was never to be cured entirely, and a few years later would reassert itself strongly. Still later it would become known finally for what it was—the first sign of a slow, wasting disease that would bring fever, and feebleness, and a creeping martyrdom.

Fortunately, young couples can foresee the future even less clearly than their elders; could they read it, how much happiness they would be denied! To Frederic and Amélie, the golden idleness of a month's rest at the spa in the Dauphiné country was unalloyed with fears for the future. It was followed by more months of transcendent happiness in Italy—in travel through Sicily, Naples, Rome, and the many towns and hamlets all the way from Palermo to Florence.

They traveled simply and—thanks in part to Frederic's knowledge of Italy and his mastery of the language—with economy. They felt themselves in an earthly paradise as they wended their way along the semitropical coast of Sicily, with its fig trees, its gigantic aloes bordering fields of cotton, papyrus, and sugar cane; its cedar, citron, and orange groves; its little palm trees along the seashore. They jaunted in native carts along roads bordered by flowering myrtle and oleander, and tall palm trees with broad-leaved crowns and ripening dates in heavy bunches. They were entranced by the wild beauty of the Gulf of Palermo, with Mount Etna raising its brow of snow against the blue Italian sky.

They wandered through Italy's Greek and Roman ruins—through empty tombs and temples, with their fragments of marble gods and pillars; through ancient theatres and baths. Frederic made copious notes; he was tracing "the progress of art from the austere nakedness of its first monuments to the somewhat over-exuberant decoration of its latest."

Most of all the starry-eyed couple were charmed by the patriarchal hospitality and simple, fervent faith of the peasants. Time after time they were pressed, almost compelled, to enter a humble dwelling, where they would find themselves surrounded by beautiful children, with the latest bambino brought proudly forward to enjoy their admiration and caresses.

In their drives from town to town in a rented carriage they visited several monasteries, where they were received with exquisite courtesy. These monastery visits afforded the couple the privilege of conversing with eminent scholars whose learning, Frederic confessed, frequently overwhelmed him.

Yielding to its charms, they lingered longer in beguiling Sicily than they had planned. It was not till November fifth that they saw from their coach on the road to Rome the vast dome of St. Peter's against the sky—"like the diadem of the papacy," Frederic said to Amélie, "suspended between earth and heaven."

In Rome they were granted a private audience by Pope Gregory XVI. The venerable pontiff, then seventy-six years old, received them with paternal kindness.

"Be seated," he said, as they entered his chamber. "You are my children; let us leave formalities aside and talk awhile."

It was, for the most part, literary talk. The pontiff, one of Europe's finest scholars, was deeply interested in Frederic's Dantean studies. He seemed genuinely grateful when Frederic offered him a copy of his thesis on the great poet.

Toward the end of November they took ship from Genoa to Marseilles, and thence a coach for Lyons.

CHAPTER 20

ARRIVING IN LYONS in the first part of December, Frederic and Amélie made their home for a few days with the Abbé Alphonse and Charles Ozanam, who, with the ever-faithful Guigui, were occupying the family apartment.

The young professor and his bride planned to remain in Lyons only a week. They were eager for Paris. To Amélie the glamorous city spelled that great adventure in a woman's life, the establishment of a home.

They packed their various treasures—the *objets d'art* that had captured their affections during their recent travels, their wedding gifts, and their favorite lares and penates—to send on to Paris. But the treasured and priceless Marie Cruziat—the beloved and motherly Guigui—she, for the time being, they must leave behind. She would remain to manage the Ozanam apartment, which was now at No. 6 Rue St. Pierre, almost directly opposite the Church of St. Pierre.

Frederic had induced his mother to move there about two years before her death, that she might be closer to the church. Growing weakness was then forcing her to count her steps, and her son knew that she could have no greater consolation than to be an across-the-street neighbor of her Eucharistic Lord, and a frequent visitor in His house.

162

Frederic told Guigui that he and Amélie longed for the time when they could all be together again, in Paris.

"You don't want such an old one as I in Paris with you," Guigui protested.

She still sewed without the aid of spectacles and was as hardy as an ancestral oak, but sometimes she required assurance that her age had not lessened her worth in the eyes of those she loved.

"It's a young one you'll want in Paris," she continued, "not one who has seen her best years."

Frederic and Amélie assumed an air of outraged astonishment.

"What!" exclaimed Frederic. "You, who braved last year's floods[1] to keep the house in food, to talk like this! You would desert us? Desert a newly married couple who so need your wisdom, your experience in running a household!"

Amélie added her entreaties. "Oh, how I wish that Charles didn't need your care while he's interning here, and that you could come with us at once," she said. Then, shrewdly appealing to Guigui's maternal instinct, she added, "I do hope you'll be with us when I'm having my first child. What should I do without you to fall back on? Guigui, dear Guigui, please think of us and of our need of you, and not of the retirement and the rest you've so richly earned."

These assurances gratified and strengthened the confidence of the stalwart retainer, to whom retirement would have been a major tragedy.

"Well, if you really need me, I'll go with you when the time comes," she agreed; then turned quickly away that they might not see her tears.

In Paris, Frederic and Amélie rented a small apartment in the Rue St. Germain, close to the Church of St. Sulpice and four or five blocks from the Sorbonne. The furnishings were somewhat sparse, but included a grand piano Amélie had received as a wedding gift. The young couple would accumulate more adequate furniture as time went on, but now they gave such material concerns hardly a thought. They were

---

[1] In November, 1840, the simultaneous flooding of the Rhône and Saône rivers brought major disaster to Lyons, necessitating the rebuilding of six hundred dwellings.

deeply happy, and life went on like a song—quite literally so, for their happiness burst out in many a gay tune, with Amélie, an excellent musician, playing the accompaniments on her cherished piano.

True, she quickly awoke to the unpleasant fact—as every bride must—that in day-after-day existence a man's work must be served, and that in Frederic's devotion to his profession she had a relentless rival. Yet she recognized that it was a rival that she, as a dutiful helpmate, must not attempt to circumvent or defeat. She was an understanding wife, with intellectual resources she could always fall back on when Frederic's labors denied her his companionship. She loved him dearly, and it was something just to be near him. She joyed in his presence even when his whole mind was so occupied with studies, speculations and creative interpretations of great literature that he worked on silently, hour after hour—conscious of her presence, but absorbed in his work.

As winter receded and blossoming spring advanced toward summer, Amélie felt growing concern for Frederic's well-being. It was a warm June for Paris, but it seemed to Amélie that the warmest apartment in the whole city was their own. They decided that they must move to less suffocating quarters.

"Père" Bailly solved their problem. When Frederic told him one night after a St. Vincent de Paul meeting that he and Amélie would probably both die of the heat unless they could find a cooler apartment, the publisher said, "I have just the place for you. It's an apartment in that old palace built for Murat, on the southwest corner of the Rue de Fleurus, opposite the western side of the Luxembourg Gardens. True, it's old, but in good condition—and I can highly recommend the landlord. I have just bought it! Let us go tomorrow, my dear Frederic, to inspect this former residence of the brother-in-law of the Emperor Napoleon—this one-time mansion of the King of Naples—this erstwhile property of the Prince de Clermont Tournerre—this fine old building whose rents, I hope, will ease my latter years."

Amélie was delighted with the apartment in the Rue de Fleurus. True, from it one could catch only a glimpse of the Luxembourg Gardens; by leaning out a window just a little,

Amélie could see the trees and the entrance to the Gardens at the end of the street.

"The entire Luxembourg Gardens will be *our* gardens, now, Frederic," she cried excitedly as, with Monsieur Bailly, she and Frederic inspected the apartment the day following Frederic's talk with his old friend.

"You must enjoy hours of its good fresh air and sunlight," enjoined her husband.

"On one condition," she answered, seriously.

"What's that?" asked Frederic, surprised.

"That you pass many of those hours there with me, even if you insist on bringing your books with you," said Amélie. "Your laryngitis is bothering you again, and you stay shut up in this apartment with your studies and your writing more than is good for your health."

Monsieur Bailly excused himself for other business, but Amélie was not half done with exploring the apartment. She flitted in and out of its vacant rooms, then went through each one slowly, planning with a homemaker's instinct the arrangement of furniture.

"Here, Frederic, we shall have the piano," she said, indicating an ample wall space. "We must have a sofa to go there," she continued, measuring with her eye another space between two windows.

Monsieur Soulacroix had recently sent Frederic the latest installment on his daughter's dowry, and part of this Frederic and Amélie planned to invest in furniture.

Amélie settled in her mind just where she would place a large armchair she had priced, and four mahogany casual chairs upholstered in deep red velvet that her heart was set on.

"You'll have plenty of wall space for the engravings we brought from Italy," Frederic pointed out.

"Yes, Frederic, and for the family portraits, too," responded Amélie, who mentally had already placed all their pictures on the apartment's walls. Her large dark eyes were dancing with excitement.

What if the apartment *were* too large by half? Charles Ozanam and Guigi would be coming to them before many more

165

months. And when their hoped-for children came, she told herself—her heart beating a little faster—every inch of the apartment would be needed. What if the rent seemed more than they could afford? The dowry would help pay for it until Frederic was a full professor with a more substantial income.

Soon they were installed in the Rue de Fleurus apartment, and Frederic, with a sigh of relief, was back at his work routine. Insofar as he was concerned, the chief article of furniture in their new quarters was a small, simple mahogany table with two drawers and two pigeonholes, at which he wrote. Always before him on this table was a very old bronze crucifix. This had come down to him through his grandparents, and through no one knew how many generations of the Ozanam family before them.

Frederic was an extremely conscientious professor. The evening before a lecture he worked far into the night preparing it and was generally up early the next morning to continue his labors.

He wrote voluminously. Although he spoke without notes, he wrote out every word of his lectures. He wrote articles, he wrote books, and he carried on a large correspondence.

Always before him on his desk were several quill pens ready to his hand, for he wore out points by the dozen. Close by was a keen penknife with which he shaped each quill to an extremely sharp point, for his writing was very small and fine. So fine, that when Amélie read his manuscript she used a magnifying glass. He wore spectacles at his work, but generally neglected to clean them. At times Amélie would lean over his shoulder, gently lift the spectacles, and as gently replace them after she had polished the glasses.

He worked at his little desk so long, and sat so still, that Amélie suggested an alternate desk at which he might stand and write. A desk made to his height was ordered, and thereafter Frederic alternated between the two—undoubtedly to the benefit of his circulation.

Amélie was typically the French housewife, not only carrying on her household tasks with skill, but keeping abreast of her husband's work, and helping him with it. All through Frederic's life, she was his secretary. She studied the subjects and the issues of the day in which he was interested and was ever able and ready to talk with him about them.

Frederic needed her help as well as her intellectual companionship, for his deep sense of duty drove him to devote to his professorship all his abilities and energy. He was never robust, and Amélie's assistance became increasingly important to him through the years.

She realized that it was imperative that her husband perform his duties as a substitute professor with distinction. Only through a display of extraordinary effectiveness as an instructor could he assure his continuance at the Sorbonne—and the continuance of the apostolate for which they had both sacrificed so much. Only by earning popularity as a professor could he attract students whose minds he desired to open to Christian truth.

If study kept his candles burning late—as it generally did —Amélie would eventually appear, persuading him to rest that he might do his *cours* justice on the following day.

Yet he never depended upon his own unaided efforts. Before leaving the apartment for the lecture hall he knelt and prayed to the Holy Spirit for light and strength. Then he bade farewell to Amélie and started for the Sorbonne. He walked through the Luxembourg Gardens with head bent, blind to the surrounding beauty, his mind absorbed still in the lecture he was soon to give.

By the time he began to serve his second term he was loved by his students as was no other professor at the Sorbonne. He was as fully idolized by students of the Collège Stanislas, at which he was now giving three senior student lectures in literature.

Every walk home from his lectures was something of a triumph. Several students generally accompanied him to his apartment, plying him with questions and listening eagerly to his comments.

Paradoxically, his popularity was in no little degree the result of his severity and exacting standard. He required his students to work and to think, and because they realized that he was devoted to their progress, they respected and loved

167

him for the demanding discipline. So did Monsieur Cousin. One day, as the latter was leaving a hall where he had heard Ozanam lecture, he turned to a companion and said, "The Lyceums and Colleges send us distinguished professors; the Abbé Noirot sends us men—men who make men of their students."

Frederic's ability to inspire his students to extraordinary effort soon made itself felt dramatically at the Collége Stanislas. Where he discovered a willingness to work he was patient and generous of his time—even with a few students at the college rated hopelessly stupid by other professors. One such young man, long a fixture at the bottom of his class, had become discouraged to the point of despair. With Vincentian charity, Professor Ozanam gave him individual instruction. Determined to prove his gratitude, the student swore to accomplish the impossible—and he did. At the end of the year, he captured first prize at the Grand Concourse, a yearly competition among all the first colleges in Paris. Nor was this an isolated instance. Before young Professor Ozanam's advent, no student of the Collége Stanislas had ever won a single Grand Concourse prize. The first year Frederic Ozanam was named professor of rhetoric at the College, his students captured all the rhetoric prizes. During this period, his classes doubled their numbers.

His approach to his students was direct, severe, and uncompromising. When he first stood before his classes at the Collége Stanislas, he introduced his policy in three sentences: "I shall never punish you. I mean to treat you as men; to do my best for you, and to trust to your doing the same. If you do not agree with this, if you behave like unruly boys, I will not waste my time with you."

Except on lecture days, he set aside two hours—from eight to ten o'clock in the morning—during which students were free to consult him; regularly through this period his study was besieged. He who mentally and emotionally had matured so early in life was ever youthful in spirit, and unfailingly sympathetic with the aspirations of hard-working students.

His influence on their spiritual life was for the most part

168

indirect, but none the less potent. Among the evidences of the fruits of his quiet apostolate which now and then gladdened his heart and Amélie's was a note handed him by a student one day on his arrival home from the Sorbonne. It read:

It is impossible that anyone could speak with so much fervor and heart without believing what he affirms. If it be any satisfaction, I will even say happiness, to you to know it, learn that before hearing you I did not believe. What a great number of sermons failed to do for me, you have done in an hour; you made me a Christian! . . . Accept this expression of my joy and gratitude.

In his continuous study and research Ozanam discovered new facts and new approaches to European history; basic knowledge and interpretations capable of contributing to the shaping of historical and philosophical thought. To make his discoveries and conclusions widely known demanded the production of various books. These appeared throughout his career.

The first of the books which resulted from his studies as a Sorbonne professor was *The Germans Before Christianity*. In this, Frederic Ozanam demolished the arguments of German philosophers, historians, and poets who sought to lead the German people in a revival of the old Teutonic pagan mythology. These writers contended that the Germans, had they been uninfluenced by Latin civilization and by Christian education, would have developed a marvelous culture unequaled throughout the world. This movement's champions aimed to divorce German thought and progress from its debt to Christianity and to Roman civilization.[2] To achieve this, they were attempting to tailor history to fit the new and narrow nationalism the French Revolution had introduced and encouraged.

To Frederic their error was painfully clear: they were confusing loyalty to country with loyalty to the abstract political man and the abstract national idea set up by the crude and

2 This movement back to paganism, and away from Christianity and European culture, had its full fruition under Hitler.

fanatical "philosophers" of the French Revolution. Ozanam had never been misled by the new doctrine, any more than he had been by those who demanded loyalty to the monarchical idea. He was not a slave to mummified traditionalism. He knew that feudalism was dead. He realized that his country, through the developments of eight centuries, had become the birthright of the whole people.

As a Catholic Frenchman he knew that everything unifying and constructive in his country's present was rooted in its past—a past in which the most powerful influences were Greek wisdom, Roman order, and Christianity. He saw the grievous wound France had suffered when her revolutionary sons repudiated the great culture that was her inheritance, and the inheritance of Europe. He loved Germany, too, and he desired to do what he could to save the German people from a similar mistake.

Passion, prejudice, and ignorance prevent most men from seeing a current historical situation in perspective; Frederic Ozanam was one of the few in his time who was able to do so. He was no friend of those who taught Frenchmen to scorn the pre-Revolutionary history of their country, and who inspired hatred of Old France and all who honored its great traditions. Yet he was able to see the tragic mistake by which the aristocratic émigrés had helped the Jacobins to take advantage of an accident of history and make the success of the Revolution synonymous in many French minds with patriotism. He hoped, ardently, that the people of France might once again be united in spirit as they had been united in periods before the Revolution. He realized that this renewed unity could come about only through two developments. First, he thought, there must be an understanding by both sides that there was nothing in Catholic dogma inimical to truly representative government. Secondly, republicanism must respect the Frenchman's age-old devotion to the land and to custom. These developments would make the French a unified people whatever their form of government.

While Ozanam held strongly to his own convictions, he was never intolerant toward those who held to opposite beliefs.

He was, in the words of Lacordaire, "just towards error." He practised justice to all men—justice founded on charity. He intensely desired mutual understanding.

This Christian forbearance was about to call down editorial thunderbolts upon his head.

CHAPTER 21

MONSIEUR FOISSET,[1] editor of *Le Correspondant,* was reading a manifesto that Count de Montalembert had written on behalf of his coreligionists, entitled *The Duty of Catholics in the Question of Liberty of Teaching.* He intended publishing it in the next day's edition.

Suddenly he paused, and reached for his pen to mark a paragraph. It was a passage in which the count attacked the University's anti-Christian professors. In acknowledging that a few Christian members of the faculty were trying to offset the great harm their associates were doing to the faith, Montalembert had singled out Frederic Ozanam for special praise.

After a moment's thought, Foisset tucked Montalembert's manuscript under his arm and set out for the Sorbonne and his friend Ozanam. He found the latter counseling a student, and waited with impatience. When the professor finally dismissed the young man, Foisset said: "I have here, Frederic, Montalembert's manifesto. It's magnificent! But it contains a personal allusion to you—an allusion I think you should know about before this appears in *Le Correspondant* tomorrow. Let's see . . . ah, here it is. While assailing the predominant skepticism of the University's faculty, Montalembert mentions that there are a few exceptions among the professors. He sin-

---

1 Foisset was not only an editor, but a distinguished judge and jurist. He and Ozanam were close friends. He was later to publish the notes on Ozanam's commercial law lectures.

171

gles you out by name as one of—and I'm quoting—'the small number of upright men who have what is greater than talent, faith, and who protest by the publicity of their Christianity and the solidity of their knowledge against the scandals of their colleagues in their lectures.'

"Here, read it yourself," he continued, placing the manuscript in Ozanam's hands, "and tell me frankly whether mention of your name might endanger your position. You have but to say the word and I'll drop it out, and no one, other than yourself and Montalembert, will be the wiser."

Frederic scanned the manifesto briefly, and handed it back to Foisset.

"Montalembert's mention of my name does me great honor," he said. "For there's certainly honor as well as the danger you point out in being named as one opposed to an abusive majority. To permit you to cross out my name would be an act of cowardice on my part. By all means, let the reference stand."

He paused a moment, a frown of concern creasing his forehead.

"Yes, by all means let the personal reference to me stand," he repeated. "However, I think you should—perhaps in the commentary you'll undoubtedly make on the manifesto—clear up a possible confusion. There are several aggressive offenders against religion among the faculty of the College of France, but here at the Sorbonne there has been a gradual change for the better. I hope that nothing occurs to befog this clearer atmosphere, although I know how easily the present comparatively friendly climate can be disturbed. Nevertheless, at the moment, there are only two active assailants of Christianity among the unbelieving professors at the Sorbonne. The others are what might be termed quiescent."

He added that there had been no disposition on the part of the Sorbonne's Catholic professors to divide the faculty into two warring groups. They wished, he said, to avoid anything that might become a detriment to education. There should be no reason, as he saw it, why scholarly conversations on basic differences could not be carried on without acrimony,

172

with mutual respect, and with hope for still better understanding.

For some time thereafter, Ozanam's hopes for a continuing atmosphere of forbearance and peace at the Sorbonne seemed to be realized.

A few days later he had reason to ask himself why all editors could not be as reasonable and co-operative as Foisset.

The young professor had been contributing to the *Univers*. But the *Univers* had suddenly changed from a policy of moderation to one of the most aggressive hostility toward all opponents of religion and the Church. It had come into the hands of the highly able and zealous Louis Veuillot, and overnight had become as brilliant, and as violent, as that dashing young lord of language.

Most people—as the youthful but experienced Veuillot well knew—love the lively entertainment of a fight, and they now found inexhaustible excitement in the pages of the *Univers*. Its witty, biting, slashing articles were skyrocketing its circulation.

Wiser, more responsible Catholics became greatly concerned. They realized that in a controversy whose ultimate aim is the winning of souls, Christian charity must prevail. To provide an organ for Christian expression of Christian truth, they had brought about the revival of Monsieur Bailly's old paper, *Le Correspondant*.

Deciding to contribute no longer to the *Univers*, but to confine his articles to *Le Correspondant*, Frederic dropped in at Veuillot's office to tell him so. He accompanied the information by a restrained statement of his desire to be associated with a publication giving more moderate and charitable voice to the Catholic viewpoint, but Veuillot listened to him in mounting anger.

Finally he arose from his chair, and standing over his desk glared down at Ozanam, sitting opposite him.

"*Le Correspondant* is welcome to your articles, and to all articles that deal gently with the enemies of truth," he said, his clenched fist hammering out the words. "You are too courteous for my policy, monsieur—too careful of the feelings of our enemies in those scholarly articles of yours."

"And you, Monsieur Veuillot," suggested Frederic quietly,

173

determined to reason with him, "do you not sometimes ask yourself whether you are not too violent?"

"I know only one method in controversy," replied Veuillot. "It is to attack with all my strength—to knock over and to destroy my opponents."

With his prominent, jutting jaw, firmly compressed mouth, and pugnacious nose Veuillot looked the able and relentless fighter all Paris knew him to be. Since he had taken over the editorship of the *Univers* in this year of 1843, his trenchant pen had developed a still keener point and had inflicted deep wounds on many.

Veuillot was thirty years old—a few months younger than Ozanam—but he was a veteran journalist. The son of a poor cooper, he was largely self-educated and had been a newspaper editor since he was seventeen. Converted several years before to Catholicism, he had thrown himself into the support of the Catholic cause with all his fiery energy.

"Your bolts of thunder and lightning, Monsieur Veuillot, have struck down many—to that all must agree," said Frederic.

"And at the same time," boasted Monsieur Veuillot, "our hard-hitting tactics have won many readers to the *Univers*."

"But have they won many friends to our cause?" asked Frederic. "Your articles are daring and witty, and everyone admires your mastery of language. But in many quarters these same articles have aroused the most inflexible hatred against religion."

"We're at war, Monsieur Ozanam," rasped Veuillot, "and insofar as I'm concerned it's a war without quarter. It's high time these enemies of the Church learn that we too can wield the weapons of ridicule and wit and vituperation as ably as Voltaire or any of his sons. We have been meek too long. So long that our enemies resent our ability and disposition to attack instead of merely to resist."

Frederic arose and faced Veuillot squarely.

"We Christians, monsieur," he said, uttering the words slowly and emphatically, "are under a most serious obligation to practise charity—and that means charity in controversy, as in every other way. Since you have made yourself responsible for the *Univers*," he added with a smile at the play on the

174

word, "you have, by the violence of your articles, offended and embittered many. I repeat, monsieur, I will submit no more articles to the *Univers* while it maintains its present policy of unrestrained invective and abuse. I hope you'll forgive me, monsieur, for speaking frankly. I do so out of a sincere desire to be helpful to you, and to the cause we both support. You realize, I know, that I have for you, personally, nothing but the greatest good will. Now, monsieur, I must bid you farewell."

He bowed and made his way to the door, Monsieur Veuillot following. "You will, then, contribute to *Le Correspondant?*" he asked.

"If its editors continue to favor me with requests for articles," answered Frederic.

"Ah, *Le Correspondant!*" Contempt tinged Veuillot's voice. "A warmed-over corpse, monsieur. It failed before, and I predict, my dear Ozanam, that it will fail again."

"Perhaps," returned Frederic. "There have been many redeeming failures in the Christian cause—that is, in the cause of charity. But to go down with such a crew as Montalembert, Falloux, Champagny, Audley and other such worthy contributors would be to fail nobly."

He again bowed, and left Veuillot staring after him, silently vowing to obtain for his paper some of the Catholic writers Ozanam had mentioned. In the meantime, he could, he promised himself, get along very well with the other young and headlong spirits who had joined him, and who were helping him make each succeeding number of the *Univers* as caustic as it was clever.

Many Catholics, including by far the greater part of the clergy, began to fear that the combative articles in the *Univers* might do the Catholic cause irreparable harm. Among these was Monseigneur Affre, who had succeeded Monseigneur Quelen as Archbishop of Paris. It seemed to that prelate highly desirable, and high time, that a respected voice be raised to counsel judicious moderation and Christian charity in the great debate between Catholics and unbelievers.

The man selected for this delicate task was Frederic Ozanam. The occasion was the regular meeting of the *Cercle Catholique*. This was an association of Catholic students recently founded under the patronage of the Archbishop, of Père Lacordaire—who had returned from Italy—and of such distinguished laymen as Montalembert and Ozanam.

On the evening of Ozanam's address, Archbishop Affre was in the audience. So, too, was Veuillot, surrounded by his supporters.

Ozanam led up to his main theme through a discussion of the relationship of science and art to faith, and went on to discuss the guidance of Christian principles in advocating the Christian viewpoint. He stressed the possibility that one could, by intemperately defending God's rights, offend God; that "the violent instincts of human nature," unless restrained by Christian charity, might "break loose."

As an example of how far astray violence in controversy can lead a Christian, he cited Tertullian, who "pursued with equal animosity the false gods, and the weak Christians who sacrificed to them"; who "could not forgive the Church for pardoning them, and ended by apostatizing out of hatred of apostasy."

"Assuredly," he continued, "when Christians embark on the painful service of controversy, it is with the firm will to serve God by gaining for Him the hearts of men.

"We must not, therefore, compromise the holiness of the cause by the violence of the means.

"Pascal understood this, and says somewhere: 'the way of God, who does all things gently, is to put religion into the mind by reason, and into the heart by grace.'

"Begin by pitying the unbeliever; he is already wretched enough.

"We must never," he concluded, "begin by despairing of those who deny. It is not a question of mortifying them, but of convincing them. Refutation, when it is conclusive, is humiliation enough.

"Whatever be the disloyalty or the brutality of their attacks, let us show them the example of a generous controversy. Let us beware of exasperating their pride by abuse, and let us not drive them to damn themselves rather than retract."

As he came to a close, the audience, with the notable exception of Veuillot and three or four friends who sat with him, arose as one man, applauding wholeheartedly. Among the most enthusiastic were many clergymen, for most leading Parisian Catholics strongly disapproved of Veuillot's passion and violence.

Archbishop Affre then spoke, and in a few significant sentences sustained and fortified Frederic's position.

Ozanam had spoken in general terms. He had carefully refrained from singling out any current controversialist or organ of controversy. But Veuillot chose to take his counsels of Christian charity as directed personally at himself and the *Univers*. The next day there appeared in the *Univers* under the heading, "Moderation and Zeal," an attack by Veuillot on the speech and speaker—an attack in which Veuillot used all his weapons of vituperation and ridicule.

He concluded his article by stigmatizing Ozanam as a "deserter."

Veuillot, who was as sincere and honest as he was violent and hasty, soon regretted his attack and apologized to Ozanam. The latter's reputation suffered little from the wild charges, which the judicious regarded as preposterous. They realized that Ozanam was daily jeopardizing his position at the Sorbonne by his vigorous defense of the Church and Christianity. In this he was aided by Professors Lenormant, Coeur, and a few others, but their opponents among the unbelieving professors were many and able. They included Michelet, Quinet, Béranger and Thiers—brilliant men whose eminence as scholars gave to their arguments an air of authority. Their power and skill were revealed by the devastating attack they led against the Jesuits, those steadfast champions of Catholic unity and Catholic education.

It was plain to informed observers that the opponents of the Church were focusing their guns on the sons of Loyola, who soon found themselves victims of various calumnies. Some accused them of working for the Bourbons—a charge calculated to arouse the enmity of the government. Others spread the charge that the Jesuits were committed, body and soul, to the support of the House of Orléans. This was intended to bring the republicans and those loyal to the House of Bourbon into the lists against them. Michelet even mistranslated phrases of the Jesuit Constitutions, causing it to appear that the order requires obedience of its members even to the commission of sin—a charge which had been conclusively refuted twenty years before.[2] So great was the power of the anti-Jesuit forces, and so widespread their attacks, that the most able confutations failed to defeat their efforts. The government of Louis Philippe asked Gregory XVI to secularize the French branch of the order. The Pope refused, but the French Jesuits, to spare the Holy See conflict with the government, temporarily and partially disbanded, and for a few years ceased to exist as a corporate body.

Taking an unmistakable stand in this bitter strife, Ozanam included in his course three new lectures. In the first, he defended the papacy; in the second, the monastic orders; in the third, monastic obedience. The relation of these lectures to the attacks on the Jesuits was indirect but obvious and added further risk to his position.

He had more than half expected his lectures to be interrupted by stamping and hissing—the students' favorite methods of demonstrating disagreement. By such tactics they had been disrupting the course of Professor Lenormant, who had deserted the skeptics and was voicing sympathy with the Christian position. In view of this opposition, Ozanam considered it more than ever desirable to emphasize his alignment with Lenormant's, and the general Catholic position. He therefore continued his course with a series of lectures on the literary history of Christian Italy. In these he took every opportunity— as he reported to friends in Lyons—"of pointing out . . . the benefits and the great works of the Church." He was surprised when the numerous unbelievers in his audiences failed to demonstrate against him. There was, in truth, a half-formed,

---

2 Michelet mistranslated the words of the Jesuit Constitutions, Pt. VI, c.5, *obligationem ad peccatum*, as if the text were *obligatio ad peccandum*. The obvious meaning and purpose of the text is that *transgression of the rule is not in itself sinful*. Thus Michelet gave the phrase a vicious interpretation sure to arouse the detestation of all who believed the erroneous version. This false charge is still revived from time to time, and will doubtless continue to be made against the Jesuits. It is a notable example of the power of prejudice to cause men to vilify the objects of their emotional antipathy.

somewhat awkward and embarrassed attempt at manifesting dissent, but the very brilliance of the lectures tended to dissolve the opposition. Even those to whose ears the truths he spoke were unwelcome were disarmed by the eloquence with which he uttered them.

Whenever Ozanam's lectures touched on history or moral values he habitually spoke from the unchanging Catholic viewpoint, and this finally brought on a feeble attempt at reprisal. As he entered his lecture hall one morning during the Lenormant troubles, he was told that someone had altered the announcement of his course from "Foreign Literature" to "Theology." He smiled, and proceeded to give a lecture on "The Church—Its Institutions, Associations, Popes, Clergy, Saints," to a crowd overflowed into the corridors. His eloquence gripped his auditors; conspirators who had come to scoff and disrupt applauded with the rest; they were, as Dufieux was later to describe the scene, "completely disarmed."

As he was about to leave the chair, he said earnestly, "I have not the honor, gentlemen, to be a theologian. But I have the happiness to believe, and the ambition to place my soul, with all my strength, at the service of truth."

Young men are quick to respond to manliness; his class greeted Professor Ozanam's statement with applause. But his position at the Sorbonne was, in fact, perilous. Some professorial skeptics could not forget that Frederic Ozanam had been the first of the faculty to champion the Christian cause. He was, therefore, a central object of their scrutiny and resentment.

It was largely the unshakable loyalty of Ozanam's students and the high regard in which much of Paris held him that protected him. For his repute extended far beyond the walls of the Sorbonne and membership of the St. Vincent de Paul Society. The Parisian public admired and loved him. His writings and his generous activities on behalf of his fellow citizens contributed toward this general esteem. He lectured regularly to young intellectuals at the *Cercle Catholique,* and to working men gathered in the crypt of St. Sulpice. Manual workers counted him as one of themselves, for he habitually described himself to them as a toiler among books as they among bricks and other material things. He believed in the dignity of labor, no matter what the work, provided it was a worthy service to the worker's fellow men, and working men recognized the utter sincerity of his conviction.

Severe self-discipline enabled him to add a continual round of activities to his university and college lecturing, his historical writings, his newpaper articles, and his domestic obligations. He was a very busy young man of thirty-one, who treasured time as a miser gold, and not because of ambition, but because time, in his mind, belonged to his Creator. He lived by a schedule, and trivialities could seldom distract him from it. Yet he always seemed to have time, and ample time, for everyone who approached him with a problem, and he was generally good-humored, even humorous. He was quick to see the ludicrous, the comical, the absurd in human life, and his wit was swift, but invariably charitable. His temper was strong, however, and he frequently reproached himself for failure to control it fully.

In his multiple activities, it was the love he found at his domestic fireside that sustained him. With Amélie he relaxed completely, finding in her the tender affection his nature craved, and in his home the spiritual and physical strength for his next day's work in the world.

Of all his "extracurricular" works, his weekly St. Vincent de Paul visits to the poor were closest to his heart. He regarded the indigent as poor only in a material sense, and was always humble in their presence. He realized that they were able to repay many times over with the alms of their prayers any material help they might receive. And he was never backward in asking them for such spiritual donations.

He considered every visit to an impoverished home a sermon preached to himself, and the strongest kind of sermon, but he never preached in return. He was, of course, always ready to offer a friendly shake of the hand and any words of consolation or advice, spiritual or material, that seemed to be invited.

"Assistance to the unfortunate," he wrote, "honors when it treats the poor man with respect, not only as an equal, but as

180

a superior—since he is suffering what perhaps we are incapable of suffering; since he is a messenger of God to us, sent to prove our justice and charity, and to save us by our works."

This he believed with all his heart, and his belief was manifest in his words and attitude.

His manner toward a family living in a cellar or a garret was invariably the same as toward the host and hostess of the most brilliant salon in Paris; with one as with the other, his courtesy never varied in degree. He greeted every tenement family with the words, "I am your servant"—and they knew his words came from his heart. He visited with them as a neighbor, because he thought of them as neighbors, and he always conversed with them on the topics important to them—their health, their livelihood, the training and the future of their children. Believing that the soul is destined to eternal life, he tried to bring all who came within his influence closer to the Creator, and he exercised this apostolate, as a matter of course, among the impoverished as well as among the well-to-do and the intellectual. He looked upon the poor with the spiritual insight of a St. Francis of Assisi, or a St. Vincent de Paul, and he urged his fellow Vincentians to treat poverty as a priesthood—"a ministry of expiation, a sacrifice whose merits redound to us"—that is, primarily, to those who sacrifice to relieve it.

"And let no one say," he cautioned, "that in treating poverty as a priesthood we aim at perpetuating it. The Authority that tells us we shall always have the poor amongst us is the same that commands us to do all that we can that poverty may cease to be."

Every Christian, he felt, was obligated to do his share to provide for his less fortunate brothers, and no matter how small Ozanam's income was, he habitually set aside a generous amount for almsgiving.

His chief contribution to the poor, as to all his fellow men was, of course, the sacrificial daily service of his mind and heart, and he deliberately spent himself.

A life lived within the narrow and spiritually enervating limitations of comfortable complacency appalled him, and in a talk to the young men of the *Cercle Catholique* he said:

"Every day our friends, our brothers, are killed as soldiers or missionaries on the soil of Africa, or in China before the palaces of the mandarins. What are we doing meanwhile? Seriously, do you imagine that God has appointed some to die in the service of civilization and the Church, while others walk about with their hands in their pockets, or lie down on rose petals?

"O gentlemen! you, toilers of science, and you, Christian men of letters, let us one and all prove that we are not so cowardly as to believe in such a division. For it would be an accusation against God had He made that division, and an ignominy on us should we accept it. Let us be ready to prove that we too have our battlefields, and that if need be we can die on them."

CHAPTER 22

"HOW FORTUNATE for me that you grew up in a university rector's home," Frederic frequently commented, when Amélie, listening to his recounting of the day's work, spoke knowledgeably about his problems.

Since she was highly intelligent and broadly educated, her intuitive judgments were immeasurably helpful to him in his teaching and writing and human relationships. But perhaps her most important contribution to his morale was her rare ability to listen attentively to his recital of his daily experiences and to his viewpoints and plans. Her scholarly background and keen interest in his work made her, also, the ideal literary secretary.

Life in the Ozanam home was serious but seldom solemn. Frederic and Amélie were both blessed with a sense of humor that saved many a situation when his naturally brisk temper rose against his cultivated patience. He laughed easily, and he could laugh at himself, for he was a humble man, and he was forever dashing off squibs of humorous verse. He worked extremely hard, but when his thoughtful wife proposed a picnic or a visit to one of the city's parks, or played a gay song and coaxed him to the piano to sing it with her, he yielded thankfully.

Frederic's brother Charles had finished his courses in Lyons, and Guigui at last had come to live with them and add to their domestic comfort. Dressed always in the peasant costume of her native village, she presided over the kitchen and directed the little maid who was the household's second servant.

Despite her age, Guigui was their highly capable cook. She did her own marketing as a matter of course, and with somewhat terrifying efficiency. When the meat and produce merchants saw her bearing down upon their stalls they knew they were in for a losing battle. Guigui bought the household food with a shrewd economy equaled only by her expert preparation of it.

On all important family problems, she was called into consultation, for she possessed in uncommon degree that uncommon asset, common sense. Nor was she altogether backward in offering her opinion unasked, particularly when Frederic transgressed the family traditions.

"Your grandfather," she would say, hands on hips and firmed lips sharpening the words, "would never have done that." Or, "Your grandmother, who was brought up before the Revolution ruined our good French customs, would have done thus and so."

When she rested, she was still spiritually active; her rosary was her silent companion, and her prayers for all she loved unceasing.

Momentous news excited the usually tranquil Ozanam household one July day in 1844. The great Charles-Claude Fauriel, who had selected Frederic to fill his chair when sickness incapacitated him, had died. For the Ozanams, his death created a critical situation.

During four years as a supply professor, Frederic's success had surpassed all his hopes. To his Sorbonne teaching he had sacrificed everything, he wrote Foisset, even in some degree his health. Yet he had held no tenure and now looked with troubled gaze toward the various university authorities who might, or might not, name him permanently to Fauriel's chair.

His concern was in large degree induced by a desire to make Amélie's financial position easier and more secure. A professorship at the Sorbonne, with life tenure, would provide an ample income as long he lived. It would give his wife, also, an honored position—one, as he described it, "worthy of her." Life tenure would give him still greater prestige with students; it would thus further his teaching apostolate.

At this critical time he wrote to Foisset, who was now serving as a judge, and whose official duties had taken him from Paris, ". . . It is hard to suppose that they would coolly dismiss me. . . . The majority of the faculty members are disposed to present me first on the list to the Minister. This would at once settle my nomination. . . . A small minority, however, opposes these kind intentions, objecting to my youth—thirty-one—my want of scientific titles, and my recent entrance into the University. They suggest that they should leave me time to win my spurs by prolonging the vacancy, and just allow me to hold the professorship next year as *chargé de cours;* that is to say, on a precarious title."

Through all the summer the uncertainty continued—then through October and most of November. Late that month he received the unanimous support of the Faculty and of the Academic Council. On Friday, November 22, the Royal Council gave its unanimous assent to his appointment.

The nomination was now before the Minister of Education, Abel François Villemain. The Minister was evidently hostile, as he had been toward all Christian influences at the Sorbonne.

Villemain ordered the paper containing the nominations

posted with the space after Ozanam's name—where the Minister of Education's signature of approval should have appeared—left blank; he declared he must have more time for reflection. It was only after Ozanam's friends had made the strongest representations and vehement demands for action, that the stubborn Minister finally yielded—at 2 A.M. on Saturday, November 23.

At breakfast next morning Ozanam received a message that he must appear before noon to take the oath of office before the Dean of the Faculty. The newspapers carried the information of his elevation that day. Hundreds of his Vincentian brothers throughout France rejoiced at the news, as did tens of thousands of Frenchmen who through his books and newspaper articles had come to know and to admire their author.

He sent off a letter about his appointment to Foisset.

"What crowns my satisfaction," he wrote, "is the way our numerous friends have shared it. One would think it was a personal success for them all. And so it is, for Amélie and I have no manner of doubt that their prayers helped, and we count on their prayers now to enable us to prove worthy of that success."

He was now thirty-two years old—the youngest full professor by five years ever admitted to teach at the University.

Amélie and Frederic shared an unspoken regret—a longing that passing time made keener: the blessing of children had thus far been denied them. As months became years, they began to wonder whether their marriage was fated to be childless. This fear was dispelled shortly before Christmas, 1844.

One evening as Frederic was writing at his desk near the hearth fire, and Amélie was sitting near him, busy with some needlework, she interrupted him with a series of questions that at first puzzled him, then made his heart sing with joy.

"Do you remember," she asked, "my old family cradle that we brought from Lyons?"

"Yes I certainly do."

"Do you know whether it's still in our storage room?"

"Undoubtedly. There was no order to get rid of it that I

know of," replied Frederic, thinking she probably wanted to lend it to one of the several families they were constantly assisting in one way or another.

"Well, Frederic—don't you think it's time we fixed it up a bit?"

"Fixed it up a bit—?"

"Yes, Frederic, I'm now sure I'll be needing it by August."

With a shout, and a leap that scattered his papers wildly about the room, he was at her side, enfolding her in his arms.

When his elated surprise had been succeeded by a deep happiness over the coming gift of a child—a happiness that was never to leave him—he said, "God has answered our prayers. Let us kneel and thank Him."

The months slipped by with the parents-to-be offering many petitions to the greatest of all mothers for a safe delivery, and in midsummer Amélie gave birth to a girl child. They named her Marie, after the Mother of God and Frederic's mother. Amélie's health was sound and she was able to nurse the infant.

In his great joy Frederic wrote to Foisset about his firstborn, his observations proclaiming the unconscious apostolate of children, which, in God's providence, is to make parents richer and stronger spiritually.

"We will begin her education early," Marie's father tells Foisset, "and, at the same time, she will begin ours; for I perceive that Heaven has sent her to us to teach us a great deal, and to make us better.

"I cannot look upon that face, so full of innocence and purity, without seeing there, less obliterated than in us, the sacred impression of the Creator.

"I cannot think of this imperishable soul of which I shall have to render an account, without feeling myself penetrated by my duties. How could I dare teach her lessons that I did not practise? Could God have found a kinder way of instructing me, of correcting me, of setting my feet on the road to heaven?"

He depended greatly on the prayers of his friends. Characteristically, he asks Foisset's family to pray for him, for Amélie, and for their child.

Like all the schoolmen, shopkeepers, and everyone else in Paris, Frederic longed to escape from the city to the cool, green country during the summer heat. But in this summer of 1845, the birth of Marie and his professorial duties kept the family in Paris.

Day after day he and two Sorbonne colleagues sat at a green-covered table from ten o'clock in the morning till seven in the evening, examining candidates for their bachelor's degrees. While his brother professors were taking their turns at questioning the candidates, Frederic dashed off letters to his friends. In some of these he commented on the work and the growth of the St. Vincent de Paul Society, which was always in his heart and mind. The Society was now in its twelfth year.

"The number of Conferences," he writes to his old friend Lallier toward the end of August, "has been increased by five new ones during this last month.

"We have six, now, in London.

"Do you remember how cross we were with you in 1833, when you brought us De la Noue, who increased our number to nine?" he adds, referring to the attitude of the majority of the Society's founding members, which he himself had taken the lead in changing. "Now we are nearly nine thousand.

"So you see Catholics are not dead yet. Now, as in the days of St. Paul, we are 'as if dying—and behold, we live.'"

Arriving home one evening early in September, he brought good news.

"We are finished—the last unhappy candidate has been examined," he said to Amélie. "Tomorrow we leave for Nogent."

Frederic had selected Nogent for a summer holiday because of its proximity to Paris. Amélie had not yet fully recovered her strength after childbirth, and he did not care to subject her and the baby to a longer journey. Yet their Nogent cottage, which was southeast of the city on the River Marne, seemed as remote from metropolitan activity as if it were a hundred kilometers from the capital.

He himself needed the country and quiet rest as urgently

as did Amélie. He was thin and drawn and enormously fatigued, and Amélie worried about his health.

Their Nogent cottage stood on a little hill commanding a rewarding view of the Marne. In its garden, shaded by trees and luxuriant with roses, verbenas, and many other flowers, they spent peaceful hours, their spirits soothed by the drowsy hum of bees. Here, resting, they recovered strength, and the baby, its proud father reported, opened out "like a little flower."

"This is one of those moments of bliss," he writes, "which are not often granted to us in life, and which make us feel more keenly the goodness of Providence."

He was at leisure, but leisure for Ozanam meant opportunity to devote himself to writing. In his garden at Nogent, he spent most of his days completing his *History of Christian Civilization Among the Germans*. It was still another book in which he sought to correct many erroneous concepts of medieval history then prevailing.

Despite almost continuous work, Frederic recovered his strength. At least, he recovered it in such degree that Amélie was reassured and, for the time being, became free of those worries about his health which had troubled her occasionally since their marriage.

CHAPTER 23

BY OCTOBER, 1845, when the Ozanams returned to Paris from Nogent, Frederic was again feeling fit, and he resumed all his former activities. More than ever his lectures were masterpieces of the teacher's art—pithy, terse, lucid, forceful and fluent. In greater numbers than ever

188

students crowded into his lecture hall. As the months wore on, however, his chief study was not the history of literature, but the unfolding personality of his infant daughter.

The learned professor had never lost his childhood sense of wonder at the mysteries and the beauty of the world about him, and for him the crowning wonder was the child God had given him and Amélie. She was his daily meditation, and his joy in her was boundless. Life held for him no sight so sweet as that of his wife tenderly caring for the infant in whom their mutual love was joined and sealed.

"She's as beautiful as apple blossoms," he would say, look-ing down upon the pink and white baby sleeping in her cradle, or playing seriously with her fingers and toes, or lustily banging a rattle against the cradle's sides.

They had purchased a baby carriage with a collapsible leather top. Pushing his infant along in this conveyance, Frederic delighted to stroll, Amélie's arm crooked in his, through the Luxembourg Gardens. On a fine day the park was always filled with children playing, their mothers and nurses following them about. Amélie, like most of the ladies strolling in the Gardens, wore a small poke bonnet, a tight bodice, slim and pointed, and a full skirt. Her husband, like most professors, wore a mustache and full beard, a cylindrical "stovepipe" hat—the style of top hat he preferred being out of fashion and production—a white pleated shirt topped by a wide stock and a frock coat.

They were greeted often by friends—a fellow professor, walking with his family, or a fellow Vincentian, or perhaps a member of the nearby Chamber of Peers in blue uniform with gold-lace-covered cuffs, some ancient order's decora-tion starring his left breast. If Frederic was ever proud, it was when friends thus met would stop to admire Marie, and Amélie would lift her from the carriage to show how she had grown, and Marie would stretch out her little arms to him, in her own baby language demanding that he, too, hold her.

Frederic's happiness found frequent expression in graceful verse in which he sang to Amélie of his love for her, and of his delight in their child. And if at times his metric lines to Marie were oversentimental, he is perhaps to be forgiven, for he wrote, after all, as an almost over-fond father to his only child. Beside this new light in the Ozanams' lives, the brilliant salons to which they were invited proved pale and artificial. Nevertheless they did attend, for it behooved a literary man to be seen at these gatherings of the great and the near-great. And here, too, one could enjoy the stimulating talk of fellow intellectuals—Frederic, as was his wont, seldom speaking unless asked a question, and then giving forth with a wholesome forthrightness and command of language that charmed the circle about him. Here also one heard news of the world, of plans and plots, and events in the making.

It was at a soirée early in 1845 that Frederic first heard rumors of a movement to unseat a fellow Sorbonne professor by classroom disorders calculated to make his chair untenable. He was deeply concerned. First, he was appalled by the planned persecution. And secondly, he saw that the reported machinations, amounting to a conspiracy, would disrupt that uneasy peace of the Sorbonne that he had told Foisset a few months earlier he was hopeful would be maintained.

The target of the intrigue was Monsieur Charles Lenormant. Professor Lenormant had long been a confirmed skeptic and a highly favored associate of those unfriendly to the Church. A comrade of Guizot, he had taken the latter's chair of history at the Sorbonne when Guizot entered Louis Philippe's cabinet.

A celebrated archaeologist, Lenormant was handsome, gifted, and married to the niece and adopted daughter of the influential Madame Récamier. In 1839 he had been elected a member of the French Academy. When Guizot became Minister of Foreign Affairs in 1841, he had sent Lenormant on a diplomatic mission to Greece, and there Lenormant used the priceless opportunity to continue his archaeological studies. On returning he had resumed his lectures on history at the Sorbonne.

In developing his lectures Lenormant made exhaustive studies of Christian sources. These explorations, continued over a three-year period, had been opening his mind, little by little, to Christian truth.

190

At first he was totally unaware that he was on the path toward Christianity. Almost unconsciously, at first, he kept his students conversant with his step-by-step progress. Humbly and lucidly, he unfolded to them the facts that these new studies made clear to his searching mind.

As his trend toward Catholicism became unmistakably obvious, the movement forming against him broke out into open warfare. His lecture hall became a scene of repeated student disturbances, which seemed to be planned and directed. Toward the end of 1845 hissing and stamping increasingly interrupted his discourses.

His former associates, the skeptical professors, had watched Lenormant's progress toward Christianity with growing uneasiness and no little anger. If he didn't know where he was heading, they knew, and they feared he would be taking many students with him. Lenormant was not only repudiating all they stood for; he was unconsciously doing so in such a way as to affect the thinking of all who sat under him. Michelet and Quinet were particularly aroused. Among the students there was much discussion as to what further measures the faculty's unbelieving majority might take, for it was thought that by their attitude, at least, some of the professors had encouraged the disturbances.

Ozanam visited Lenormant and pledged his support.

"Why risk your own position, which now seems comparatively secure?" Lenormant objected. "Why needlessly identify yourself with one who has deserted the ranks of those he previously supported? I have become a reproach and a loathing to my old comrades. But you, my dear Ozanam, have incurred no such stigma. So why risk becoming a victim of the same punishment my former associates in skepticism seem determined to visit on me?"

"And let you bear the brunt of their attacks alone?" said Frederic. "No Lenormant, never! If I can't do much to help repulse the assaults, I can at least stand with you against them. I intend to identify my position with yours as publicly and as positively as possible. As long as the disturbances continue I'll try to be present at your lectures."

"I hear that my former friends have been referring to me

as 'the convert of the Sorbonne,'" observed Lenormant. "They are incensed against me, and some influence is inflaming the students. Yet I have, as you know, scrupulously refrained from directly, or even indirectly, refuting the abusive attacks that so many, especially at the College of France, have made upon me."

Frederic, agreeing, shook his head sadly.

"These noisy upheavals," he said, "are certainly calculated. Monsieur Bailly informs me that student meetings directed against you are being called in the offices of the revolutionary newspapers. So you see, you have become a target of national as well as university politics. Your enemies are determined, it seems, to make your chair untenable. I'm sure that you'll experience increasingly violent classroom demonstrations. And I fear the government will sacrifice you, for it is unprincipled and opportunistic and therefore spineless. When do you resume your lectures?"

"January eighth," replied Lenormant.

"Good! That will give me time to alert our Christian students to be present. They can at least take up some of the room that would otherwise be occupied by those who want to prevent your lecturing."

As the audience gathered in the lecture hall on January 8, 1846, for Lenormant's appearance, Frederic Ozanam was sitting in the front row.

A flurry of catcalls greeted Lenormant's entrance. He began to speak, but his voice was lost in continuous hissing and stamping, which the applause from the Christian students could not drown.

Ozanam arose, advanced to the lecture platform, and stood beside Lenormant. An outburst of applause acclaimed his action; it came from Christian students and from others who resented the brutal unfairness of their school fellows.

For a moment Frederic gazed earnestly into the faces of those who, now silent, had a few seconds before been hissing and meowing.

"So these," he said, "are the friends of freedom of expression."

He paused while his words sank in.

192

"So these," he continued, "are the followers of Voltaire, who so eloquently proclaimed the right of his opponents to disagree with him."

Another pause.

"No one is so unfair as he who would silence those whose opinions he opposes.

"No one is more tyrannous and cowardly than he who prevents freedom of speech.

"No one is so dedicated to ignorance as he who permits passion and prejudice to shut the doors of his mind against another's opinion and viewpoint.

"If you believe in freedom of the intellect, you will hear Professor Lenormant without further disturbance."

Delivered by a professor celebrated for his patience and forbearance, these words were effective. The audience remained respectfully quiet during the lecture.

But the disturbances had already served the purpose of their instigators. The government, always worse than weak when called upon to protect religious freedom at the University, had given willing ear to claims that the rows at Professor Lenormant's lectures would be repeated.

The day following the lecture, it closed his course.[1]

Busy days pass swiftly, and the 1845–46 university term was moving rapidly toward June, when Frederic noticed that he was tiring more quickly than usual. His enervation increased, and soon only his strong will enabled him to drive himself to performance of his professorial duties. He was forced to curtail most of his other activities. He looked forward impatiently to the long vacation and a thorough rest.

With the coming of the baccalaureate examinations in the sultry heat of August, his work became an almost unendurable burden. Craving the green and open countryside, he wrote to a friend of his yearning for "the woods and fields, the

[1] Lenormant resigned from the Sorbonne faculty, and took over the editorship of *Le Correspondant*. This he held for the next nine years. He also served as director of the Commission of Historical Documents. In 1849 the Academy appointed him to the chair of archaeology in the College of France. His writings bore constant witness to his deep Catholic faith, and greatly influenced public thinking in the much discussed question of academic freedom.

balmy air, the very odors of the farmyard. All these are conducive to health."

Like most Frenchmen he had a peasant's love for the land, but his eagerness for the country at this time was induced chiefly by a physical decline. A continuous low-grade fever was dissipating his strength.

Toward the end of the examinations, the fever suddenly flared up. Utterly exhausted, Ozanam had to be helped from the table of the examining professors. One of them called a carriage and rode home with him.

For several days he was confined to his bed. He had spent himself too generously; he was, the doctors said, a victim of overwork.

His physicians prescribed the country, and absolute rest. Amélie quickly selected a retreat close to Paris, a cottage in the woods near Meudon, to the southwest of the city. Though only six miles from their home, it was surrounded with the green and growing beauty and unbroken tranquility of a wilderness.

For nearly a month Frederic lay inert, ministered to by Amélie and Guigui. He ate well and slept long and soundly, but his physical exhaustion continued, and the physicians finally decided that only a year's rest could give hope of recovery. So informed, the new Minister of Education, Monsieur Narcisse-Achille de Salvandy, promptly ordered Professor Ozanam on a literary mission to Italy, the Mecca of health-seekers. He was commissioned to gather *Notes on Unpublished Documents to Serve for the Literary History of Italy from the Eighth to the Thirteenth Century.* So Frederic was to entitle the work he eventually produced.

The Minister's intentions were excellent. He expected that Frederic would make a leisurely tour of a few Italian libraries, doing only as much research as an invalid's need of rest permitted.

They left Paris—Frederic, Amélie, and Marie—in November, and relaxed pleasurably in southern France. He was enjoying complete rest, and he gained strength. When, however, their slow-paced travel brought the little family as far as Genoa, he began to busy himself with the work of his mission. The scholar forgot the invalid; he worked enthusiastically, and he worked hard. In the libraries and museums of Genoa and Florence and the cities between he spent the morning hours copying ancient Latin and Italian manuscripts and making notes; in the afternoons he classified and arranged.

He overworked, and his health broke again. On his arrival in Rome early in 1847 he was too lacking in energy to work at all.

The Ozanams found the Eternal City in festival mood. Republican enthusiasm for Pope Pius IX, elected only seven months before, was at its height.

Frederic's health seemed to reflect the universal optimism; resting again, he soon regained sufficient strength to get about Rome and to observe the dramatic events of which it was the center.

He was a republican in a day when most upper and middle class people considered representative government a sure road to rule by the rabble. Now he beheld the people of Rome, under the direction of the Supreme Pontiff, marching toward self-government "through streets garlanded with flowers, resounding with choirs of music and hymns."

Thus eloquently did Ozanam write to his friends in Paris, not suspecting that the Pope's courageous approach to republican rule—taken in the face of adamant opposition from the Roman nobility, and from most European governments—was foredoomed to fail. The French professor could not know then that the demands of the radical adventurers whose past treasons the Holy Father had pardoned were merely pretexts for rebellion and abolishment of the temporal power. He could not foresee that they would not be satisfied with the establishment of constitutional government; that they would stab to death the Pope's prime minister; and that, when the Father of Christendom refused to belie that title by declaring war on Austria, they would drive him from the Quirinal and institute a reign of terror in the Eternal City.

In this springtime of 1847 the success of the pontiff's

experiment was to Frederic all but certain, and he ardently desired the effort toward democracy to succeed. He felt that its attainment would cement an alliance between republicanism and Christianity in every European nation, and he was sure that republicanism was the government of the future. He was even more certain that only Christianity could inspire and nourish in a people the virtues necessary to self-government in the complicated modern state.

Buoyed by this vision of the future, he joined wholeheartedly in the fiestas and fetes at which the Roman populace showed its affection for Pius IX. He was among twenty thousand who assisted at the Papal Mass in St. Peter's on Easter Sunday. Later during his Roman visit, he and his family were received by the Holy Father in private audience. The saintly pontiff conversed at length with them, Frederic relates, about "France, the youth of our schools, the duties of professorship, with a nobility, an emotion and a charm which are indescribable."

Marie quite won the Holy Father's heart. Seeing her parents kneel for the Pope's blessing, "she knelt down, too," her father recounts, "and clasped her small hands with an air of veneration. The Holy Father was so delighted that three or four days afterward he condescended to allude to this little scene in speaking about us to a French priest."

Frederic's research into the literary history of Italy required travel to Monte Cassino. The round-trip journey by carriage to Naples and the famed Abbey necessitated two wearying nights and days on the road. He remained at the Abbey only a day and a half, making extracts from precious manuscripts which the learned sons of St. Benedict showed him. Their hospitality was warm, but the monastery, like the weather, was cold. Their visitor reported: "These good monks, who know so many things, don't know how to warm themselves. I nearly died of cold among their fine archives."

This exhausting journey resulted in a return of the fever, but the alarming symptom lasted only a day after he returned to Rome. He considered himself doubly fortunate to escape more serious sickness, for the second day after

196

his return he was scheduled for a second audience with Pius IX.

His audience did not begin until nine o'clock in the evening; the Pope had been in conference for hours and showed signs of fatigue. Nevertheless he received Frederic with unhurried cordiality, inquired about his health and that of Madame Ozanam and Marie, and visited with leisurely friendliness and familiarity.

The pontiff had aided Frederic in his researches by a word here and there that opened the proper doors, and Frederic, thanking him, presented him with a copy of his *History of Christian Civilization Among the Germans.* He also delivered to the Holy Father letters from the Society of St. Vincent de Paul.

He referred to these letters in recounting for the Pope the dramatically rapid growth and spread of the Society both in the old world and in the new. The Holy Father listened with paternal satisfaction to the story of how the Society had become established in England and in Ireland in 1844; in Germany, in Scotland, and in the United States in 1845; in Canada and in Mexico in 1846. It was now rooted in cities and towns throughout France; the membership there was numbered in thousands. During this very journey, Frederic informed the pontiff, he had been acquainting "zealous and influential men" in Italian cities with the objectives and the operation of the Society.

Just before the Ozanams left Rome, on April 21, Frederic and Amélie were among eight hundred guests at a banquet celebrating the twenty-six hundredth year of the foundation of the Eternal City. The following morning the Pope took the first concrete measures toward actualizing representative government in the Papal States. That evening his action was acclaimed by the entire populace. Pouring into the streets and squares, Roman citizens swelled a mammoth torchlight parade in celebration of the pontiff's progressive step. The Holy Father gave his benediction to the huge assemblage from the Piazza of Monte Cavallo; then the thousands extinguished their torches and dispersed.

Frederic lingered after most of the paraders had departed.

He felt that he was standing at one of the pivotal points of history. Here, he told himself, beneath this starry Roman sky, the papacy had turned away decisively from the false and shackling friendships of the absolutist monarchs; here it had embraced that representative government that Ozanam was sure meant freedom for both the people and the Papacy.

Like nearly all Catholics of his time, Frederic was keenly aware of the powers and influences threatening the Church throughout the Italian peninsula and in many European nations. With them, too, he was to suffer almost continual disappointment as the political fortunes of the Vatican declined. Yet during the long period of these political defeats, the spiritual strength of the Church steadily increased. It was to seem, as the years rolled on, as if He who had promised that He would be with His Church always, had called a term to its dependence upon the material powers of this world, that it might be free to serve with greater zeal the spiritual realm from which it receives its mandate.

As if in anticipation of that new day, an increasing fervor had for some years been evident, animating clergy and laymen. Of this regenerating spirit Frederic Ozanam's cherished Society of St. Vincent de Paul was one of the many results.

Immediately after Holy Week, the Ozanams left Rome to visit Siena, Bologna, Padua, and other Italian cities, in all of which Frederic promoted the establishment of Vincentian Conferences. Both he and Amélie were busy writing as they traveled. She was authoring a French version of the *Little Flowers of St. Francis*—that charming collection of legends about St. Francis and his early disciples. Her rendering of the *Little Flowers* into French preserves the unaffected simplicity and the sweet, fresh delicacy of the original.

Frederic was engaged in writing *The Franciscan Poets*, a scholarly work of great poetic insight and equally poetic expression. In this he established the shaping influence that the Franciscan friar-poets, and notably St. Francis himself, had on the Italian language.

Arriving in Paris in the autumn of 1847, Frederic felt almost like his old self again. Despite his sickness, he could look back upon a year of important accomplishment in author-ship. And he now felt sufficiently strong to look forward to all his former activities. He possessed, after all, a young man's recuperative powers; he was only thirty-four years old. And so with a high heart he entered upon another year at the Sorbonne.

There were no portents to warn him that this calm and peaceful prospect was about to be shattered; that within a few weeks a storm of personal accusations and condemna-tions would break about his head. Nor at this time did any immediate signs indicate that within a few months the bloody struggle of "those who had too little, against those who had too much"—of which he had so long forewarned—would threaten another reign of terror, and that he himself, a musket in his hands, would be serving in the ranks of an army pledged to save a new republic.

CHAPTER 24

"THE TRAITOR!" cried the editor of the *Univers.* "The revolutionist! He wants us to surrender to the godless rabble!"

Louis Veuillot, shouting to his assistant, had risen from his chair. His accusing finger was pointing to *Le Corres-pondant's* full-length report of a talk Frederic Ozanam had given the previous day before the *Cercle Catholique.*

"Read here," he continued. "Ozanam wants us to put our-selves in the hands of those who hate God and the Church—the scum of Paris, who'd cut our throats with delight. He says—'Let us go over to the barbarians!' Meaning, my friend, the savages of St. Antoine, of the Rue Mouffetard. Does this trusting fellow want to bring back the Terror? Does he want

199

to deliver us into the hands of the foes of society and of all morality?"

"He should be denounced!" urged the assistant, seemingly oblivious of the fact that this was exactly what Monsieur Veuillot was doing.

"And denounced he shall be—this very day," answered Veuillot. "This is too much! Go over to the *sans-culottes*, indeed. This Frederic Ozanam will find himself answered in the columns of the *Univers* in language that can't be misunderstood."

Seating himself, he began to write furiously. The next day the *Univers* carried his vitriolic attack. Other papers supported Veuillot in his heated condemnation of Ozanam for his plea that the "barbarians" he conciliated. In the first few days of Feburary, 1848, Frederic found himself the most roundly abused man in Paris.

Ozanam's words had struck the raw nerve of fear in the body politic, for the Parisian middle and upper classes dreaded these "barbarians" with whom he had counseled friendship. They regarded them as implacable enemies. Had they not—in the Revolution, and again in 1830—twice wreaked vengeance upon Paris, and France, for their real or fancied wrongs? Were they not ready to strike again—to plunder, burn, rape and kill on a monstrous scale? Did they not hate the "rich"? And in their eyes was not everyone who wore a coat "rich"?

Ozanam, familiar with the poor in the most miserable sections of the city, was more realistically aware of this hatred than most of his fellow Parisians. But he also knew that the antagonism was exaggerated—not in depth, but in extent. In a large percentage of tenement dwellings he had seen the crucifix upon the wall, and knew that many of the poor were Christian and forgiving. He realized, however, that the other thousands of ignorant, half-starved Frenchmen in the poorer quarters were godless, seething with resentment, and ready to follow any agitators who might spring up to lead them. These, truly were the modern barbarians who, as savage and ruthless as the invaders of the Roman empire, had helped to despoil the imperial domain of the monarchs of France, and were impatient to despoil France again. Now it was high time, he had boldly declared, for the Church, under the leadership of Pius IX, "to go over to the barbarians," even as the Popes had turned to the barbarians of ancient times. The Church, he said, must advocate more insistently than ever social and economic justice for all; must strive to free the poor from the grinding oppression of exploiters, and through the love of Christ manifested in the charity of His followers, must raise them from ignorance and despair, and win them to herself.

In the early days of the St. Vincent de Paul Society, he had seen "the division which exists among men growing deeper and wider every day."

"Here," he had said, "is the camp of the rich; there, the camp of the poor. Only one means of salvation remains to us. It is that Christians, in the name of love, interpose between the two camps . . . teaching them on both sides to look upon each other as brothers."

Twelve years before he had said, "A struggle is preparing between the classes, and it threatens to be terrible. Let us precipitate ourselves between these hostile ranks so as to deaden the shock, if we cannot prevent it."

Unfortunately he and the many Catholic laymen who thought as he did were a minority—too pronounced a minority among the twenty-five million people of France to bring about a peaceful, Christian revolution in the minds and hearts of men. Now, because of his attempts to reconcile the opposing classes, he was under the furious attacks of Veuillot and others. He remained impassive and silent, but his friends ably defended him. His supporters included the Archbishop of Paris and Père Lacordaire.

Finally, on Feburary 22, urged by Lacordaire and others, he himself answered his critics.

"When I say," he wrote in an article published on that date, " 'let us go over to the barbarians,' I mean that we should do as he [Pius IX] has done; that we should occupy ourselves with the people whose wants are too many and whose rights are too few; who are crying out, and fairly, for a share in public affairs, for assurances of employment, and against distress; who follow bad leaders because they have no good leaders . . ."

He was not, of course, advocating weakness toward those who, misled by agitators, might attempt to destroy society. He was, rather, urging remedial measures that would deliver the masses from their miseries and from their false leaders, and assure permanent civil peace.

At is happened, he had made his answer to Veuillot on the eve of a revolution.

The pleas of Ozanam and others for distributive and social justice had made little impression on the ultra-conservative members of the King's Cabinet headed by the former Sorbonne professor, the learned Guizot. The upheavals they had predicted began now to agitate the nation. Dissatisfaction with Louis Philippe had unsettled France for several months, and on February 24, 1848, the revolution broke.

An infantry company, startled by an explosion, fired on a menacing mob. Barricades arose immediately in many parts of Paris, and soon members of the National Guard refused to serve, or went over to the revolutionists. The Citizen King quickly abdicated, a republic was proclaimed, and a provisional government was installed.

In major degree it was a revolution of patriotic, enlightened, temperate and even conservative Frenchmen. It promised reforms long overdue. But the leaders of the revolution had made one tragic mistake. They had admitted two hundred thousand *sans-culottes* into an enlarged National Guard. These potential enemies of orderly revolution were soon disbanded, but they retained their rifles. For this blunder Paris was to pay four months later with blood.

"My knowledge of history," Ozanam declared, "leads me to the conclusion that in the nature of mankind democracy is the final stage in the development of political progress, and that God leads the world in that direction."

He considered the overthrow of Louis Philippe as fundamentally a social revolution, and the establishment of the

Republic as a realization of the democracy to which all nations were destined. He desired with all his heart that it be a Christian republic, and he saw that there was imminent danger it might degenerate into a communistic dictatorship.[1] While Catholic leaders such as the Abbé Gerbet and Père Lacordaire accepted and advocated sound political progress, each according to his individual ideas, Catholic monarchists, including some members of the clergy, were clinging to the ancient order. A vast number of Frenchmen distrusted popular government. Many of them, including the editors of the *Univers,* assailed anyone who dared support advanced political views. The Abbé Maret, founder of the *Univers,* had long since been forced by his progressive political principles to sever all ties with it. The champions of social, economic and political justice enjoyed the approval of the Archbishop of Paris, Monseigneur Affre, and of the Pope himself, but they were without a newspaper to advance their ideas.

Ozanam, with his usual clear-sightedness, saw the need for a new publication, (from various causes *Le Correspondant* had become moribund), and with his usual quickness in meeting a need, he sought out the Abbé Maret. The Abbé possessed friends with progressive ideas and money. The priest assured Frederic that he could round up financial support for a newspaper, and the two then called on the Abbé Lacordaire. The latter's name, as well as articles by him, could contribute immensely to a publication's success.

"To take up a journalistic pen is the last thing I want to do," said the great Dominican. "But if you think I can add strength to your publication, I will write for it—for in doing so I know I will be writing for religion, for order and for liberty."

The newspaper, called *The New Era,* was launched on April 15. The following day, the Archbishop of Paris wrote to the editors, giving his hearty approval to the journal. Ozanam worked mightily, turning out several articles a week

1 Not the pseudo-scientific communism based on revolutionary Marxist socialism but a system of social organization in which all goods were to be expropriated and all wealth shared in common, according to the ideas of such visionaries as Charles Fourier and Etienne Cabet.

while fulfilling his professorial duties with his customary conscientiousness. *The New Era* struck a popular chord, and circulation climbed. Frederic's articles pleaded with the rich and the powerful to help "seek the justice of God and the welfare of the country"; he appealed to parish priests to seek out the poor and preach the gospel to them, and to use all their influence with Christian families to bring relief to the indigent.

He was calling upon Christians, also, to stand for election to the new National Assembly, and when his own friends in Lyons proposed to nominate him for the Assembly from that city, he felt himself forced to accept. He did so reluctantly, for he felt that he was ill-fitted for politics. He could not go to Lyons to campaign, and to his brother the Abbé he wrote about his hope that he should have an honorable number of votes, and that Providence would spare him the perilous glory of being a representative. He received an "honorable" sixteen thousand and some-odd votes, and was defeated.

The struggle he had so long foreseen and warned against, "of those who have nothing against those who have too much," was now impending. He realized the immediate danger, and continued desperately, but with increasing hopelessness, to urge responsible Frenchmen "to bring about as general an equality as possible among men," and "to make charity accomplish what justice and law alone can never do."

Now, in the spring of 1848, he was more certain than ever that the remedy for a sick France was a social and religious remedy. "Do away with misery, Christianize people, and you will make an end of revolutions"—thus he pleaded as he had been pleading, unavailingly, for many years. But now it was too late; his prophecy of an uprising of the underprivileged was about to be fulfilled.

When the National Assembly began to sit in Paris several weeks later, it proved to be conservative rather than radical. The extreme radicals began to agitate among the wild, irresponsible men of the tenement quarters, thousands of whom had their National Guard rifles ready for trouble. The demagogues raised the red flag, demanded abolition of private property, and led a mob onto the floor of the National Assembly. They threatened the lives of its members, and the life of the infant Republic.

All parties other than the fanatical factions rallied around the tricolor. Even the chief Socialist leaders refused to lend themselves to the insurrection.

The insurgents, armed with thousands of National Guard rifles, were confident of success. Under threat of those rifles, every responsible Frenchman felt another reign of terror impending. Only one course was open to those who dreaded the wrecking and ravaging of Paris—they must join in repelling the assault now preparing against the infant Republic.

The rebellion of the downtrodden did not lessen Frederic Ozanam's sympathy for their sufferings. No one understood better than he why so many of these dwellers in the economic dust were moved to rise against the government. He knew the callous indifference of many of the wealthy and the unbroken misery that caused the poor to take counsel of despair. For the previous fifteen years he and his fellow Vincentians had been devoting themselves to relieving that misery, to combating the causes of hopelessness and despondency, and to unifying all men in the brotherhood of Christ. In this work they considered themselves the most humble instruments of parish priests, and minor co-operators with the self-sacrificing members of religious orders working heroically among the people of the slums.

Now, with other citizens, they had no choice but to defend their families and their city against an incensed, loosely organized army of wretched men who were being incited to take over the national government by force.

Determined to save Paris and France from another reign of terror, thousands of Parisians joined the reorganized National Guard, and Frederic was one of them. The mission of these amateur soldiers was to support and relieve the regulars and the Guard Mobile—that highly effective force of youngsters recruited from the streets of Paris by order of Lamartine. Like other National Guardsmen, Frederic supplied his own uniform, down to its yellow gloves and patent leather boots.

His health, still delicate, would have amply justified his being excused from service. But he insisted on serving, for he realized that every man might be needed to repel the threatening danger. Among those enlisting with him were many Vincentians, including his friends Cornudet and Bailly.

One of his first military assignments was guard duty at the entrance to the National Assembly. He was, it seems evident, already suffering from the weakness and fever attendant on tuberculosis, for he found this duty extremely fatiguing. He reports that one day early in May while on guard duty at the Assembly, he "barely missed perishing from weariness and heat."

It was generally felt that the insurrectionists would be defeated, but not without many men on both sides killed, and Frederic and Amélie were too clear-sighted not to face the possibility that he might be among those slain. The thought weighed on their spirits; the knowledge, too, that he might be called upon to take the lives of others added to Frederic's mental burden.

Amélie, in her concern for her husband's safety, had recourse to her "other mother"—the Mother of God—under her ancient title of Our Lady of Mount Carmel. Frederic constantly wore that Lady's badge, the brown scapular, but Amélie decided he must have a new one that she herself would make.

"Wear Our Lady's pledge of protection," she said to Frederic, as she placed over his shoulders the new scapular that was her handiwork. "Marie and I will pray to her to guard you."

Amélie knew he would need guarding, for the insurrection was reported to be gaining in strength. A little later, as the danger to the city increased, Frederic and his fellow Guardsmen were ordered to live in barracks. He prepared to leave his family for he knew not how long a time, and with gravest apprehension for its safety. True, the insurrectionists were being contained behind their barricades, and the section of the city where the Ozanams lived was not at the moment under fire. Yet all knew that the thousands of reckless men behind the barricades were planning to break out and sweep the government forces before them. If they succeeded, the city would be subject to savagery, atrocity, and terror.

Before leaving for the barracks, Frederic donned his uniform and said his farewells. He held Marie close to him for a long time, talking to her a little more maturely than her four years warranted. He could not brush from his mind the thought that he might never see her, nor Amélie, nor Guigui, again. A large number of the National Guard had already been killed in assaults upon the barricades, and he expected that his own company would soon be in the midst of the fighting. He embraced Guigui, who clung to him with the feeble protectiveness of the aged, and Amélie, who clung to him with all the strong, matronly love of her heart, while trying to hide her concern and keep back the tears.

Frederic had tried to persuade Amélie to go to Versailles, where he had arranged quarters for the family. She objected, desiring to remain near him in their apartment on the Rue de Fleurus. She argued that the government forces, according to all reports, were now after a period of weakness gathering strength, and that every day thus lessened the possibility of a successful insurrectionist breakthrough. It was agreed, however, that at serious signs of an impending insurrectionist triumph, the family was to set off at once for Versailles.

In barracks, Frederic heard alarming rumors. These mushroomed daily; there seemed to be a new crop every morning. The young professor calmed his comrades as best he could, but he himself knew that with thousands of armed insurrectionists manning the barricades, defeat of the government troops was always a possibility.

His worry over his family's safety increased. Finally he dashed off a note to Amélie and sent it by a friendly dispatch-bearer.

> Shut up here [he wrote her], I know nothing. But I hear some very alarming reports circulating. Send to the offices of *The New Era* to ask what they know. If the

207

news is not serious and the streets are passable, come to speak with me, or write me.

If, on the contrary, the news is threatening, leave while you can still get carriages, for it may not be possible later to walk.

I give you my word that I will rejoin you at Versailles.

Please give the bearer fifteen francs in a little package that may not be recognizable.

Precautions—but no trepidation. I am all yours.

Frederic

Before handing the note to the dispatch-bearer, he reflected on Amélie's insistence that she remain in Paris, and to assure her he added a postscript:

If absolutely necessary, I can depart for Versailles on foot, but you could not walk as far as Versailles, and I cannot support the idea of knowing that you are all shut up here while they besiege us.

On receiving this message Amélie set off at once for the office of *The New Era*. There she learned that the government military leaders were confident of their ability to repel any attack. Within hours additional National Guard regiments summoned by semaphore telegraph from other cities would begin arriving in Paris. The insurrectionists, she was assured, would be overwhelmed.

On this welcome news, Amélie decided to remain in Paris, and she had no difficulty in making her way to Frederic's station to tell him of her decision. She found his company patrolling a section the center of which was the corner of the Rue Garancière and the Rue Palatine. This was near the Church of St. Sulpice, less than half a mile from their home.

A few days later Frederic's company was transferred to the corner of the Rue Madame and the Rue de Fleurus. It was now possible for her to look out of their apartment windows and see her husband on duty in the street below.

As it happened, Frederic's battalion was employed exclusively on guard duty during the entire period of the insurrection. Describing his military experience to the Abbé Alphonse, who was at that time in Lille, Frederic wrote: "There were excursions and alarms, and bad patrols on the boulevards. But, thank God, we did not fire a cartridge. My conscience was easy, and I should not have quailed from any danger. However, I am free to admit that it is a terrible moment when a man bids what he thinks may be his last farewell to his wife and child."

While his company and his family were in comparative safety, the fighting only a few blocks away was bloody. Finally, in a desperate series of assaults the government forces defeated the insurrectionists at several points. Within ninety-six hours more than sixteen thousand men were killed or wounded on both sides.

The insurrectionists, though badly mauled, remained dangerous. Fighting continued at some of the principal barricades, notably that of St. Antoine. Many of the rebels, it was felt, would welcome a peace offer. But any such offer must be made over the heads of desperate and irresponsible leaders. For the most part fanatics were in command, and for an insurrectionist to utter a word for peace was to be shot on the spot.

Continuance of the civil war had now become a senseless tragedy. The conflict continued only because there seemed no way peace proposals could be made. This impasse troubled every humane man on the government side, Frederic among them.

On a Monday morning in June—it was the twenty-sixth— during guard duty on the Rue de Fleurus, he found himself discussing the hopeless stalemate with his fellow soldiers, Bailly and Cornudet. They were particularly concerned with the terrible suffering prolongation of fighting would visit upon the poor. Many women and children behind the barricades, they were certain, must be facing starvation. As they talked, there gradually evolved a conviction that the one person who could successfully broach terms of peace to the

209

insurrectionists was the Archbishop of Paris. Even the rebels, all three agreed, would trust Monseigneur Affre.

"Let's ask the Abbé Buquet what he thinks of the Archbishop approaching the insurgents with a peace offer from the government," suggested Frederic. "No one knows the Archbishop better than he."

Frederic happened to know that the Abbé Buquet was that morning in the vicinity of their post. The three obtained leave, and were soon talking with the Archbishop's friend. The Abbé approved, and gave them a letter to the prelate.

"This will recommend your suggestion to him, and will also serve as a safe-conduct," he said. "You'll need it to get through the fortifications protecting the Ile St. Louis."

It was noon before they made their way to the Ile St. Louis and the Archbishop's residence. Monseigneur Affre listened with deep interest as they advanced their proposal.

"Your suggestion is, perhaps, realistic," he said when they had ended. "My mind has been urgently assessing this very idea since yesterday—but how can the idea be actualized? Will General Cavaignac[2] permit me to go to the insurrectionists with terms? And how can one penetrate the barricades? Supposing the General agrees that I should be entrusted with a peace offer—is the insurrectionist leadership sufficiently responsible to give the offer authoritative consideration?"

To these questions the Archbishop's visitors could answer only by voicing their confidence that he would be received everywhere with respect and trust.

"Well, I am going to General Cavaignac, and if he approves, to the insurgents," said the prelate. "But first, I must put on a common *soutane* [cassock] so as not to be too conspicuous. And then you will show me the way to the General's headquarters."

As the Archbishop was about to leave, a priest entered, apparently intensely agitated. Only a few minutes before he had witnessed a butchery perpetrated by the insurrectionists, and he described it in detail.

Monseigneur the Archbishop listened with visible abhor-

2 General Cavaignac had been appointed military dictator.

210

rence, then he left the room. After several minutes he reappeared garbed in an inconspicuous *soutane*. As they looked at him, a thought struck the three Vincentians at the same instant—the Archbishop should wear clerical garb that would identify him unmistakably as a dignitary of the Church. This would dramatize more forcefully his mission of peace.

They made the suggestion, and again the Archbishop complied with almost childlike simplicity.

"You think more conspicuous dress would be better?" he said. "Well, I will put on my violet *soutane*."

When he again appeared—a noble figure in the long violet robe, with the pectoral cross gleaming upon his breast—they set off at once.

As they made their way through the Rue St. Louis to the bridge that connected the Ile St. Louis with the right bank, citizens uncovered and soldiers presented arms; the prelate was greeted everywhere with the utmost respect and reverence.

"The men behind the St. Antoine barricade may not show you as much reverence as the people now greeting you," observed Frederic, "but many of them are Christians at heart. And no one, I feel sure, would commit a hostile act against your person. Your Grace, nevertheless, runs great risk. With rifles in the hands of so many men under tension, anything can happen. But then, no one needs inform Your Grace of the inherent danger—for you know it as well as any man in uniform."

The Archbishop did not respond at once. He walked rapidly, with downcast eyes. Were they, Frederic asked himself, resting on the figure of the Crucified on the Archbishop's pectoral cross?

They had proceeded for some minutes in silence, when the Archbishop said: "Granted the danger, and the possible failure of my appeal, I am nevertheless convinced that this attempt must be made. Somehow, this civil war must be brought to an end, and quickly. Class hatred mounts with every government soldier, and every insurrectionist, killed or wounded. And back of those barricades, how many children and frantic mothers must be without food!"

As they progressed toward General Cavaignac's head-quarters, the Archbishop's presence on the street became more widely known, and the people hurrying from all directions to greet him made his walk a triumphal march. Everyone sensed that the prelate was on a mission of great moment.

General Cavaignac welcomed Monseigneur Affre warmly, and listened with evident agreement to his suggestion that he carry the government's peace terms to the barricades.

"I have the deepest admiration, Your Grace," he said, "for your willingness to risk your life for peace. But I have just now received news which causes me to hesitate to authorize such a mission. Only a few hours ago, General Bréa undertook a similar mission. Word has come that the insurrectionists disregarded his flag of truce and have taken him and his escort prisoners. We are dealing with savages, and I fear that we will never see General Bréa alive again."[3]

"My life is of little value," replied the Archbishop. "I will gladly risk it."

The general argued no further. Sitting down at his desk, he wrote out a proclamation for the Archbishop to carry to the insurgents. It was a guarantee of mercy if they would put down their arms.

The Archbishop had offered his life to his Creator as a sacrifice of atonement, that peace might be quickly restored, and he felt that the sacrifice might be accepted. He decided to make a general confession and to set his episcopal affairs in order. For this purpose he must return to his residence. Ozanam, Cornudet and Bailly accompanied him, expecting to return with him to the barricades. But when they arrived at the Bridge of the Saints-Pères he stopped them and asked them to permit him to go his way alone.

"You are in uniform," he told them. "Your presence has the semblance of a military escort. It might, messieurs, create a false impression. I understand that the insurrectionist in-

---

[3] General Bréa had long been honored as a national hero. He volunteered to inform the insurrectionists that the National Assembly had at last voted relief for the unemployed. After seizing him, they insulted and beat him, and finally buried his sword in his body. It was a sword presented to him in memory of his gallantry at Waterloo.

telligence is excellent. Now that I have decided to approach them, they will undoubtedly be watching every move I make. Therefore I must proceed from now on as one being observed, and with nothing to destroy the idea that mine is a mission of peace."

Unwillingly the three heeded his request, and returned to their company.

Arrived at his residence, the Archbishop took a brief rest, made his confession as if about to die, met with his secretaries over some necessary ecclesiastical matters, and then left for the Place de la Bastille. He was accompanied by the Abbé Jacquemet and the Abbé Ravinet, his grand-vicars, and by his devoted servant, Tellier.

As Monseigneur Affre advanced through the streets, the Guards presented their arms to be blessed. A group of officers approached and begged him not to go to his death.

"My life is a little thing," he replied.

As he moved forward he quoted to the priests with him the Saviour's words: "The good shepherd gives his life for his flock," and commented on them as he walked along. At the Place de l'Arsenal he stopped and chatted a few moments with wounded soldiers, and blessed them. Then he hastened on, for the day was dying and he must reach the barricades before dusk obscured his identity from the men behind them.

There was heavy firing on both sides, and the Archbishop asked the colonel in command to order the sounding of a "cease fire." As the firing from the government troops ceased, that from behind the barricades slackened and then stopped entirely as the Archbishop moved out into the square and toward the frowning barriers looming before him.

Out of nowhere there now appeared a young man carrying a long branch, at the end of which, among a few green leaves at the tip, there was tied a white handkerchief. A citizen who was a member of the St. Vincent de Paul Society recognized him as a fellow Vincentian by the name of Brechemin. He strode rapidly, far ahead of the Archbishop, who now walked forward alone, having ordered his attendants to leave him.

The prelate's pectoral cross glittered on his breast in the last rays of the setting sun as he reached the corner of the Faubourg St. Antoine, and turning, passed through a shop and thus arrived at the large barricade that closed up the area.

A few insurgents descended to the square and stood before him. He held up the written pledge of pardon he was carrying in his left hand, gestured toward it with his right, and then began to read it amid a silence disturbed only by faintly heard rifle fire in distant parts of the city. He had not quite finished when a single shot rang out, followed instantly by heavy fusillades from soldiers and insurgents.

The Archbishop was seen to pitch forward—he had been facing the barricades—and a man in a laborer's smock rushed to catch him, then lowered him gently to the ground. Firing again ceased, and the Archbishop was carried into a neighboring house.

He had been wounded seriously, and his wounding was a tragic irony. For he had been shot in the back, probably by a bullet from a badly handled government rifle.

For the moment, insurgents and soldiers alike lost appetite for fighting. They stood about in silent and sorrowful homage.

Ozanam, Bailly and Cornudet had, perforce, returned to their command when the Archbishop dismissed them.

Not until several hours later did they learn that he had been struck down, and they then heard the details from the lips of Frederic's brother, Dr. Charles Ozanam. He had been on duty with an ambulance corps, and it was his ambulance that had been rushed to the Archbishop's aid. Dr. Charles, after giving first aid, had ordered him placed on a litter and carried into a nearby house.

Some time later, he was borne to his residence in the Rue St. Louis, and there, about forty-eight hours later, he died.

His sacrifice hastened the end of the fighting. The insurrectionists realized that the Archbishop had offered his life for peace, and the fact that he had been stricken in the cause of peace softened their hearts. Within a few hours of the Archbishop's appearance before the barricade, they forced the more ruthless and obstinate of their leaders to open negotia-

214

tions. The parley ended in failure, but following it most of the insurgents fought with little heart for slaughter. The morning after the prelate had been wounded, a final assault on the barricades swept away the last show of resistance.

The Archbishop's death had been an accident, but it seemed to many that the sacrifice of this innocent victim was an expiation for the hatred of man for man. He himself had thought of it as such. He had offered his life for that intention and for peace, if Divine Providence desired the sacrifice.

Thousands had died in the conflict; he was the only one to die willingly, without attempting or desiring to kill or to protect himself; the only one to die for love of God and man.

CHAPTER 25

ON THE evening of August 2, 1848, Professor Ozanam brushed and combed his hair and his full beard and mustache, adjusted his cravat, kissed his wife and little daughter Marie, donned the top hat which was the usual headgear of a gentleman, and after a three-block walk, came to the parish hall near the Church of St. Sulpice. Here he fell in with a stream of Vincentians entering the hall, where presently the St. Vincent de Paul Society would hold its quarterly general meeting. It was a Wednesday—selected to avoid interference with the regular Tuesday meetings of the parish conferences.

Arrived in the hall, Ozanam seated himself in the president-general's chair. As vice-president of the General Council he was to preside in the absence of President-General Adolphe Baudon.

At the stroke of eight, Frederic called the meeting to order. His audience was expectant; its several hundred members felt privileged that he was to address them. They greatly respected Ozanam as chief founder of the Society, as a historian and an educator, and as a journalist who currently, in the Paris press, was a leading defender of the Church and of the poor.

"Most of you know," he began, "why President Baudon is unable to be present this evening. While defending the republic in the June fighting, a bullet shattered the bone in his left leg. Your prayers are asked for his complete recovery and that of other members injured in the fighting, and also for the souls of our brothers who died to save France from anarchy."

Then he talked of the poor, many of whom had been amongst the insurgents in the June fighting, and who were now even more miserable than before the insurrection. Through ringing appeals in the columns of *The New Era,* he had been bringing their desperate condition to the attention of all political parties. Today, in his words to his Vincentian brothers, he re-emphasized those eloquent pleas.

"Now that peace has succeeded the storm," he said, "it is right that we should proclaim certain truths that can now be voiced without fear that agitators may use them to instigate bloody insurrection."

He pointed out that though two months had passed since restoration of peace, 267,000 workers in Paris out of a total population of 1,500,000 were idle.

"People of property will tell us," he said, "that these individuals receive ample public assistance—but we who have the privilege of distributing this public help are less assured."[1]

He described conditions in the twelfth arrondissement, which had been one of the strongholds of the insurrection and whose population numbered 90,000. Here 8,000 families were entirely dependent on charity, and 21,992 families were receiving some assistance.

"Our Society has developed rapidly," he said, "perhaps that it might be ready for the important work of bringing

[1] Funds under the control of several mayors were at this time entrusted to the St. Vincent de Paul Conferences for distribution to the destitute.

216

material and spiritual aid to such as these victims of starvation and disease. We Vincentians, who have seen these poor fellows on the barricades, now see them at their own hearths, disarmed and surrounded by their wives and children. Even we are astonished to find how much Christianity there still is amongst these people—and consequently, how much there is to work upon. Ah, if only we had some saints! But can we doubt that God has a few in reserve for a century to which He has given Pius IX and the Archbishop of Paris?"

The business of the quarterly meeting concluded, a member asked Ozanam to comment on the general attitude of French citizens toward the poor since the suppression of the insurrection.

"I need only sum up," Ozanam responded, "what I have been writing the last several weeks in *The New Era*. In our publication, we have sharply challenged Frenchmen who, claiming that their less fortunate brothers were 'hopeless,' washed their hands of all responsibility for their moral, physical and economic condition."

He laid bare the fact that the lower economic classes of Paris were being vitiated, morally, mentally and physically, by the unrestrained wine, distilling and amusement industries. While the poor were encouraged to debauch themselves, pauperism was multiplying. Many well-to-do, whose avarice fostered these conditions, blamed the poor for the vices their industries promoted.

"God did not make the poor," Ozanam now told his Vincentians. "He sends few human creatures into this world without providing them with those two basic sources of riches—intelligence and will. But we allow intelligence to be quenched in ignorance and will to be weakened by vice."

He reproved what he considered a reactionary parliament for its lack of action in the crisis.

"When it was a question of crushing out the last embers of the insurrection," he declared, "there were no delays and formalities to the pitching of twenty camps on the boulevards of Paris, and up to the very doors of the Hotel de Ville. And here we are, after four months, when in the twelfth

217

arrondissement alone there are four thousand children without shelter—here we are, our parliament still struggling amid adjournments, motions and debates, fighting to overcome I know not what scruples of committees, boards, administrations and the rest of it. Here we are, with many legislators terrified that the state will be ruined and overturned if the education of young working men is confided to Sisters and Brothers—to teachers, that is, capable of teaching them something more than how to spell out the syllables of the newspaper, and to scrawl the 'order of the day' on the barricades with a piece of charcoal."

His Vincentian brothers applauded. For most Frenchmen, however, his demands for social and political justice were too advanced.

Despite its first months of popularity, *The New Era* began to decline. Not a few Frenchmen confused democracy with demagoguery, and the genuinely democratic *New Era* was misunderstood by both Catholics and unbelievers. The bloody insurrection in Paris and uprisings in other Continental nations had filled most Frenchmen—and indeed, most Europeans—with fear that any representative government might degenerate into a despotism of the proletariat. The Italian revolutionists, who through intrigue and assassination had recently driven the Pope from Rome and now ruled despotically in Italy, also helped to destroy confidence in the "rule of the people."

Ozanam, convinced that only a republican form of government could assure freedom for both the people and the Church, fought on with the quiet courage, the courtesy and charity, and the bulldog tenacity characteristic of him. But he fought against hopeless odds.

Yet Ozanam and those who served with him on *The New Era*'s editorial board—the Abbé Lacordaire, the Abbé Maret, Audley, Eugène Rendu, Gouraud, Feugeray, and L. F. Guérin—refused to give up the unequal struggle. To Ozanam particularly, the issue was too important to permit surrender; the flag would be lowered only when he and his friends had no more resources to continue the fight. For he saw in a

Christian republic—which in his opinion was the only kind of republic that could ultimately succeed—freedom for the Church from the secular claims and restrictions that had impeded her and obstructed her mission through generations past. In France these secular pretensions of despotic rulers had even threatened the papal authority in matters of faith. If the Church were to fulfill to the utmost her destined work of bringing souls to Christ, he considered it imperative that she be freed from her galling chains. But not even all clerics in France agreed with him.

The *Univers* fulminated, and referred to *The New Era* as *The New Error*. Other editors of less vitriolic papers joined Veuillot in his attacks. Even Ozanam's good friend Montalembert assailed *The New Era* and its doctrines in both speeches and articles. Lacordaire, whose prestige and pen had been invaluable, resigned from the board of editors because he felt that the interests of his order and his religious ministry made withdrawal prudent. He continued, however, outspokenly in favor of *The New Era's* objectives. Lacordaire's resignation brought a crisis; the board voted four to three to discontinue publication. But some influence—probably Ozanam's—induced reconsideration, and publication continued.

By now republicanism was generally held in such contempt that when Ozanam appealed through *The New Era* for contributions to a fund for relief in the Venetian Republic —then under simultaneous attack by Austrian cannon and cholera—few responded. His appeals for subscriptions to a fund for Pius IX, then a fugitive in the stronghold coastal city of Gaeta, were far more successful.

For six months after Lacordaire's resignation *The New Era* fought a valiant rear guard action on behalf of the fading French Republic, the application of Christian principles to modern society, and the liberty and the dignity of man. Ozanam had for some time realized that the Republic's cause was hopeless, but he continued the unequal struggle that it might not be said that Catholics were "a band of timid times-servers" for the Republic when it seemed strong, but turned from it when it became weak. In April, 1849, he finally agreed to *The New Era*'s discontinuance. Its publishers, with Ozanam at their head, drew up *A Declaration*, which concluded: "We resign in consequence of material difficulties, in which God has perhaps hidden His design for the fructification of our doctrine, even as the very hoarfrosts, which drive the sower home, fructify the wheat."

Writing to Madame Soulacroix on Holy Thursday, shortly after *The New Era*'s discontinuance, he said: "When the head is worn out with work, and the heart is embittered by controversy and disappointment, one leaves the petty rivalry of man, and the contacts with wicked passions, to aspire to the peace of these holy days! How good it is to come to the feet of the kind Master, who awaits us tomorrow morning."

The Republic was about to collapse, but though humiliated and frustrated, Ozanam's spirit would not collapse with it. Taking the long-range view of the historian, he wrote to a learned friend in Venice voicing present dejection, but confidence in the future: "See how little the great lesson of 1848 has taught men! . . . Behold how they resume their old hatreds . . . their sloth which recoils at any new idea! . . . I have but one hope—which is, however, great—that amid the general decay, Christianity will assert itself."

With the new Archbishop of Paris, Monseigneur Sibour, lending his support, those who had stood with Ozanam founded a new journal, the *Moniteur Religieux,* and Frederic was invited to become a regular contributor.

He longed to accept, but his health was failing. His physicians ordered him to conserve his strength—above all, to get out and to keep out of the political and editorial arenas, with their endless demands on time and energy. He obeyed reluctantly. For he realized more than ever the importance of publicizing Catholic truth and of offsetting the activities of the comparatively few, but narrow and violent, men to whose views Louis Veuillot and his *Univers* gave acrimonious expression.

He had seen religion gain back many hearts, and he was fearful that the intemperate defenders of the Church might start an unfavorable reaction and cause a new upsurge against religion.

"I ask myself," he said, "if, when our hair has grown gray, we shall be able to kneel before the altar without hearing on every side those hisses which, twenty years ago, pursued the Christian to the door of the Church?" With St. Francis de Sales, he was convinced that a spoonful of honey catches more flies than a barrel of vinegar.

With him, winning souls to Christ was not a mission only for his pen and the lecture platform. He continued, as a member of the St. Vincent de Paul Society, to visit the poor through all the busy years of his professorship and his history and newspaper writing.

Toward the end of 1849 all activity, including his Vincentian work, became a burden. He began to tire quickly. Nearly every day now, mid-afternoon found him drained of energy. Obeying his physicians, he was refusing all requests for newspaper articles and appearances on the platform. But he continued his attendance at the Tuesday meetings of the St. Vincent de Paul Conference of his parish and his weekly visits following the meetings.

Desperately fatigued though he frequently was, he would set out with Cornudet for the noisy and noxious Rue Mouffetard and the dark, narrow, crooked streets that led off it from either side. His weary body would be crying out for rest—for fever and weakness increased as the day lengthened—but there was no scientific authority to order the complete, prolonged rest that might have cured him. A few passersby would greet him, for he was a familiar figure in the cobblestone streets with their filthy open sewers, the teeming, five-story tenements and the scurrying rats as big as small cats.

He had asked that his team of two be assigned families in the vicinity of the Rue des Lyonnais, for here lived the poorest of the poor, and perhaps there might be people from Lyons among them. One Tuesday evening in the spring of 1850, Ozanam and Cornudet sought out a destitute couple living in this street. They found them in a cellar—a black, unhealthy hole. A little straw served as a bed, on which was lying a sallow, hollow-eyed woman. Her husband, sitting beside her on a box, stood in silent welcome as the visitors entered.

"We bear you greetings from your pastor," said Frederic. "He tells us that you can perhaps direct us to some in this quarter who might be in need of a little assistance—as which of us is not, in one way or another, now and again in this life?"

In the Vincentian spirit, Ozanam was most careful to respect the sensibilities and the dignity of those he came to help, and he frequently adopted an indirect approach. He realized that most people resent having to accept assistance, even when they need it the most, and that a strategic word or two can do wonders to save a needy person's natural pride. In the present visit, he achieved this result by making the man confronting him an associate in his benefactions to others.

"There are many in this quarter who could use assistance," answered the man. "Our neighbor in the next room has lost three children by consumption, and she has three more who suffer from it. Ah, there's much misery in this tenement, messieurs—and we ourselves could do with a little help."

"If we can aid you in any way, my dear sir," replied Ozanam, "please consider Monsieur Cornudet here, and myself, Frederic Ozanam, as your servants."

Learning that the woman was consumptive, they informed the couple they would arrange for nursing care, and gave the husband—he was almost penniless—money for a week's rent and other necessities. This, with tickets for food, assured the couple immediate relief.

"We will try to help you find more healthful quarters and some kind of work," added Frederic. "By the way"—pointing to a rope running from wall to wall—"may I inquire as to the purpose of this rope?"

"On that," explained the man, "we hang bags of food—when we have any. You know—so rats can't get at it."

Ozanam and Cornudet decided to canvass the entire building.

In a windowless garret that received light through two small holes in the wall, they were greeted by a tailor, his wife and their eight children. The roof of their "apartment"

222

slanted from a six-foot height to three feet, and under the lowest part of the roof were some piles of straw. To these "beds" the father, mother and children would crawl on hands and knees when they wanted to sleep.

In one room they met a half-crippled cooper who gave his age as seventy-two. He was hard at work shaping staves; his wife and a grandson—a deaf and dumb lad of twelve—depended on him for a living. Despite the boy's handicap they had succeeded in teaching him to read; they had also managed to teach him his religion and his prayers. When they had left the workshop-home, Ozanam remarked to Cornudet upon the cleanliness of the cooper's quarters.

"In spite of their difficulties in obtaining water and cleaning supplies," he said, "haven't you often noted, Cornudet, the cleanliness that the poor are frequently able to attain? Under such circumstances thorough cleanliness is heroic—and we've encountered it more than once today."

The next poor room they entered was another example of this "heroic cleanliness." In it the mother, clothed in the costume of her native Auvergne, was working away with her four young daughters at some piece-sewing for which they would receive a few sous a day. Their garments were threadbare but immaculate. The room's one window was tiny but spotless, and its light disclosed religious pictures, carefully arranged, pasted on the walls.

In the rooms of the better-off families, six people had two beds to share; in these the sick and the healthy must huddle together. In this entire tenement, which sheltered forty-eight families, there was not an adequately fed man, woman or child.

Their visits concluded, Ozanam and Cornudet sought out Sister Rosalie to report the sick cases they had encountered. They found her in the same little office where Frederic had met her seventeen years before when he was accompanied there by Jules Devaux.

The years had added to her fame, and to her burdens, but to Frederic her step seemed as light and decisive as ever. Her heroism during the recent street fighting had already become a legend, and all parties were deeply grateful to her and her Sisters for their care of the wounded.

As had Archbishop Affre, Sister Rosalie had risked her life on a barricade to stop the fighting—and in the Faubourg St. Marceau she had succeeded. She had further endeared herself to the people of the quarter by saving many insurrectionists from execution, for she had powerful friends. Also, it was characteristic of her universal charity that not a few of her friends were former soldiers whose lives she had saved by defying the insurgents and sheltering them in her convent.

"You Vincentians," she told them after they had given her information about the sick they had visited that day, "are truly good neighbors to the poor—and that's the best and most direct apostolate. After all, messieurs, how can a family fail to trust those who for their sakes accept all kinds of inconvenience to bring them their friendship and kindly help?"

There was further talk, during which she studied Frederic's face with growing concern. His long evening had exhausted him, and he looked haggard.

"You must rest more, Monsieur Ozanam," she urged. "I am a nurse. I know a sick man when I see one. And you, monsieur, are a sick man. You must obey nature; you must stop driving yourself. You have done much for the poor—do not neglect your duty to yourself."[2]

The need for Sister Rosalie's warning was sadly demonstrated soon after Ozanam and Cornudet bade her farewell. As they worked their way up the crowded, boisterous Rue Mouffetard, Frederic grew so weak that Cornudet felt it necessary to support him. Arms interlocked, they walked on till they came to a vegetable stall before which was a little bench. Here Frederic rested until he had regained sufficient strength to set out again, and finally they came to the vicinity of the Pantheon, where Cornudet was able to hail a cab.

Cornudet called at the Ozanam apartment the next morn-

2 Sister Rosalie failed to apply this advice to herself. Worn out by her ceaseless work for the poor, she died in 1856. In 1852 the government, against her will, had awarded her the Cross of the Legion of Honor. All Paris mourned her passing; she was venerated as a saint. Her cause for beatification is now being promoted.

ing. Frederic was about to leave for the Sorbonne, and his friend, who walked with him through the stately Luxembourg Gardens as far as the University, was reassured. Ozanam looked about as well as usual, and Cornudet felt that his weakness of the night before might be merely the result of overwork.

Neither he nor anyone else realized that any work, for one in Frederic's condition, would have been overwork. The disease that had fastened upon him could have been cured only by complete inactivity—if, indeed, at this stage it could have been cured at all.

CHAPTER 26

PAUSING in the courtyard of the Castle of Truscat, Frederic and Amélie looked out over the Atlantic sparkling in the morning sunlight, and the sawtooth coastline of Lower Brittany with its granite rocks and cliffs and little sandy beaches.

"The island of Artz is over there to the northwest," said Monsieur de Francheville, pointing. "And that sturdy boat you see below," he added, directing their eyes downward toward the little dock at the foot of a long flight of stone steps, "will sail us to it in less than an hour if this southerly breeze holds."

Marie overheard the words and squealed in delight as she tried to hug all the four Francheville daughters at one time, for she loved to be on the water.

The Ozanams were in Lower Brittany for rest and ocean air and visits to some of its celebrated shrines. Frederic's health had again broken, and his brother Dr. Charles had ordered complete abstinence from work.

Following the tragic times of 1848 Ozanam had enjoyed two peaceful and productive years, but in the early summer of 1850 he had suffered another serious physical setback.

A little before his physical decline he had been the victim of another unrestrained attack by the tempestuous Louis Veuillot. This exponent of an intensely personal journalism was in the habit of taking personally any general criticism that appeared in print. Reviewing a volume of poetry by his friend Monsieur de Francheville, Ozanam had referred to a group of Catholics that "presents truth, not in the form that attracts, but in that which repels; that has not before its mind the idea of bringing back unbelievers, but of inflaming the passions of believers."

Veuillot pounced on this mild and impersonal statement as one directed against himself, and in five columns of bitterly personal vituperation went so far as to accuse Ozanam of apostasy. The latter understood Veuillot's nature, and forgave him even as he read the attack. He was hurt, but decided, in the interests of peace and after consulting his friend Cornudet, who was then a Councillor of State, to throw the reply he had written to protect his reputation into the fire. But when a letter from his cherished friend Dufieux arrived from Lyons, informing him that his friends there—including Dufieux—were confused and upset by Veuillot's accusations, he was deeply grieved and responded eloquently and at length. In the course of his reply he asked: "Would I be, my dear friend, exhausted with fatigue at thirty-seven years of age, and reduced to a state of premature infirmity if I had not been driven on by the desire, by the hope—if you wish, by the illusion—of serving Christianity?"

Whatever the cause, it was soon after the Veuillot attack that the "premature infirmity" he mentions became total exhaustion, and early September found him in St. Gildas de Ruiz. The rest, the baths and quiet strolls beside the tranquil sea brought peace and a restoration of strength. Francheville had been insistent that he visit him, and so too had another old friend, Monsieur Rio, to whose native island they would soon be sailing. The Franchevilles and Rios were among several Breton families who extended the patriarchal hospi-

226

tality of their old castles and mansions—in Monsieur Rio's case, of his peasant home—to the Ozanams as they leisurely toured picturesque Brittany.

"A perfect day on land or sea," said Ozanam, as he and his host helped the women and children into the boat. "I'm looking ahead eagerly to renewing with Monsieur Rio the good talks we used to have in Paris. He was one of our great history professors, and he stands alone as France's leading exponent of Christian art."

"History, and Christian art, and the island of Artz are his life," answered Francheville. "His people have made the island their home for generations untold, and he was, of course, born there."

They reached the island in the company of many sailboats from up and down the coast, for this was Artz' religious feast-day, and scores of guests were coming from the mainland to take part in the celebration.

After the Solemn High Mass at the island's church, Monsieur Rio received the Ozanams and Franchevilles in his family's ancient cottage, where his mother, dressed in her native peasant's costume with its lace headdress, presided in the midst of her devoted family.

Late that afternoon the feastday procession formed and wended its way across a huge plain sloping down toward the shore. The low afternoon sun cast long shadows across the greensward as the double line began to move, led by a score or more of little girls in their gaily starched dresses, as snowy white as the clouds drifting against the blue Breton sky.

Frederic and Amélie watched eagerly as the children approached for among the little girls was Marie. Soon they saw her, almost at the end of the girls' section, walking with the conscious gravity of her six years. She smiled shyly as she noticed them amid the onlookers; then recollected herself and became again a picture of dignified solemnity as she walked on with the four Francheville girls.

Next came the small boys in their holiday best, women in the traditional costumes and lace headdresses of their locales, fishermen and sailors in their distinctive attire, and priests bearing on a litter a statue of the Blessed Virgin. Every section of the procession bore banners, now billowing in a stiffening breeze which seemed to carry the voices of the marchers heavenward as they chanted the litanies, the thin trebles of the children forming a delicate obbligato to the heavy notes of the men and the round, full tones of the women.

As the party embarked for the return trip to the Castle of Truscat, their craft was surrounded on every side by sailboats bound for the mainland. The stiff wind that had made marching difficult for the procession's banner-bearers had died to a gentle breeze; the bay's waters were as blue as a mountain lake, and flocks of sea gulls rose from the water and flew before their boat as it bore them toward the castle's beach. It was, thought Frederic, one of those serene and beautiful moments of life that is always remembered.

In the fall Frederic returned to his professorial duties at the Sorbonne. He carried on, doing his best to conceal from his students, and from Amélie, the physical weakness that came and went, but from which he was never entirely free.

His brilliance and eloquence blinded his students to occasional indications that his energies were nearing exhaustion. But Amélie knew, and her heart bled for him when she saw the recurring fatigue and feebleness he tried so valiantly to hide under a cloak of simulated unconcern and gaiety. It seemed to her that the crushing burden of physical weakness was the cruelest form of bodily suffering.

His weakness brought on moments of depression and sadness which he was sometimes unable to conceal; he was concerned, most of all, for his family's future. But his mental and physical suffering never destroyed his soul's deep hope and happiness. He became a more frequent communicant; he prayed still more for himself, his family and his friends, and earnestly asked their prayers; he added to his customary half-hour morning reading in devotional books. In these he marked passages for the "daily bread" of his later meditations. Peace blessed his home, and honor attached to his position as a professor of the Sorbonne. He was still, at thirty-seven, the youngest member of the University's permanent faculty, and still the idol of the students.

The summer of 1851 came, bringing the "long vacation," and Amélie hastened to move the family to a house they had rented in the country at Sceaux, six or seven miles to the south of their Paris home. Here they would have the seclusion that would allow Frederic continuous rest.

He could not rest mentally, however, and he welcomed the visits of Jean-Jacques Ampère, who came for a few days every week during the summer. Ampère was working on a new novel, some chapters of which had already met with warm approval of literary men at Madame Récamier's soirées in the Abbaye-au-Bois. His writings had long since won the acclaim of intellectual Europe. Yet in his heart was a spiritual void that could be filled only by the faith he had carelessly lost in his youth.

At Ozanam's country house the two friends applied themselves to their writing in the mornings—for Frederic some months before had persuaded his physicians to lift their ban against literary work—and gave themselves to walks and conversation in the afternoons. Ozanam, sympathetic and understanding, did his best to help his friend overcome theological difficulties, for none knew better than he how sweet and priceless was the treasure of faith.

The great Crystal Palace Exhibition was drawing the world to London, and Ampère pressed Frederic and Amélie to visit it with him. The doctors agreeing, they set off during the first week in August.

In England Ozanam spent little time at the exposition, but was much with his London brothers of St. Vincent de Paul, visiting the tenement dwellers.

London overwhelmed him with its wealth, appalled him with its poverty, and—except for Westminster Abbey and the Houses of Parliament—disappointed him with the crudity of its monuments and architecture. St. Paul's he describes as "an icy edifice to which even Catholicism could give warmth only with difficulty."

He explored what he termed "a second city of London"—

the docks and countless huge warehouses crammed with the world's wealth. Beside this fabulous wealth he beheld pauperism such as he had never seen in Paris, even when revolutions had caused economic collapse. He saw half-naked beggars "pursuing the stranger, rushing under the very wheels of the carriages, and bearing on their countenances the traces of a fixed despair . . . women in rags . . . little girls in frocks tattered up to their waists, with naked feet in the cold, black mud . . . narrow little alleys, dark and foul."

He admired "the fine qualities of the people" and found them "full of respect for the law and the order of their country . . . indefatigable in their industry . . . religious, too, if we may judge from the immense number of church steeples that soar above London." But he was dismayed, though grimly amused, by the rigid class distinctions observed by "upper class" Englishmen, who held proudly aloof from contacts with the "lower classes," and who even expected shop clerks to hand them their change folded in a bit of paper (that they might not be defiled). He observed with gratification, however, that English Vincentians did not think themselves contaminated when they clasped the hand of a pauper. "Our confreres of St. Vincent de Paul have . . . overcome the prejudice of their birth," he writes. "They do a great deal of good, and it was a joy to pass an evening in the midst of them."

Leaving London's misery, fog, and smoke for Oxford University's cloisters and gardens, he and Amélie were charmed by the colleges of Christ Church and Magdalen. Charmed so completely, indeed, that he wrote: "We were seriously tempted to take up our abode there; for though celibacy is the rule in these communities, there is an exception in favor of the canons of Christ Church."

Ampère left London for the United States, while the Ozanams returned to Sceaux. From there Frederic wrote to his wandering friend at length, striving to inspire him to return to the faith. With characteristic delicacy, he urged on Ampère the spiritual humility and the generosity with God that would open his heart to receive the grace of belief. "We must give our soul to God," he told him, "and then He gives us the fullness of light."

There is a note of urgent pleading in this letter. Ozanam feared that his beloved friend might take sick and die in some distant American town without an opportunity of becoming reconciled to the Church. He advised Ampère: "If some day you fall ill in a distant city in America without a friend at your bedside, remember that there is not a town of any importance in the United States where the love of Jesus Christ has not guided a priest to console the Catholic traveler."

Ampère's response brought Frederic reassurance. The novelist was grateful for his friend's solicitude. He promised to pray perseveringly for the fullness of light.[1]

CHAPTER 27

STUDENT demonstrators were crowding about the door to Professor Ozanam's classroom. The door was closed; it had been closed for many days past.

The professor, it was rumored, was in his apartment across the Luxembourg Gardens on the Rue de Fleurus, denying himself to all callers while feverishly engaged in finishing the manuscript of a book. His publishers, hearsay had it, were insisting that he complete the manuscript by the deadline specified in their contract.

The students were now vociferously demanding his appearance in the lecture room.

"He should at least appoint a substitute!" declared one in the crowd.

[1] Ampere's petitions were finally answered, but not until shortly before his death fifteen years later.

"Who wants a substitute?" objected another. "We want Ozanam."

"Let's demonstrate here every day till the faculty wakes up and takes action," cried a third. "That'll bring back Professor Ozanam to his lecture platform!"

"I'm for that!" another shouted. "Who has more right to the professor—his publishers or his students?"

It was true that Ozanam was confining himself to his home, but he was not writing, and he had been too sick even to think of the business of hiring a supply professor. After having taught the 1851–52 term without interruption until the last part of March, he had been stricken with pleurisy, and weakened by a high fever. For some time his life had been in danger.

He had partially recovered, but the fever continued. He was still confined to his bed when, on this particular morning, reports that dissatisfied students were accusing him of malingering came accidentally to his ears.

Astounded, his chief concern was that such rumors might reflect on the faculty. He forced himself from his bed, announcing that he was going to his lecture room, and demanded his clothes. Fearing that such an effort might bring a relapse, Amélie and Dr. Charles strove to dissuade him.

"I am going to the Sorbonne," he insisted. "I must protect the honor of my profession."

Surrendering finally to his iron determination, they assisted him to dress, and Dr. Charles, summoning a cab, accompanied him to the Sorbonne.

The student crowd before his classroom had grown larger. Speakers were denouncing professors for "taking it easy," and for dropping lectures they were "well paid to give." One hot-eyed young agitator had just started to propose a march to Ozanam's apartment, when suddenly the speakers fell silent, and all eyes turned in one direction. Down the corridor, Ozanam's familiar figure had appeared.

Leaning heavily upon his brother's arm, he advanced upon them, his thin pale face set in the effort he was making to overcome his weakness and pain.

The silent crowd drew back, and Ozanam walked through

232

their midst and into the lecture room. After he had passed, the students looked at one another, and each saw his own reproach and self-contempt in the others' eyes. Their beloved professor's ghostly countenance accused them, and they were filled with remorse and repentance. They felt they were looking on a man on his way to the grave.

The hall quickly filled, and ashamed silence hung over the audience as Ozanam mounted the platform. Then as he stood gazing down at them, gathering his thoughts, a spontaneous tumult of applause broke out.

His voice was thin but as clear and penetrating as that of a silver trumpet as he addressed them, though he had to pause and catch his breath after every sentence.

"Gentlemen," he began, "our age is accused of being an age of egotism. We professors, it is said, are tainted with the general epidemic. Yet it is here, in these halls, that we use up our health. It is here that we wear ourselves out.

"I do not complain of it. Our life belongs to you. We owe it to you to our last breath. And you shall have it.

"For my part, if I die, it will be in your service.

"I will now proceed with the lecture for today."

He delivered the lecture prepared the night before he had been stricken. Perhaps apprehending that this might be his last lecture in the Sorbonne, he was inspired as never before. As he concluded the students crowded about him, acclaiming him, marveling anew at his erudition and his eloquence.

It was, in fact, his last classroom lecture. The next day he suffered a relapse. His condition became so alarming that Dr. Charles feared that death might be but a few days away. But, attended constantly by Charles, and tenderly nursed by Amélie and Guigui, he passed the crisis.

He recovered slowly, but by late spring he was able to walk to a nearby church in the mornings to assist at Mass. He favored the Church of the Carmelites, where so many had been martyred during the Terror.

One morning, despite the fact that he was still running a temperature, he insisted on going to the church as usual. He was very weak, and his feebleness filled Amélie's heart with anguish. She could not rid her memory of a few words that had slipped from him the previous evening when they were discussing the possibility of a journey to Italy. "If I should die in Italy," he had said, "let me be buried there."

Almost before the sentence was completed he was biting his lips in vexation at the inadvertent disclosure of his inmost thoughts. But it was plain to Amélie that death had been heavily on his mind.

As they entered the chapel this morning she was fighting back her tears, and that he might not note her grief she did not enter the pew with him, but slipped into the one behind. She tried to pray, but a feeling of desolation swept over her. A vivid premonition seized upon her mind; she felt distinctly in that moment that she would never again accompany her husband to that chapel, but that he would die in some far-off place.

Drained of energy, she arose with difficulty as the Mass was concluded, and as she did so happened to look toward the left wall of the chapel. On it she seemed to see the words: "Here rests Anthony Frederic Ozanam."

Shaken though she was by the vision, she was able to control her emotions, and when Frederic arose to leave, she seemed as calm as usual.[1]

In mid-July, Dr. Charles and the consulting physicians considered Frederic sufficiently recovered to travel, and the family set off for Eaux-Bonnes in the western Pyrenees. Medical practitioners placed great faith in the sulphur spring water of Eaux-Bonnes, and in truth the health resort boasted not a few cures of consumptive patients. In these, complete rest and the town's pure, dry mountain air were doubtless the essential factors, but importance was ascribed to drinking the unpleasant sulphur water from the crystal springs. So Frederic Ozanam held his nose, imbibed the bitter potion, and consoled himself with viewing the beautiful mountains that rose on either side of the town.

From Eaux-Bonnes he and Amélie and a former student and old friend, the Abbé Perreyve, made a pilgrimage to

[1] Appendix 1 relates the strange sequel to this experience.

234

the ancient shrine of Notre Dame au Rameau d'Or. The Abbé was young, but he, also, was consumptive. He was devoted to Ozanam and sought his company at every opportunity. In this retreat, where each sick man was moved by his weakness to contemplate the brevity of his earthly journey, the talk of the professor and the priest touched often upon the life to come. Each, however, hoped to continue his work in this world; both felt that Eaux-Bonnes was helping them, and the fact that many who had "taken the cure" there had been restored to health tended to build their confidence.

Frederic noted that only the well-to-do came to the spa; the poor could not afford the journey and the months of rest required. But why, he asked himself, should not the consumptive poor also have the advantage of Eaux-Bonnes? They surely had the greatest need of such a resort, for among them the incidence of the disease was higher than among those better housed and nourished. He became absorbed in plans for building a hospital for the sick poor at the watering place, and in establishing a system among St. Vincent de Paul Conferences to support those who might take advantage of such a hospital. His own illness forced him to leave to others the carrying forward of this project.

In September, the Eaux-Bonnes season having ended, the Ozanams and the Abbé Perreyve went on to Biarritz for the sea air and sea bathing. The Abbé's health had improved to such degree that in Biarritz the doctors told him he was fit to return to Paris. Ozanam accompanied him to nearby Bayonne, where the Abbé was to take the Paris-bound stage.

On the way to Bayonne, Frederic spoke of spiritual values, with particular reference to his own life as a layman and the Abbé's as a priest. He discussed, also, the state of the world and of the Church, and talked optimistically of the promise of the future. "But when we reached the highroad of Spain," the Abbé later related, "that point where the towers of the Cathedral of Bayonne become visible in the distance—Ozanam changed his tone. He told me he knew the hand of death was upon him, and that we should doubtless never meet again. . . . I tried to combat his sad forebodings. But he was not to be shaken; he spoke to me of his approaching death with

235

a conviction that bore down all my suggested motives of hope. When our carriage drew up before the coach that was to take me to Paris, he grasped my hand in a long pressure.

"We alighted, and I had barely time to get my little luggage secured in its place, when it was time to start. He embraced me fervently, and said, 'Henri, bid me a good farewell.'

"I felt my heart breaking, but not a tear came. I followed him with my eyes as long as that consolation was possible; at last, a turn in the road suddenly hid him from me, and I never saw him again."

Despite his prediction of impending death, Frederic again regained much of his former strength, and with it hope returned. He began to speak of his recovery by summer.

Enforced idleness and separation from his Parisian friends were heavy burdens. At times he became depressed, and then blamed himself for not being thoroughly happy.

He had been devoting himself to Marie's education during this long undesired vacation, and he continued to do so at Biarritz. She was now nearly nine years old—as delicately fine in form and feature as a Dresden china figurine, but merry and mischievous and full of fun. She adored her father and entered into his playful moods with hilarious delight. To please him, she strove to be a worthy pupil. She was his whole school now, and he taught her languages and history and arithmetic and sciences as gravely as if she were studying for a doctorate.

In his professional way, his brother Charles was equally devoted. He left his practice in Paris to come to Biarritz and care for him, arriving, Frederic reported, "like a rainbow," in a torrent of rain.

"After examining, thumping, feeling and sounding me, he declares that Eaux-Bonnes has done wonders, and that I am well!" Frederic wrote exultingly to a friend, Eugène Rendu, toward the last days of October. "How can I, in the face of this verdict, permit myself to catch the shadow of cold or fever?"

With what they thought would be a complete recovery in view, Frederic and Amélie's minds were concentrated on preventing any setback; in this, the doctors considered the choice of a winter residence of first importance. The weather growing colder, they moved from beautiful Biarritz to a warmer apartment in Bayonne. But they knew they must soon seek a milder climate, and Spain seemed to assure sun and warmth. It would also bring new interest, for they had never traveled in that country.

During the first week of November Frederic and Amélie risked a journey of a little over a hundred miles to richly storied Burgos, the home of the Cid and a storehouse of pure Castilian art. They had had some fear that the trip might cause a relapse, but Frederic was able to write joyfully to Dr. Charles, now back in Paris, that the journey had been without accident and without fatigue. The riches of Spanish history and legend fascinated him, and he made copious notes for a book about his travels there.

So confident was he now that his health would be as good as ever that he suggested a pilgrimage of thanksgiving. Soon after arriving back in Bayonne he journeyed with Amélie and Marie to the shrine of Notre Dame de Buglosse, visiting also the nearby village of St. Vincent de Paul—renamed after the "father of the poor" who had been born there nearly three hundred years before.

Shortly after arriving at the shrine he received the sacrament of penance. In the confessional he found himself before an aged priest who, without any reason apparent to Frederic, entered into an eloquent exhortation, encouraging him to accept suffering and sorrow patiently and to bear them with courage.

Astounded, the penitent observed the saintly-looking priest with new interest and not a little bewilderment. The confessor's mixture of childlike simplicity and forceful counsel reminded him of what he had read of the personality of St. Vincent de Paul. But he was completely nonplussed by the good father's homily. Here he was, feeling unusually strong and well. Yet— as he was later to write to Lallier— the confessor "spoke of nothing but patient acceptance of pain, and submission to the will of God."

As he set out on his return to Bayonne, Ozanam pondered

the spiritual counsel he had received. Here was a priest he had never seen before, speaking to him of sickness and pain at the very time he felt better than he had in months. He shook his head in puzzlement. Finally he gave up the mystery, and joined Amélie and Marie in enjoying the scenery as their carriage rolled through the countryside behind its two sturdy horses.

About two weeks after returning to Bayonne, Frederic experienced a new and far more severe recurrence of weakness and fatigue.

The old priest at the shrine had been a true prophet. As he had implied, Frederic Ozanam would need immeasurable patience and resolute endurance in the eleven months now left to him.

CHAPTER 28

IN THEIR drives about Bayonne the Ozanams talked much with the shrewd and knowing peasants, and Amélie showed worried interest in their predictions of an extra-harsh winter in that far southwest corner of France.

She knew that if the Bayonne winter threatened to be unusually severe they must go to Italy. The doctors had recommended Pisa—and that meant a six-hundred-mile journey, much of it in a lurching mail coach.

Continuously inclement weather finally forced a decision, and early one morning in December the Ozanams set off for Italy.

The mail coach driver, whose practised eye could tell much about his passengers at a glance—even by the very manner of their boarding his vehicle—stood by to help them up the step. Eight-year-old Marie literally bounded in. Her mother ascended gracefully and gravely; here's a woman greatly troubled, thought the driver. For a worried frown fretted the fine, broad forehead beneath the waving combed-back hair. The father—ah, thought the driver, here's the reason for the woman's anxiety—a very sick man indeed. Distinguished, yes—with his studious bearing, his full beard, his greatcoat and his professorial top hat. But so thin and hollow-eyed! And evidently so weak. The driver wanted to assist him, but he knew from experience that a male invalid might resent a helping hand.

Marie carried a little basket of fruit, from which, leaning out the coach window, she offered an apple to the driver. She was joyously elated. Ahead was a thrilling ride, new scenes and continuous, exciting adventure—and at the end a milder climate that would soon make papa as well again as ever. Frederic, smiling fondly at her, found cheer in her innocent optimism, but Amélie was pensive and depressed as she looked at her child and her husband. She had long since noted the physical changes his sickness had worked in him. His features had become somewhat heavy; his bearing, stiff and feeble, was that of an elderly man. Their fellow passengers would have been surprised to learn that there was but seven years' difference between him and his beautiful young wife of thirty-two.

A few days before Christmas they arrived in Marseilles. There by prearrangement they met Amélie's mother, who was on a pilgrimage to Rome; she would travel with them as far as Pisa. In Marseilles they stayed at the home of relatives, with whom they celebrated Christmas.

At Toulon they saw the French fleet riding to anchor in the harbor, and Frederic thrilled with patriotic pride. While in Toulon another complication was added to his physical burdens; he suffered a seizure which physicians diagnosed as a heart attack. They prescribed digitalis. He recovered quickly and was soon able to continue the journey.

The little party, increased to four, was now traveling in a private carriage from which they could enjoy at leisure the scenic thrills of mountainous Italy. One day there was a thrill of another kind, when hatchet-armed men of villainous aspect drew close to their carriage as the horses were laboriously pulling it up a mountain road. Amélie and Marie and Madame Soulacroix shuddered when the brigands—as they thought them to be—cast toward the carriage what the frightened imaginations of the ladies interpreted as the most ferocious and menacing glances. But Frederic, somewhat to the indignation of the women, only laughed.

"These good fellows," he insisted, "are not one tenth the brigands we've been encountering at inns all along the way. We've been fleeced and despoiled far more, I assure you, by innkeepers these two hundred leagues than we'll ever be by such hard-working woodcutters as these."

Nevertheless, the women were only half reassured, and sighed in relief when the "brigands" turned off into the dark forest that bordered the road.

At last they arrived in Genoa, happy to rest for a few days before continuing on to Pisa. In Genoa Frederic sought out members of the St. Vincent de Paul Conference and met with them—as he had in Marseilles, Toulon, and Nice. In all four cities the Society was flourishing.

On a January day in 1853 the Ozanam party, long since tired of tedious carriage travel, boarded the *Marie Antoinette,* a small coastal vessel sailing from Genoa to Livorno. It was a rough crossing. With about eighty other passengers they arrived thoroughly drenched, even to the garments in their trunks.

The rain followed them to Pisa, and fell incessantly.

The weeks of travel had sapped his strength, but a meeting with the Pisan Vincentians now spurred Frederic on to a new activity despite his diminished reserves. The Vincentians informed him that the Grand Duke of Tuscany was suspicious of the St. Vincent de Paul Society, and had refused to sanction it. His opposition had stopped its growth, and was threatening its extinction throughout his dukedom. Ozanam felt defeated; he himself had sown the seeds of the Tuscan Conferences five years before.

The Grand Duke, whose rule was absolute, had been told

that some of the Society's members were in favor of a more representative government. Besides, had it not originated in France, that birthplace of all kinds of radical movements?

Ozanam determined to test the duke's opposition. He would help establish new Conferences, and encourage the growth and the increased activity of Conferences already established. Soon the Grand Duke would be faced with the necessity either of condemning the Society to prevent its further spread, or of sanctioning it.

It wasn't long before the Grand Duke acted. He sent his mother, the Dowager Grand Duchess, to Pisa. She arrived in the afternoon, and sent word to Ozanam to wait upon her that evening.

Such a summons amounted to a command, but Ozanam was very weak, his fever was high, and he had been ordered to bed. He would have sent his regrets to the great lady had he not been driven by devotion to the Society—that is to say, to charity. Against Amélie's pleas, but with her help, he arose, dressed, and was driven to the ducal residence. The Dowager Grand Duchess received him kindly. She was a motherly woman, as well as a cultivated aristocrat. She perceived that Frederic Ozanam was a sick man; that he had evidently come to see her at great sacrifice, and her heart went out to him.

She began by extolling Ozanam's work on Dante, and compared two Italian translations of it, with which she seemed thoroughly familiar. Her literary judgment commanded her guest's admiration. Almost imperceptibly she came to the subject that had brought her to Pisa—the St. Vincent de Paul Society.

"I have no doubt," she said finally, "that the objectives of your Society in France are most laudable. But here in Tuscany you are in a hotbed of radicalism and political intrigue. The enemies of the government know how to seize upon even an organization as beneficent in purpose as yours. They know how to make it a front and a cover for their designs. The Grand Duke is convinced that such men are among the members of your organization here in Tuscany. How then, monsieur, could my son be expected to sanction your Society?

Of course, if these suspected individuals were dismissed—well, that would, we feel, put a different face on the matter."

With this, the duchess produced a paper, from which she read several names. Ozanam recognized some of them. He knew they were the names of sincerely charitable men whose political views, evidently, were at variance with those of the Grand Duke. Aroused, his expressive blue-gray eyes glowed with indignation as he answered the duke's mother. He began by describing the birth and early years of the Society in France, and its rules—particularly the rigid rule against political activity within the Society.

"The essential point," he said, "is whether the rule is effectively applied within the Conferences of Tuscany. Fortunately, I can speak for the Conferences in Pisa; I have been attending their meetings. They are wholly devoted to charity. Never once have I heard politics mentioned by any member. Some of the men you name perhaps hold political views differing from those your son entertains. But I cannot believe they are intriguing against the government. And they certainly are not doing so within the membership of the Society of St. Vincent de Paul.

"I would recall to Your Grace that the Society's chief work is the saving of souls. Our members join out of charity toward others—but first, out of charity toward themselves. They find in their work for the poor a means to holiness. In political opinion they may not all be rigidly conservative. But all—as you and I—are trying to work out their salvation. When a man desiring to advance his spiritual welfare seeks to be admitted to our Society, it is incumbent upon the Society not to deny him what may be to him a great means of grace. Our only qualification is that he be a sincere Christian. And sincere Christians, as you well know, respect the authority of their rulers when it is exercised in accordance with justice and morality."

Before he took his leave the Dowager Grand Duchess, now completely won over, assured Frederic that she would report favorably to the Grand Duke. Within a few days the Government sent its formal sanction to the Conference at Florence.

It was not many weeks later that Frederic wrote to his old

Vincentian friend, Cornudet . . . "we now behold a new proselytism multiplying our Conferences. The ecclesiastical authorities lend it [the Society] their countenance. Religious orders commend it. Fervent laymen enroll in it. The Conferences are flourishing at Leghorn [Livorno] and Pisa; they are beginning to prosper at Florence and Pontadera; they are being established at Prato, about to be so at Volterra and Porto Ferrajo. Here, then, we shall have seven families of St. Vincent de Paul in this fair Tuscan land, where Catholicism was languishing, stifled, as it were, under the golden chains of Josephism."

Ozanam agreed to speak at the first meeting of the Florence Conference held after the ducal sanction had been received. His talk was a masterly exposition of the aims, the spirit, and the policy of the Society.

In Florence, the sanctioning of this new Catholic organization was important news. Journalists interviewed members of the new Conference, managed to obtain a full report of Ozanam's talk—which had been given in Italian—and published lengthy accounts of his address. The publicity surprised and displeased Frederic, for publicity violated the Society's rules and spirit. When he protested, the members agreed in principle, but advanced good reasons for an exception. The Society, they pointed out, was comparatively new in Italy, and newspaper reports of his talk might well sow the seeds of Conferences in other Italian cities.

Several weeks later, when their numbers had greatly increased, members of the Florence Conference again requested him to address them. He agreed on condition that his talk would be given no publicity. In his second address he discussed the true meaning of charity, and its spiritual benefits to those who practise it. So impressed were the members that they implored him to permit publication.

"We want to distribute copies in Loreto," they told him. "It will help us interest many good Catholics there in forming a Conference."

"How many copies would you require for Loreto?" Frederic asked.

"One hundred," was the response.

"Then print the needed one hundred copies," said Frederic. "They will, after all, be privately circulated."

But Tuscans are strongly individualistic, and readily disregard rules and prohibitions that seem to them unreasonable. "If," these Florentines argued among themselves, "one hundred copies of Ozanam's address are good, twelve hundred should be twelve times as effective." So they printed that number for distribution in several other cities.

Later, Frederic could not deny that this refusal to abide by his restriction seemed justified. For the wider distribution of his address had helped in the forming of Conferences in Sardinia, at Macerata, and in other cities.

CHAPTER 29

LIVING in Pisa, Frederic daily passed its celebrated leaning tower and thought of it as symbolizing his own condition.

"Since I left France," he wrote to Foisset in the first part of February, "the fatigue of traveling has broken my strength, and I am here, suffering, tottering, but without falling—almost like that tower that I pass daily. Its example should reassure me, and instruct me—because, leaning as it does, it has not ceased during some seven hundred years to serve God in its own way."

Measured by the degree of his physical weakness, his efforts on behalf of the St. Vincent de Paul Society were heroic. To visit the Florence Conference, for example, called for a round trip of a hundred miles by carriage—highly formidable to one enervated by continuous fever. Yet it was during this time that he made several onerous journeys to

Florence and other Tuscan cities to aid in the formation of Vincentian Conferences. All this time he was alternating between hope of recovery and despair of recovery, but in his recurring periods of hopelessness Amélie was an unfailing source of comfort.

Writing to Ampère he calls her his "visible guardian angel," and adds: "Since my sickness has become grave, you can hardly conceive the shifts and expedients she has, in her goodness of heart, discovered—not merely to relieve, but to cheer me. With what ingenious, patient, tireless tenderness she surrounds my life, divining, foreseeing every desire! Happily, God fortifies her for her burdens; she and my little Marie are in perfect health."

He was cheered also by many letters from relatives and friends. Madame Soulacroix, who was now in Rome, wrote frequently, as did his brothers, and his many cherished friends, including Ampère. The latter was still traveling in the United States, and sent him books by Everett, Agassiz, and Longfellow.

His will to live was strong, for he had much to live for and much work to do. This included, particularly, completion of the history which had so long occupied his mind.

Frederic's failing strength brought home to him, as his fortieth birthday approached, the brevity of man's sojourn in the material world and the vanity of human ambitions. For divine light he had recourse more than ever before to sacred scripture. From his youth he had been a daily reader of the Bible, and in its inspired words he now found new meaning and comfort.

This solace he desired to share with other invalids. With Amélie acting as his amanuensis, he began compilation of a book, *Le Livre des Malades*, consisting of scriptural passages that had brought him spiritual strength and consolation.

Seated in his Pisa apartment on this fortieth birthday, his mind dwelt on one of these selections—the Canticle of Ezechias, that king of Judah who dying had prayed to God for "the residue of his years," and to whom God had granted an added fifteen years of life.

Reading it, Frederic too longed with a great human longing for "the residue of his years." So intense became his desire for more earthly days in which to complete his work, to watch his child grow to womanhood, and to cherish the wife he loved so devotedly, that he was moved to counteract what seemed a temptation to rebellion. Grasping a quill pen in fingers that now held it less firmly than ever before, he began to copy the first verses of the Canticle as an introduction to a written act of resignation to God's will. In this he would have no immediate interruption, for Amélie and Marie were busy in other parts of the apartment with preparations for the celebration of his birthday.

Resting the Bible, which he had opened at the Canticle of Ezechias, against another book on his writing table, he copied the following verses as an appropriate preliminary to the act of resignation he was about to write:

I said in the midst of my days: I shall go to the gates of death. I sought for the residue of my years: I said, I shall not see the Lord God in the land of the living. I shall behold man no more. My life is at an end; it is rolled away from me, as a shepherd's tent. My life is cut off, as by a weaver; whilst I was yet but beginning, He cut me off. My eyes are weakened looking upward. Lord, I suffer violence; deliver Thou me. What shall I say, or what shall He answer me, whereas He Himself hath done it?

I shall recount to Thee all my years in the bitterness of my soul.

He paused awhile, sitting back and resting; then his pen began again to move deliberately over the paper as he set down his act of resignation to his Creator's designs for him, whatever they might be.

"Thus begins," he wrote, "the Canticle of Ezechias. I know not whether God will permit me to apply to myself the end of it [i.e., recovery from his sickness]. I know that I complete today my fortieth year, more than half the full period of a man's life. I know that I have a young and beloved wife, a

246

charming child, excellent brothers, a second mother, many friends, an honorable career, studies brought precisely to the point where they might serve as the foundations of a work long dreamed of. And yet I am a prey to a long and grievous malady, the more dangerous in that it conceals perhaps an utter exhaustion.

"Must I then leave all these things, Lord, that You Yourself have given me? Will You not be satisfied with a portion of the sacrifice? Which of my irregular affections must I immolate to You? Will You not accept the holocaust of my literary self-love, of my academic ambitions, of even my projected works, wherein perhaps there is mingled more of pride than of pure zeal for truth?

"If I sold half my books and gave the price to the poor and, confining myself to the bare duties of my position, were to devote the rest of my life to visiting the indigent, and teaching apprentices and soldiers, would You be satisfied, Lord, and would You leave me the happiness of growing old beside my wife, and of finishing the education of my child?"

Not in many weeks had he written so many words without pause. His strength spent, he put down his pen and stretched himself out on a nearby couch. Resting, he thought back through the years to his earliest memories of childhood, of his brothers and sisters who had died in infancy, of his own childhood sicknesses, and of how marvelous it was that he had been one of the three of his parents' fourteen children who had survived.

Soon he sat up again and resumed his writing.

"Perhaps, Lord, You do not will I should live much longer," he wrote. "You do not accept these interested offers; You reject my holocausts and sacrifices. It is myself You demand.

"It is written in the beginning of the book that I must do Your will, and I now say, 'Lord, I come.'

"I come, if You call me, and I have no right to complain. You have given forty years of life to a creature who came into this world sickly, fragile, destined to die ten times, if ten times he had not been rescued by the tenderness and intelligence of a father and mother. Let not my people be scandalized if You do not think meet now to work a miracle in order to save me! . . . Five years ago You did bring me back from close to death, and was not this delay granted to me to do penance and become better?"

He thought of all those praying for his recovery—his relatives, his friends, his Vincentian brothers, many priests and members of religious orders, and he continued:

"Ah! the prayers that were sent up to You then were heard. Why should those that are being offered now, and in so far greater number, on my behalf, be lost? Perhaps You will answer them, Lord, in another way. You will give me courage, resignation, peace of soul, and those indescribable consolations that accompany Your Real Presence. You will enable me to find in sickness a source of merit, and of blessings. And those blessings You will cause to fall on my wife and my child —and on all those to whom my labors perchance would have been less useful than my sufferings.

"If I express the years of my life with bitterness before You, it is because of the sins that have sullied them; but when I consider the graces that have enriched them, I look back upon them, Lord, with gratitude to You.

"If You chain me to this sickbed for the days that I have yet to live, they would be too short to thank You for the days that I have lived. Ah! if these pages be the last I ever write, may they be a hymn to Your goodness!"

He sought his couch again, and lay still a long time, meditating on the ways of Divine Wisdom. How frequently, he thought, did God permit unforeseen events to turn aside His servants from their most cherished projects. Even—and he smiled wanly at the memory—even as he himself had often diverted Marie from her childish concerns to more serious interests, closer to her father's heart.

True, everything he himself had desired and striven for and done, including his writings, had had for ultimate objectives the winning of souls. Yes, even his desired election to the Academy of Inscriptions; it would, he had thought, have added prestige to his books. However, the election to that body was, after all, a vanity—and he had given up hopes of it almost with a sense of relief. But to give up what was to have been the crowning achievement of his scholarship—his projected *History of Literature in the Middle Ages*—this was hard indeed. It had been so long contemplated. And nearly all his life had been, consciously or unconsciously, a preparation for the writing of the several volumes which would have comprised it. Into this great work he had planned to put all his learning and logic. He had hoped that it would bring the light of Christian truth to many unbelievers.

It had been thirteen years earlier that the concept of the *History* had first formed in his mind. And today only two of the several volumes he had planned were completed. One of these, *Dante and Catholic Philosophy in the Thirteenth Century*, had brought to scholars a new realization of the towering genius of Dante, of his loyal adherence to the Church, and of the learning and culture of the Middle Ages. This—though written first—was to have been the *History's* concluding volume. The other, *Civilization in the Fifth Century*, was to have been the first. And while this too had been completed, and published serially in *The New Era*, it would be several months before it appeared in book form.

Two years before he had determined to work very hard on the *History* and bring it to completion. He remembered himself as he had arrived home Good Friday afternoon from services at St. Sulpice. Standing at his writing table, he had written the preface to the *History*, setting forth its scope and objectives. He intended, he had stated in the preface, to refute Gibbon and other unbelieving historians who had sat in judgment on the Church; to show how Christianity had enabled love to triumph over brute force and, in the midst of the wreckage of the barbarous centuries, had saved the human mind.

Now these objectives of his *History*, unrealized, weighed heavily upon his spirit. His mind's eye saw a bookshelf sufficiently long to hold several volumes, but containing only two set far apart. The great gap between them was for those volumes that should have covered the seven centuries from the fifth to the thirteenth, and which must now remain unwritten.

His mind roamed back over the years and brought before

249

him the memory of precious hours that might have been devoted to the writing of his *History*, and were not. There were the many nights he had used up in giving talks to the working men in the crypt of St. Sulpice. And those lectures to the young men of the *Cercle Catholique*. And the endless hours he had given over to his newspaper articles, and to his Vincentian work. Some of his colleagues had been astonished at such prodigal "squandering" of his energies and time.

Well, that was all past now. Perhaps he should have thriftily conserved those hours so lavishly spent in day-to-day activities for his fellow students, for the workmen, for the poor of the Faubourg St. Marceau. Yes, that certainly would have been the course of worldly wisdom. It would probably have assured completion of what was to have been his life's great work, which now would never be completed. But, he asked himself, was the writing of history truly his life work, after all? The printed word could be powerful, yes; but it was potent only in the degree to which it inspired action. And were not the Lenten lectures at Notre Dame, and the day-after-day, week-after-week work of the humble members of the St. Vincent de Paul Society, that very action itself? Were not these activities—both originating, as it were, on the spur of the moment and in quick spontaneous response to the needs of his fellow men—were they not reaching and influencing thousands and tens of thousands of human hearts each year? In God's eyes were they not more valuable than authorship of a thousand books?

He felt sleepy, and as drowsiness crept over him he was thinking how well God plans men's lives for them when they give Him their best service from day to day—yes, infinitely better than they could plan them for themselves.

Solaced and strengthened, he slept peacefully, and when Amélie and Marie came to awaken him, they noted how serene he looked. He awoke as they stood silently gazing down at him. They brought him gaily to the table, and all during the birthday dinner he was as lighthearted as a boy.

CHAPTER **30**

SPRING advanced, turning to blue the gray skies above the brown city of Pisa, and the sun shone brightly nearly all day long. On his better days Frederic was now able to stroll with Amélie and Marie along the Arno and its borders of ancient, ruinous palaces. In obedience to medical directions he remained out of doors as much as possible, trying to be as inactive as the doctors and Amélie desired. But for him inactivity was virtually impossible. He was unhappy unless working at his writing, or laboring to spread the spiritual influence of the St. Vincent de Paul Society; these were his apostolate. He felt that he must work while yet there was light, even at the expense of his depleted health.

His activities were largely confined, now, to talking with those seeking guidance in St. Vincent de Paul work, to visiting and counseling Conferences of the Society in and about Pisa, and to his writing. Amélie understood how consoling to him these occupations were, and objected only when he overdid. When he wrote too long, she would place her hand gently on his brow and bid him rest.

To such counsel he resigned himself easily when it concerned his professional writing, which now was devoted solely to the completion of his *Pilgrimage to the Land of the Cid*. But he would not curtail the writing of letters that might advance the spiritual good of others.

With Jean-Jacques Ampère, particularly, he continued his correspondence long after writing had become an exhausting effort. Ampère he considered his special problem, and his letters disclose how eager he was that his friend should apply to himself what Frederic wrote about his own uncertainty of life.

Sea air was thought beneficial to such invalids as he, and so with the coming of May the Ozanams moved to San Jacopo, a sleepy seaside village near Livorno. It was an ideal spot in which to drowse away the days, yet not even here would Frederic's apostolic spirit let him rest. He found the energy to write a long, encouraging letter to a Monsieur Jérusalémy, a Jewish convert to Catholicism. He had met him in Pisa, and had given him introductory letters to friends in Paris.

> I should be inconsolable for my feebleness [he tells Monsieur Jérusalémy] if I did not find in the Psalms those cries of sorrow which David sends up to God, and which God finally answers by granting him pardon and peace. Ah, my friend, when one has the happiness to have become a Christian, it is a great honor to have been born an Israelite; to feel oneself the son of the patriarchs and prophets whose words are so beautiful that the church has found nothing more noble to put in the mouths of her children.
>
> During the long weeks of languor the Psalms have hardly been out of my hands. . . . The Gospel alone is superior to the Psalms of David . . . it is their fulfillment. . . . Such is the bond between the two Testaments that the Saviour Himself had no name dearer to Him than that of Son of David.

He mentions to Monsieur Jérusalémy his own remote Jewish ancestry. He names various friends to whom he has given him letters of introduction, but he voices the hope that his brother Charles will have introduced him into company which, Frederic says, he himself has found even better than the society of the salons, namely, the Vincentian Conferences.

The cause of the St. Vincent de Paul Society—that is, the cause of the love of Christ—continuously inspired and stimulated him to achievements that otherwise would have been beyond his strength. He visited various Conferences near San Jacopo, and to San Jacopo, too, Vincentians came to visit him, and to ask his counsel.

It was at San Jacopo that he heard how greatly a Conference was needed at Siena. The Grand Duke of Tuscany had recently divided the University of Pisa, ordering that half the students—mostly young noblemen—be located at Siena. These aristocrats were heirs to a tradition of exclusiveness. If ever students needed to develop greater love of God, through humble service to His poor, thought Frederic, they surely were the students at Siena.

To Siena, therefore, Ozanam decided to go. He would see Padre Pendola and lay before him the need of a Siena Conference. The padre, a professor at the University, was Frederic's warm, enthusiastic friend. Open-minded and progressive, he was a highly influential factor in the school's life, and noted, too, for his unbounded charity. Frederic pleasantly anticipated that once he had fully outlined the Society's work and worth, Padre Pendola would enter wholeheartedly into promoting a Conference for the Siena students.

Amélie pleaded, and Frederic's physicians warned, against the fifty-mile carriage journey to Siena. But Frederic persisted.

"Since God gives me the strength," he said, "I ought to employ it in His service." Perhaps it would be the last service, he told himself, that he would be able to perform for his Vincentians.

Amélie took over the management of the journey. She obtained the use of a large, comfortable carriage and a reliable driver. She engaged an excellent woman, skilled in nursing, from the seaside town of Antignano, a few miles distant. Marie, who loved to travel, would go along also.

Very early in the cool of a May morning they set off, driving past orchards and vineyards and forests, cottages and castles, seen clearly and vividly through the delicate transparency of the Tuscan air. About midway they dined and rested at a little inn, and arrived in Siena in the late afternoon. Here high, severe Gothic buildings had shielded the pavements from the blazing sun, and the coolness of the city's streets was a welcome relief from the heat of the long country road.

The padre, a vigorous fifty-three, welcomed them with open arms. He saw to it that they were lodged immediately, that food and drink were supplied, and that his good friend Professor Ozanam was thoroughly rested before settling down to a visit with him. He insisted that the Ozanams must remain for a leisurely period and declared himself completely at their service. They must see, he said, many things, including one of the two schools he had founded for the deaf, in whose education he was a pioneer.

When Frederic took up the matter of a Vincentian Conference at Siena the padre listened with deep interest. He deliberated long before he answered. And then he was entirely negative.

"Our Siena students," he explained, "are for the most part young nobles brought up in an aristocratic tradition and atmosphere that disincline them to consider any but their own narrow interests. They lack the primary requisites of membership in a Vincentian Conference—which are, as you have said, willingness to sacrifice self, and genuine humility. These attributes, my dear Ozanam, are, sad to say, quite foreign to our students at Siena."

All of Frederic's logic and eloquence failed to move the padre from his position. After a four-day visit he left Siena defeated, and low in spirit. At parting the padre had said that he would give the matter further thought, but it seemed to Ozanam that the good priest was merely being polite.

"What good am I any more in this world?" he said to Amélie, as they were driving out of the city. "I know how greatly Siena needs a Conference. And yet I have been unable to convince so charitable a man as Padre Pendola."

"Why, you were wonderfully persuasive!" reassured Amélie. "It isn't that the good padre lacks faith in you, or in the Society, but in the Siena students."

"I felt sure of success here, because I was sure I could not fail in the face of so clear a need," answered Frederic. "This is a service I very much wanted to do for the poor people of Siena, and for the spiritually poor students of Siena's University."

Amélie, standing beside Frederic as he lay on his couch, gazed from the terrace of their new home looking out over the blue Ligurian Sea. They had left San Jacopo, and moved

254

to the little village of Antignano, to a villa pleasantly situated beside the rocky coast. It provided more comforts than their quarters at San Jacopo, and commanded an inspiring view of shore and sea.

During these long, light, radiant July days in Antignano songbirds made melody everywhere, day and night, and flowers were blooming as if the summer season would never end. Now Amélie and Frederic watched, out on the blue sea, the fast *feluccas* with their lateen sails and narrow hulls silhouetted against the crimson glory of the setting sun, as they beat into harbor against a spanking offshore wind.

"What beauty!" exclaimed Amélie. "And the people are so much a part of it—so warmhearted, so lighthearted. And so generous, too—and each one so much himself. They're as picturesque as their sailboats, and as graceful. It seems to me that all this beauty surrounding them enters into every fiber of their being."

"I also love this gorgeous land, and these simple fishermen and peasants," answered Frederic. "But our work, Amélie, lies in Paris."

He had been feeling more poorly since his journey to Siena. The physical strain had told on him. He had suffered a psychological letdown, too, at his failure to win over Padre Pendola.

"There is so much to be done in Paris," he continued. "And here I can accomplish nothing more, not even for the Society. I fear I was too insistent during my talk with the padre; I probably offended him. It seems that God no longer desires to bless my efforts."

He had talked thus once before, in San Jacopo, and Amélie had sought to cheer and distract him with a whimsical plan that for the moment had then succeeded in diverting him.

"Don't forget my plan for living in Italy, Frederic," she now said, putting an arm about his shoulders. "God wants you to rest your mind and body, and to be carefree from now on. So when you recover we must sell all our books, and with the money buy a good, solid boat, and with Marie sail along this coast until we find the village that suits us best. And there we'll live in peace and beauty, utterly free from thought of tomorrow."

"Ah," she thought, dreading the future and the inevitable, "if only there could be no tomorrow."

The fishing boats were close to shore now, and the fishermen's voices were heard faintly against the wind, singing a lilting folksong of the district.

"Yes, we must buy a boat," continued Amélie, "and go off singing with these fishermen of Antignano—or, if you'd rather, among the coral fishers of Sicily or Sardinia."

"I have another dream," said Frederic, smiling. "It's about a boat that will bear us back to *la patrie*."

"Ah, you are hungry for the salons," said Amélie, teasing. "You are a victim of the Marquis de Salvo's eloquence," she said, referring to a letter Frederic had received the day before. "He made you wish you were present again among the intellectual celebrities foregathering at his place. Yes—and at Madame Swetchine's, and at Madame Récamier's."

But Frederic was not at all preoccupied with thoughts of Parisian salons. He was a Frenchman, and he longed to see his country once again—Paris and his Vincentian brothers, the Sorbonne and his students. That longing, he feared, might never be satisfied, and he wasted no further time thinking about it. Instead, his apostolically practical mind continued to pursue the idea of a Siena Conference.

"Do you think Padre Pendola would think me too persistent were I to write him another plea for the founding of a Conference?" he asked Amélie.

"How could he blame you for being ardent in such a cause!" she answered.

"Then I shall write to him at once," said Frederic.

Amélie wanted him to dictate the letter to her, to save his energy, but he preferred to write it himself.

"The padre knows my hand," he said, taking one of his quill pens and dipping it in the ink. "And there's something about one's own handwriting that makes a message seem more personal and direct."

The letter was to be Ozanam's last testimony to the spiritual benefits that membership in the St. Vincent de Paul

Society had brought to him, and can bring to those who sincerely engage in its work.

He began by paying eloquent tribute to the padre's character and works, and to his generosity in burdening them with gifts at the conclusion of their recent visit to Siena. From this he passed to his objectives.

"Ah, well, my Reverend Father," he wrote, "all that you have done for me and for my little family touched me less than the hope"—*was the padre just being polite?* Frederic asked himself—"you held out to me at the last for [the Society of] St. Vincent de Paul. This dear Society, also, is my family. It was the means, next to God, of preserving my faith after I had left my good and pious parents. I love it, therefore, and cling to it with all my heart. And it has been a joy to me to see the good seed growing and prospering in Tuscan soil.

"Above all, I have seen it do so much good, sustain so many young men in the path of virtue, and inspire a smaller number with such wonderful zeal! We have Conferences in Quebec and Mexico. We have them at Jerusalem. We most certainly have one in Paradise, for during the twenty years that we have existed at least a thousand members have taken the road to a better world. How, then, is it possible that we should not have one at Siena, which is called the antechamber of paradise? How is it possible that in the city of Our Blessed Lady a work whose chief patroness she is should not succeed? . . . You have rich children. O my Father, what a useful and beneficent lesson—and how strengthening to enervated hearts —to show them the poor; that is, to show them Jesus Christ not only in images painted by the great masters, but to show them Jesus Christ in the persons of the poor."

He paused to trim his quill with the very sharp penknife which always rested conveniently on the desk, and resumed: "We have often talked together of the frailty, the frivolity and the emptiness of even Christian men among the nobility of France and Italy. . . . It is necessary that these young noblemen know what hunger and thirst, and an empty breadbox are. It is necessary that they see the miserable poor, the sick children, the children crying from hunger. It is necessary for them to see them, that they may love them. The sight would awaken their hearts, else they are a lost generation. But we should never permit ourselves to believe in the death of a young Christian soul. 'She is not dead, but she sleeps.' "

He lacked strength to go on, and was compelled to lie on the couch and rest awhile. When he arose and again took his seat at the little writing desk, the concluding words flowed quickly from his pen.

"Before long," he assures Padre Pendola, "your better young men, divided into small groups of three or four, and accompanied by a master, will be ascending the poor man's stairs. You will see them returning sad, and at the same time happy; sad at the sight of the wretchedness they have seen, happy at having been able to relieve it, even if ever so little.

"Some will go about it coldly; perhaps without intelligence; others, on the contrary, will take fire at the work, and will pass on their heat to places where no Conferences now exist. . . . And out of all these good works a share will be taken, and added to the crown which God is preparing for Padre Pendola, but which He will give him, I hope, as late as possible.

"And now I realize that I am practising the old French proverb, 'the sexton preaches to his pastor!' No, my Father, I am not preaching; it is your example, it is your own words, it is your charity that are preaching to me, that bid me leave this good work confidently in your hands."

He signed and dated this eloquently persuasive letter, and asked that it be sent off at once.

The date was July 19, the feast of St. Vincent de Paul.

Frederic had expected several days to pass before arrival of an answer from the padre. But the very next day, the post brought him a brief note from Padre Pendola!

"At last, my dear friend," the padre had written, "yesterday, the feast of St. Vincent de Paul, I founded two Conferences —one in my college, the other in the city."

Frederic was momentarily puzzled.

"How could the padre have acted so quickly?" he asked Amélie, rereading the note to her.

Then, a great light flooding his mind, he burst into laughter.

258

"Why," he exploded, "the padre obviously sent this *before* receiving my letter! And that means he must have been in-augurating those two Siena Conferences during the very hours I was so laboriously writing him yesterday. And doesn't that mean, Amélie, that for some days past he must have been busy promoting the Conferences? Note that he doesn't acknowledge my letter—which he certainly would have done had he received it. Yes, he must have started several days ago to organize the two Conferences he speaks of."

"Why two?" asked Amélie.

"I suggested one in the city, as well as one in the university," said Frederic. "The city Conference will have a nucleus of day students."

He looked at his wife with a weary smile.

"To think of all that labor the letter to the padre cost me!" he said ruefully. "Well, again Providence teaches me a lesson in humility and faith. My long letter to the padre, with all its persuasive pleas and arguments, might just as well have not been written. When will I learn to depend on Our Lord and His saints more, and on myself less?"

"That good letter of yours will serve a purpose, have no fear," Amélie assured him. "It will be treasured by the Siena Conferences, and will inspire them." Then, ever quick to fortify his morale, she added: "You are not at all the unprofitable servant you accused yourself of being. Your talks must have won over the padre, else there would have been no Conferences established in Siena."

"It was St. Vincent de Paul, rather, who with God's permission changed the padre's mind," declared Frederic. "Undoubtedly the good Lord prefers our humble prayers to heaven rather than our clever pleas to our fellows here below.

"Now the young Tuscan noblemen will see for themselves the results of social injustice. In a few years they will be in positions of leadership, and through the lessons they'll learn as Vincentians they'll be better able to help solve the problems of their less privileged brethren."

CHAPTER 31

DESPITE steadily declining health, Frederic Ozanam continued optimistic about his recovery though now in ever lessening degree. His was the optimism that seems to accompany tuberculosis, the patient's hope persisting even as the ravages of the disease increase and the possibilities of regaining health become less and less.

In early June, when he had felt considerably stronger, he had even cherished the thought of returning to Paris by summer. Now, only three weeks later, he gave up the idea, for new and alarming symptoms had developed. He had begun to suffer severe intermittent pains. Though neither he nor his physicians were aware of the cause, the tuberculosis had attacked the kidneys.[1] Every new day the pains recurred with increasing severity.

He made known through Ampère that he was abandoning his candidacy for election to the Academy, describing himself as a hermit who had no business to think of such preference.

Ampère ceased promoting Frederic for membership in that distinguished body, but in the *Revue des Deux Mondes* he brilliantly reviewed Frederic's *Poètes Franciscains*. In thanking him, Ozanam wrote: ". . . your regrets for the absent professor"—referring to himself—"touched me to the heart." He informs Ampère that "the General of the Franciscan Order, from the silence of his cell in the Ara Coeli, has addressed his gratitude to me with a diploma which is not the least pre-

---

1 This was the diagnosis made many years later by doctors in the Ozanam family. In the light of more advanced medical knowledge than was available in 1853, they were able to study the record of an autopsy made by Dr. Charles Ozanam, Frederic's brother.

cious of my titles. He places me on the list of benefactors of the Franciscan family, and associates me with the merits of the Friars Minor, who work and pray for all the world."

Among the other "precious titles" to which he refers was membership in the Academy de la Crusca of Florence, to which he had recently been elected.

The sick and suffering man maintained a cheerful attitude, and his letters reveal his good spirits and good humor. In one to his friend Eugène Rendu he even managed to be merry. Toward the middle of July Rendu wrote Frederic that he had at last become engaged and was to marry a lovely young lady. Ozanam replies with a recital of the delighted remarks he and Amélie voiced on hearing the news: "Now he's caught, that uncatchable," he reports them as saying, "and that free heart is bound in chains! . . . The good spirits who intended to bestow this wife upon him took care to load her with their gifts. . . . Is it due to our example that you choose the twenty-third for your wedding? The twenty-third brings happiness," he adds, referring to his own wedding date.

He was more cheerful than his health gave him right to be, thought Amélie, as she sat beside his couch on their terrace overlooking the Ligurian Sea. He was dictating to her the last part of the *Pilgrimage to the Land of the Cid,* which he was determined to complete. He was able to work only a few minutes without rest, for he was very weak; sustained intensity of thought was becoming as difficult as sustained physical activity had been these many weeks.

The sun was sinking in golden glory beneath the watery horizon when he stopped dictating and said: "I've troubled you enough for the present. Shall we go over to the church?"

Amélie helped him to arise from the couch. He was glad to lean on her slightly as they walked the short distance to the ancient fortress which dated from the Saracen invasions and which housed the church. There they knelt and prayed, and Frederic thanked his Sacramental Lord for all the blessings he had known in life, and for his sickness too, and asked Him again, as he had so often from his youth, to do with him as He would.

They walked back through the soft purple of the Tuscan twilight to the terrace of their home. Again, with Frederic reclining on his couch, they gazed on the sea and the sky and watched the shadows deepen over land and water, as the eloquent, wordless stars took their accustomed places in the darkening firmament and commenced their unhurried progress toward a new dawn.

"When one looks at God through His creation, how can one fail to realize that His paradise must begin now, in this world!" Frederic exclaimed. "How can we have any fear, excepting the filial fear of offending the God who loves us so much as to surround us with majestic beauty? And how can one doubt that he who lives with the love of God in his heart is already enjoying here, on this earth, a foretaste of heaven? Suffering, yes, we all have, and in God's mysterious providence, we must have. But how insignificant, Amélie, that suffering is, compared to the glory that is to come—and which we see reflected in these countless suns that sing of their Creator!"

He went on to mention that their Tuscan neighbors were ever singing, too, because they were good and happy, and to marvel at their unfailing kindness as well as the deep personal interest in his welfare shown by his brothers of the St. Vincent de Paul Society.

"I fear one of our Tuscan noblemen was disappointed in not being permitted to pay you his respects personally this afternoon," said Amélie.

"I saw his carriage through my window," replied Frederic. "I must admit that its crest was most impressive. He did me great honor in desiring to make my acquaintance. But I was too exhausted to engage in social conversation."

Again leaning on Amélie's arm, he went inside, and was about to retire for the night when a knocking was heard on the outer door. It was a young man, their little servant girl reported, who had walked there from Livorno. He wanted to speak to the Signore, to learn how to establish a Conference in his parish.

"Show him in," said Frederic instantly.

He talked with the young man for an hour, seeking to instill in him the Vincentian spirit.

262

He was ever ready to welcome his Vincentian brothers, though every effort was now a severe strain on his feeble resources. Afternoons brought higher temperatures and greater weakness, and the infection's continuing inroads caused increasing pain.

The hot weather of July and August intensified his suffering. The fever could be alleviated by ice applications, but ice was unknown in Antignano's primitive economy. The nearest source was Livorno. Two Vincentians there, the Benilacqua brothers, realizing that ice packs would relieve the sufferer, took it upon themselves to carry daily a supply of ice all the way from Livorno to the Ozanam villa. They always brought, also, a floral bouquet. To their sensitive Tuscan minds, the comfort of beauty was also necessary to the sick.

CHAPTER 32

IN PARIS, Dr. Charles Ozanam was becoming increasingly alarmed over his brother's condition, for Amélie's letters during the first days of August were a succession of adverse reports. Finally, a telegram from Antignano caused him to hurry there by the new railroad and by carriage; it stated that Frederic had become extremely weak.

He found the patient shockingly debilitated, with legs swollen, and painful seizures becoming more frequent and more intense. The day Dr. Charles arrived in Antignano was hot, and fever was torturing the invalid.

Early that evening the Benilacqua brothers had, as usual, brought ice from Livorno. Seeing how desperately the sufferer needed its cooling comfort, they decided between themselves that a much larger supply was required.

About midnight Dr. Charles and Amélie, sitting by Frederic's bedside, were startled by the sound of pebbles rattling against the windowpane. Dr. Charles looked out and saw the two Vincentians—a great basket of ice, covered with sawdust, between them. They had made a second journey on foot all the way to Livorno and back.

They brought the basket into the kitchen, and were about to start out again on the three-and-a-half-mile return walk to their home, when Amélie remonstrated. She insisted that they rest the remainder of the night in Antignano. There was a small cabin on the villa grounds, and she prepared beds for them there. From then on the Benilacquas, after bringing ice from Livorno, remained on duty in the cabin, ready to perform any service Professor Ozanam's condition might require. Other friends and acquaintances from Livorno and from nearby villages also desired to do something for the sick man. The sympathetic people of Antignano brought flowers and fruits and prize fish from their catches.

Frederic was deeply grateful. One morning he opened his will to add a codicil acknowledging the charity of the villagers and of benefactors in Livorno. He had written the will on his birthday the previous April, at the time he had written the prayer of resignation commencing with the lines from the Canticle of Ezechias.

Now, lying on his couch, he perused the will again, looking for the proper place to insert an expression of gratitude to his Italian friends.

"In the name of the Father, and of the Son, and of the Holy Spirit, Amen," he read. "Today, the twenty-third of April, 1853, at the moment of completing my fortieth year, in the anxiety of a grave sickness, suffering in body, but sound in mind, I write in brief my last will and testament, proposing to set it forth more fully when I shall have the strength."

He smiled now at his optimism of only four months before. Wondering whether he would have the strength to add even an additional line of thankfulness to his Antignano and Livorno benefactors, he read on: "I commit my soul to Jesus Christ my Saviour, fearing because of my sins, but trusting in the Infinite Mercy. I die in the bosom of the Catholic, Apostolic, and Roman Church. I have known the misgivings of the present age, but all my life has convinced me that there is no rest for the mind and the heart except in the faith of that Church, and under her authority. If I attach any value to my long studies, it is because they give the right to entreat those I love to remain faithful to a religion in which I found light and peace.

"My supreme prayer to my wife, my child, my brother and brothers-in-law, and all those who may be born of them, is that they persevere in the faith in spite of the humiliations, the scandals, and the desertions they shall witness."

He paused in his reading to sip water, for fever was parching his lips, and then resumed his scanning of the will: "To my tender Amélie, who has been the joy and the charm of my life, and whose devoted care has consoled all my sufferings, I address a farewell—short, like all earthly things. I thank her, I bless her, I await her. It is only in heaven that I shall be able to give her back all the love she merits. I give to my child the blessing of the patriarchs, in the name of the Father, and of the Son, and of the Holy Spirit. It grieves me not to be able to carry on further the dear labor of her education, but I confide it without reluctance to her virtuous mother."

He scrutinized that part of the will in which he named his brothers, other relatives and his friends. Among the last he had mentioned Noirot, Ampère, Pessonneau, Lallier and Dufieux, and in this section he wrote in the words: "I thank once more all those who have been kind to me," inserting the names of the brothers Benilacqua, of Dr. Prato and of the Reverend Père Massuces, superior of the Lazarists of Livorno, who was his confessor.

He rested a few moments, and then read the will's concluding sentences: "I implore the prayers of my friends of the Society of St. Vincent de Paul, and of my friends in Lyons. Let not your zeal be slackened by those who say, *He is in heaven.* Pray unceasingly for one who loved you all much, but who has sinned much. Aided by your supplications, dear, kind friends, I shall leave this world with less fear. I firmly trust that we shall not be separated, and that I shall remain in the midst of you until you rejoin me.

265

"May the blessing of God the Father, and of the Son, and of the Holy Spirit rest upon you all. Amen."

He put down the document, his strength thoroughly spent.

"There are so many things one desires to say to those he is about to leave," he thought. "Now I lack the strength to write them."

He heard Amélie coming, and fearing that the sight of the will might sadden her, slipped it into a drawer in the little table. He picked up his Bible, which more than ever now was his daily companion.

As Amélie stood over his couch, he read aloud from it a passage he had recently applied to himself: "It has been written at the beginning of the Book that I should do Thy will, my God. I have willed it, and placed the law in the midst of my heart."

From the beginning of August he had been unable to assist at Mass. But when August fifteenth brought the feast of the Blessed Virgin's Assumption into Heaven, he arose and dressed, and announced that he would go to Mass. Refusing a carriage for the short distance, he said to Amélie: "This may be my last walk in this world, and I desire to make it a pilgrimage to Our Lord and His Blessed Mother."

The aged parish priest of Antignano, too, was bedridden with a sickness that must soon bring death, and for a long time had been unable to celebrate Mass. But when the old padre heard that Frederic Ozanam was on his way to the church, he arose and dressed.

"I'm too weak to celebrate Mass," he said, "but I'm not too weak to claim the privilege of giving Holy Communion to this man who has been the instrument of so much good in our poor world."

Meanwhile Frederic, supported by his brother Charles on one side, and Amélie on the other, with Marie walking solemnly beside her mother, was slowly making his way to the church. As he neared it, he passed by little knots of villagers in fiesta attire. They greeted him with low-voiced salutations, for they regarded this learned and humble man with respect approaching reverence.

266

As the Ozanams entered the ancient edifice they beheld, behind the lambent, mellow flames of hundreds of candles, a gorgeous array of flowers about the altars. From chancel to vestibule, the whole church glowed with color as the villagers in their gala costumes filled the nave and transept.

When time came to approach the Communion rail, the congregation with a fine, natural delicacy remained kneeling, waiting until the emaciated savant arose and, helped by Charles and Amélie, went forward and knelt before the altar.

The old priest, summoning all his strength, walked unassisted to him and administered the sacrament. Then the padre's strength gave out, and he was forced to lean heavily on the acolyte's shoulder as he handed the ciborium to the waiting celebrant and then made his way to the sacristy.

It was to be the last time the aged priest would appear before the altar, and this was the last Mass at which Frederic would assist.

Late that afternoon, Frederic and Amélie were on the terrace of their villa, he reclining on his couch, and she sitting a little behind him, as was now her habit, that he might not see the tears that so frequently these days welled into her eyes. So was she sitting now, gazing upon her husband, holding close to her spirit the pure, unselfish love with which he had blessed her life through twelve devoted years. The sun was sinking into the sea, and far away the lateen-rigged fishing boats were sailing before a light breeze toward the shore. The day was dying in calm splendor, and there was serenity, too, in Frederic's countenance. God, she reflected, had enriched him with many spiritual gifts, including wisdom, and thinking thus she was moved to ask, "Which of God's gifts, Frederic, do you think is to be prized the most?"

His answer came instantly.

"Peace of heart," he said. "Without peace of heart we may possess everything else, yet be unhappy. With it, we can bear the most difficult trials, and the approach of death."

There was a long silence.

Then Amélie said—for she thought to cheer him: "How few of us achieve so much good for the world as you have since you were a very young man in Lyons. That 'little Society' you helped to found and guide is spreading all over the world, and growing daily. And the Lenten lectures at Notre Dame—the Abbé Noirot tells me that they are the greatest single force in Paris against the spread of skepticism. The books you have written, too, and the students you've taught—they're carrying on your work, day in and day out."

"Ah, my teaching," sighed Frederic, and he remained silent awhile, thinking of his beloved University.

"My poor Sorbonne!" he exclaimed, longingly. "How often my thoughts go back to it—to its blackened walls, its bleak courtyard, its begrimed halls. To those halls, Amélie, that I've so often seen filled with the generous youth of Paris! . . . My darling, next to the infinite consolations a Catholic finds at the foot of the altar, and"—turning and placing a thin, pale hand on hers—"next to the joys of family life, I know of no greater happiness than that of addressing young men who have heart and intelligence. How I have longed to return to my dear Alma Mater and to my students."

"Frederic," said Amélie, "your books will continue teaching for you, even if you never return to the classroom."

He shook his head sadly.

"What a grand scheme I laid out for my literary history," he said. "And how short I've fallen of its accomplishment! No, Amélie, from the literary viewpoint I fear I've lived to little purpose. But if anything consoles me for leaving this world without having achieved what I wished to do, it is that I've always worked in the service of truth."

In their twelve years of married life, Frederic and Amélie had celebrated one hundred and fourty-four "wedding anniversaries"—for on the twenty-third of each month Frederic unfailingly made some special commemoration of their wedding day.

This August "anniversary," he felt, might be his last, and with special care he had selected a memento. The Abbé Alphonse had arrived the morning before, and later in the day had driven Frederic in a carriage along the seashore. Frederic had observed a beautiful myrtle tree in flower and made a mental note of its exact location. On the morning of the twenty-third, he asked the Benilacqua brothers to bring him a flowering branch from the tree. They selected a particularly full branch, rich with pure white flowers nestling among its ovate leaves.

Presenting this to Amélie, he said: "This is from the tree the ancients considered sacred to Venus—but I convert it from paganism by making it the missionary of my love for you."

Her smile at his fancy answered his, and she embraced him. Then he added, still lightly, but with a serious undertone: "Indeed, my darling, you are a myrtle tree—thoroughly Christianized, of course—for its ever-green leaves speak of the eternal springtime of your spirit, and its snowy blossoms of your soul's white beauty. May every myrtle tree you ever come upon tell you once again how I have loved you."

That afternoon after all had left his room that he might rest, he lay for some time contemplating a copy of a painting by Fra Angelico, depicting guardian angels welcoming into heaven the souls they had protected on earth. He had often derived consolation from the thoughts the picture suggested, and now the idea came to him of making it a last memento, a final farewell gift, to Amélie.

Taking up the pad at his bedside, he wrote a note directing that after his death the picture be presented to her whom he had so often referred to as his "earthly guardian angel." Then, after lengthy concentration, he added three stanzas which had been writing themselves in his mind during his previous contemplations, and which he now set down that she might share those sentiments the Fra Angelico had suggested to him. It was to be the last of all the strong and graceful poems he had written to her over the years. Indeed, these words, which she was to read only after his death, were the last that were to come from his pen:

> These guardian angels welcome souls that gain
> To Paradise, who here were in their care;
> But you, my guardian angel, will remain
> To open heaven for me with your prayer.

You will remain a few, fast-fleeting years
To guide and guard the child who was our joy.
Teach her to think of me. All that endears
Your soul to mine, make hers.—This will employ

Your life and love until we meet once more
In Love's abode. Ah, love there will transcend
As heaven, earth, all it had been before
—And in God's sight will never know an end.

He read the verse over, then folded the paper, and extracted his will from a drawer in the bedside stand. He opened it, and refolded it with the farewell poem inside.

Despite his gracious reference to his wife as his "guardian angel," Frederic knew he had a heavenly guardian angel, also—and he humbly feared that this angel would have a long wait for him in heaven. All who knew him considered him a person of extraordinary virtue, but he thought of himself as a great failure in the eyes of God. This resulted from his deep realization of the infinite perfection and generosity of the Creator, and of man's limitless obligation to Him. Only his appreciation of the fact that that Creator is Love itself enabled him to face the thought of the Divine judgment.

One evening, shortly after he had written his poetic farewell to her, he and Amélie were on the terrace, and he was accusing himself of many times having fallen short of what God had a right to expect of him.

"Why do you trouble your mind with such self-accusations," remonstrated Amélie, gently, "you who have always been such a zealous apostle of charity and truth?"

Frederic looked at her long and sadly.

"Ah, Amélie," he said at last, "as one draws nearer to the judgment of all his earthly actions, how much more clearly he sees eternal values. How much more he realizes his own sinfulness, and the holiness of God."

He was, indeed, fast approaching the judgment of his earthly actions.

Two months before he had written to Ampère, "If July and August, who pass for being great physicians, treat me well, I shall be cured this autumn." He had even resumed, though against Amélie's protestations, his professional writing, and he had been able to summon the strength to travel to Siena. Long before the Siena journey, his disease had probably developed to a point that made recovery impossible. But the strain of the Siena trip undoubtedly weakened him. It was now nearly the last of August, and July and August had proved but poor physicians.

During August his suffering increased, and toward the end of that month the full realization came to him that he must soon die. He desired to die in France, and he asked his brothers to hasten preparations for his journey home.

They learned that a good ship was scheduled to sail from Livorno on August 31, and preparations for departure were hurriedly made. Early on the morning of the sailing day, when the carriage that was to carry the Ozanams to the Livorno docks drew up before the villa, Frederic asked his brothers to wait. With Amélie assisting him, he walked slowly out to the terrace and once again gazed on that rocky shore where he had so often sat long hours in the sun, contemplating the timelessness of man's soul as he listened to the ceaseless cadence of the timeless sea. Lifting up his hands, he said, "O my God! I thank You for the afflictions and the sufferings You have sent me in this place; accept them in expiation of my sins."

Seeing the heartbreak in Amélie's eyes, he put an arm weakly about her and continued, "My dear, I bless Him for all the consolations He has given me through you—and I should like you, too, to give thanks with me for my sufferings."

Then he turned slowly and, with Amélie supporting him, walked toward the waiting vehicle. His brothers assisted him into the carriage, and after they had seated Amélie and Marie, the party set off along the seashore road toward Livorno. The morning was radiant, the air heavy with the fragrance of the blooming hedges bordering the road, and in every tree gaily feathered songsters piped their liquid music. It seemed as if Italy, the land of Frederic's birth, the foster-mother of his intellect, had donned her most gorgeous attire, with perfumed flowers on her breast and a plumage of songbirds in her hair, to bid this illustrious Christian son of hers a fitting, fond farewell.

When they arrived at the Livorno docks and waiting ship, the Abbé Alphonse and Dr. Charles carried Frederic up the gangplank to the deck; their burden was pitifully light. He asked not to be taken below at once, but reclined in a deck chair, facing the shore of the beautiful, warmhearted Italy he loved. Many friends were waiting to say adieu, including priests, religious, and members of the St. Vincent de Paul Society. Farewells were brief; the sick man was close to exhaustion. As the visitors made their sad departure, many were weeping silent tears. Soon the anchor was weighed, and the ship began to slip out of the great Livorno harbor. Frederic remained on deck till the shore was a hazy outline; then his brothers carried him below.

It was a smooth, rapid voyage, with following winds. They put in at Corsica's port of Bastia, landed and received cargo, and were off for Marseilles.

At the dock in Marseilles, Madame Soulacroix and others of Amélie's family were waiting. Their presence seemed to lift a load of concern off Frederic's mind, and his tone of voice was almost buoyant as, calling upon all his little strength, he said: "Behold one journey completed. I shall make another. But I shall make it in tranquility. Now that I've placed Amélie and Marie in your arms, God may do what he sees fit with me. . . . A few days in Marseilles," he added, "and we'll be off for Paris!"

One earthly hope still was left to him—the hope of dying in the city which had been the scene of most of his unceasing apostolate.

Relatives living in Marseilles had provided living quarters for the Ozanams, and members of the city's Vincentian Conferences came, offering their services. Told of these visits, Frederic smiled his appreciation; he spoke very seldom now. A smile, a nod, the pressure of a hand made known his gratitude to those waiting on him.

Dr. Charles, commenting to the Abbé Alphonse on Frederic's optimistic declaration that he'd soon be on his way to

Paris, gave it as his opinion that Frederic would never leave Marseilles alive.

"I think Frederic was trying to cheer us," replied the Abbé. "If he was serious then, I'm certain that now he's not thinking of journeying on to any earthly city."

The next day Frederic made plain to all his realization that death was now quite near. He asked for a priest, that he might receive the last sacraments. When the priest came, he made his last confession, received Viaticum, and was anointed with the consecrated oil of the sacrament of Extreme Unction.

Afterward, the Abbé Alphonse, remembering Frederic's overpowering consciousness of God's justice, and how often he had spoken of it during their conversations in Antignano, commenced to talk to him of God's goodness and mercy.

"Offer your soul to Him," advised the Abbé, "confidently, trustingly, without fear."

"Why should I fear Him?" asked Frederic, with a note of surprise that indicated all his former dread had been forgotten. "Why should I fear Him," he repeated, "when I love Him so!"

During the next few days his weakness increased.

Shortly before eight o'clock in the evening of September 8, he lifted his hands, and gazing as if startled by a presence only he could see, cried out in a penetrating voice, "My God, my God, have pity on me!"

He fell back with a deep sigh. There followed the brief inward struggle that marks that separation the Creator never intended—the rending of the human soul from the body.

The Abbé Alphonse was leading Amélie and the other relatives in prayers for the dying. In the next room, a group of Vincentians was praying silently.

Frederic Ozanam's long martyrdom was ended.

It was the feast of the birth of the Mother of God—and he, newborn, was in the presence of his Maker.

APPENDIX

1.

Frederic Ozanam's burial place.—After a Solemn Requiem Mass in the Church of St. Sulpice in Paris, the body of Frederic Ozanam was placed temporarily in the crypt of that church.

When the time came to remove the coffin to a permanent burial place, Madame Ozanam ardently desired that it be entombed in another crypt instead of in the earth. This preference she made known to Père Lacordaire, then Dominican Provincial, and he said without hesitation: "You must transfer the body to the 'Carmes,' "—then under Dominican supervision. This was done.

This crypt was within cloistered precincts, to which at that time Madame Ozanam did not have the special permission necessary for entrance. She learned, however, that her husband's tomb was exactly under the Chapel of the Holy Angels, where a few months before she had seen the vision of an inscription on the wall, reading: "Here lies Anthony Frederic Ozanam."

Vincentians have erected a monument over the crypt. It bears the words: "He recalled the souls of young men to the Faith."

2.

The cause for beatification of Frederic Ozanam.—On July, 2 1956, Canon Geraud, Superior of the Institut Saint-Sulpice, as Postulator of this cause, placed it before the Sacred Congregation of Rites in Rome. This action followed two official investigations of Ozanam's life. The first was a diocesan process. The second, while under authority of the Holy See, was still a preliminary informational process.

Should Ozanam's beatification eventually be decreed it

would not, of course, be in recognition of his achievements—of which the founding of the St. Vincent de Paul Society is today the most noted. It would, rather, result because the Church, after most thorough investigation, finds that he was a person of heroic virtue, and that there exists unmistakable proof of a miracle, or miracles, obtained through his intercession.

For many years Vincentians, at every Conference meeting, have offered the following ecclesiastically approved prayer for the beatification of Frederic Ozanam:

O God, Who filled the hearts of Frederic Ozanam and his companions with a love of the poor and inspired them to found a Society for the relief of the needs of the suffering, bless this work of Christian charity. If it is Your Will that the Church should honour Frederic as a Saint, we ask You to show by miracles how pleasing he was in Your sight. Through Christ Our Lord, Amen.

3.

The St. Vincent de Paul Society today.—The Society spread rapidly in Frederic Ozanam's day, and continues to grow.

When Ozanam died in 1853—twenty years after the founding of the first Conference—the Society had become operative in sixteen countries, including the United States and Australia.

Today, in 112 countries circling the globe, Vincentian membership totals more than 750,000 men and women who, organized into 38,000 Conferences, continuously serve the poor.

The aggregated Conferences number 15,500 in Europe, 16,800 in the North, Central and South Americas; 1,250 in Africa, and 4,450 in Asia.

Joining in the work, chiefly in Asia and Africa, are an estimated 12,000 Conferences not yet aggregated, making a total of 50,000.

The percentage of women is increasing, now numbering, worldwide, 15%, or 113,000 members.

In the pattern of the first Conference, members meet once a week throughout the year, report on their previous week's activities, obtain counsel, accept new assignments. Assistance to those in need varies endlessly, for no work of charity is foreign to the Society. Assistance is given, usually, during neighborly visits to people in their homes. Some may require emergency aid; others, extended rehabilitation over months or years; still others, merely a friendly visit to relieve long days of loneliness.

Each Conference, also, may help support summer camps for underprivileged children, programs of work rehabilitation, or other projects which are under supervision of a District Council—the Society's central governing body for a city or district. The District Council is formed by the Presidents of the parish Conferences.

In each nation, a National Council unites all branches of the Society. An International Vice-President is assigned to and is the responsible representative for each Continent, reporting to the International Council General. The latter body is composed of the Presidents of the National Councils, and members appointed on a personal basis.

An International President General directs the International Council. He is elected for a six-year period to coordinate the action of the Society at the international level.

As an international organization, the Society encourages linkages between Conferences of the more affluent nations and those in developing countries. A United States Conference in Chicago, for example, may be "twinned" with a Conference in Lima, Peru. The twinned units seek to establish ties of deepening friendship. They regularly correspond; they pray for one another; the financially advantaged Conference shares in the work of its twin by providing regularly a modest degree of assistance.

In this way Australian Conferences help those of Thailand, of India, and the Philippines; New Zealand, those of Korea, Sri Lanka, and Samoa; the Irish Conferences, those of English-speaking Africa; those of France and Belgium help those of French-speaking Africa; U.S.A. Conferences give aid to those in Latin America.

A major catastrophe anyhwere in the world activates the Society's emergency program to relieve victims of flood, earthquake, drought or war. Funds for immediate needs are

276

sent directly to the stricken population's National Council, or its Conferences. Thus in recent years the Society has responded to calamities in Biafra, Vietnam, Pakistan, Bangladesh, Nicaragua and Sahel.

Wherever established, the Society works to relieve poverty while studying how to remedy conditions which cause it. To this end it collaborates with peoples of all races and faiths who uphold the dignity of man. For the Society of St. Vincent de Paul is simply men and women trying to live more fully the great commandment to love and to help all men, of all nationalities, classes and faiths, particularly those who need help most.

In obedience to this teaching, Vincentians act with unfailing respect for all they serve, regarding them as their brothers and sisters united, explicitly or implicitly, in the fellowship of Christ.